12-92
16.⁰⁰
B+T
VER

MORAL RESPONSI
THE BOUNDARIES O

BJ   Smiley, Marion.   27563
1451
.S65 Moral responsibility and
1992   the boundaries of
        community

DATE DUE

Moral responsibility and the boundaries
BJ1451.S65 1992   27563

Smiley, Marion
    VRJC/WRIGHT LIBRARY

                                    DEMCO

MARION SMILEY

MORAL RESPONSIBILITY AND THE BOUNDARIES OF COMMUNITY

Power and Accountability from a Pragmatic Point of View

VERNON REGIONAL
JUNIOR COLLEGE LIBRARY

THE UNIVERSITY OF CHICAGO PRESS
Chicago and London

Marion Smiley teaches moral and political philosophy
at the University of Wisconsin, Madison

The University of Chicago Press, Chicago 60637
The University of Chicago Press, Ltd., London
© 1992 by The University of Chicago
All rights reserved. Published 1992
Printed in the United States of America

01 00 99 98 97 96 95 94 93 92   5 4 3 2 1

ISBN (cloth): 0-226-76326-9
ISBN (paper): 0-226-76327-7

Library of Congress Cataloging-in-Publication Data

Smiley, Marion.
    Moral responsibility and the boundaries of community : power and
accountability from a pragmatic point of view / Marion Smiley.
        p.   cm.
    Includes bibliographical references and index.
    1. Responsibility.   2. Blame.   3. Pragmatism.   I. Title.
BJ1451.S65   1992
170—dc20   91-37468
                                                                    CIP

⊗ The paper used in this publication meets the minimum
requirements of the American National Standard for Information
Sciences—Permanence of Paper for Printed Library Materials,
ANSI Z39.48-1984.

To Adele M. and E. Forbes Smiley

Contents

Preface

This study began wtih a practical dilemma that rapidly became philosophical. In thinking about how to create a framework for arguing openly about responsibility in cases such as third world starvation and apartheid in South Africa, I was forced to confront two rather troublesome aspects of the prevailing view of responsibility. The first was its dependence on a notion of free will that probably does not exist. The second was its rejection of social and political considerations as irrelevant to responsibility. How, I asked, can we ever hope to develp a serious practice of responsibility if free will does not exist? What sense, moreover, does it make to invoke responsibility in a social and political context if responsibility is itself construed as independent of all worldy contingencies?

Since I began with cases that were clearly social and political, I found it necessary not only to show why the prevailing view of responsibility is flawed, but to reconstruct the concept of responsibility as part of social and political practice. Likewise, since I wanted to do so without sacrificing the moral aspects of responsibility to pure power politics, I found it necessary to talk about morality and politics together in a way that respected both. I chose to do so by developing a pragmatic approach to the study of responsibility that understands morality and politics not as polar opposites, but as mutually determinant aspects of our practical life.

In developing such an approach, I was greatly aided by a number of moral philosophers and political theorists. Don Herzog, Amy Gutmann, Judith Shklar, and Sheldon Wolin provided very helpful comments on particular chapters of the manuscript. Charles Anderson, Elizabeth Anderson, Joseph Carens, Don Downs, Booth Fowler, Nancy Hirshmann, Timothy Kaufmann-Osborne, Diana Myers, Thomas Scanlon, Elizabeth Spelman, and Dennis Thompson read very different versions of the entire manuscript and provided suggestions that were of great use along the way.

E. Forbes Smiley, my father, read each chapter with enormous care and intelligence. The resulting manuscript may not live up to his physicist's standards. But it owes its inception to a man whose intellectual honesty and curiosity about the world proved impossible to resist.

Bernard Yack contributed to the manuscript in so very many ways. He read and helped clarify arguments in every chapter. He shared with me his own insights while encouraging me to speak in my own philosophical voice. And—perhaps most important of all—he taught me through his own example what it means to exercise personal and intellectual integrity. I cannot imagine a more intellectually stimulating colleague or a more loving friend.

1

Introduction

The Political Context of Moral Responsibility

Questions of responsibility lie at the heart of many of our most heated social and political controversies. Who, we ask, was responsible for the deaths of Vietnamese children at the My Lai massacre? Does it make sense to blame officials at the Pentagon or supporters of the war in general for these events? How are we to apportion blame in cases of inner city drug addiction and teenage violence? Can we really hold members of the entertainment industry responsible for the drug addiction of inner city youths or the violence of those who watch heavy metal rock videos? What, moreover, are we to make of the debates surrounding the responsibility of U.S. investors for apartheid in South Africa? Are antiapartheid activists correct to point their fingers at U.S. investors, or does responsibility for the suffering of South African blacks stop at the borders of South Africa itself?

In cases such as these, what catches our attention is often the spatial distances that exist between those suffering and those being held responsible. But physical space is not the only controversial aspect of responsibility. Nor could it be, since questions of responsibility arise much closer to home all the time. Take, for instance, the case of unemployment in U.S. cities where women and/or persons of color have "taken" jobs once held by white males. Here the spatial distance between those suffering and those being blamed is as a close as a single job, but we nevertheless disagree a great deal among ourselves about responsibility. While many among us feel free to blame employed women and minorities for the high level of unemployment among white males, others contend that the causal connection between the two groups is indirect (or highly mediated) and hence irrelevant to blame. Which side is correct? Who is to blame?

Not surprisingly, in cases as socially and politically charged as those

1

cited here, we often differ among ourselves—sometimes violently—
about who is to blame. But we do not, contrary to the image that we may
have of ourselves, argue openly about our differences. Nor do we try to
develop criteria for evaluating each other's judgments of responsibility.
Instead, we generally impose our judgments of responsibility on others
and then retreat back into groups who agree with us or else resort to
political bullying if we are so inclined. Both moves are clearly well
suited to partisan politics. But neither—as we learned in Vietnam—
can sustain moral communication in an area where such communication is so desperately needed.

Moreover, even if we now tried to argue openly about responsibility
in controversial cases, it is not clear what such an argument would look
like in practice. As things now stand, we know how to counter facts with
other facts when talking about responsibility. ("Pentagon Official X
signed Document Y." "No, he did not.") But we do not know how to
respond to those who claim, for instance, that our candidate for blame
was only indirectly responsible for harm or that she was only following
orders. Nor do we know how to respond to those who acknowledge a
causal connection between the individual's action and harm, but claim
that it was a laudatory action in other respects and hence not blameworthy.

If such claims were unusual or not taken seriously by the rest of society, we might not have to worry about them in our discussions of responsibility. Likewise, if responsibility itself were simply a matter of
moral conscience, or in Robert Goodin's words, a mere "problem of
getting one's hands dirty,"[1] we might not have to ask about the consequences of our moral judgments for the community at large. Indeed,
we might, as Goodin himself suggests, be justified in treating the issue
of responsibility as a mere "narcissistic fixation on moral character."[2]

But claims about responsibility are made in almost every social and
political controversy that we can think of and are the crux of the matter
in those cited above. Moreover, whether or not we decide to hold a particular individual responsible for harm makes a great deal of difference to whether or not the harm is eventually prevented—not only
because blame itself is powerful, but because our judgments of responsibility often guide, and are sometimes used to justify, both social exclusion and legal punishment.

Since our judgments of responsibility are so important to social and
political practice, we might expect ourselves to have developed a frame-

1. Robert Goodin, *Political Theory and Public Policy* (Chicago, 1982), 12.
2. Ibid.

work for arguing openly about responsibility in controversial cases. But no such framework is now to be found. Why is it that we are not now able to argue openly about responsibility among ourselves? What, moreover, would it mean to argue openly with one another about responsibility in cases such as those cited above?

I focus on both questions throughout this study in an effort to provide a basis upon which we might communicate openly about responsibility in cases where we disagree about who is to blame for various sorts of harm in the world. I argue that our present difficulties lie not, as we often assume, in the complexity of the causal relations that exist between us and those suffering. Nor do they lie in the blatantly political nature of the controversies themselves. Instead, they lie in the particular understanding of moral responsibility that we bring to bear on our judgments of responsibility in both controversial and noncontroversial cases.

In the cases cited above, we do not always acknowledge that what we have in mind is *moral,* as opposed to purely *causal,* responsibility.[3] But we do clearly have moral responsibility in mind, since we almost always attach blame to our causal discoveries. In some cases we make our concern for blame explicit and condemn those individuals who caused the harm in question. In other cases we treat our judgments of blame as incidental to more purely factual inquiries into the causes of harm. But even in these cases, we generally conclude from our factual discoveries that particular individuals are or are not to blame.

Not surprisingly, our willingness to appear morally detached is most apparent in cases where our analysis is supposed to be scientifically based. Take, for instance, the debates surrounding the responsibility of U.S. investors for apartheid in South Africa. If we are participants in these debates, we may think of ourselves as pursuing a purely causal analysis of the relationship between those who invest in multinational corporations and the suffering of South African blacks. But we do not take a morally neutral stand on U.S. capitalists themselves. If we consider them to be causally responsible for the suffering of South African blacks, we not only blame them for such harm, but try to shame them into changing their economic practices. If, on the other hand, we consider the South African government to be solely responsible for the apartheid system, we insist that U.S. capitalists be exonerated from blame and perhaps even praised for their positive contributions to the reform movement.

---

3. I argue in part 3 that the differences between causal and moral responsibility are not as great as is often assumed.

While we do not make our concept of responsibility explicit in such judgments, we do lay bare two controversial assumptions about the nature of responsibility itself. One is that individuals are blameworthy not in virtue of a decision on our part that they are worthy of our blame, but in virtue of their having themselves caused that for which they are being held responsible. The other is that responsibility is a fact about individuals—that they caused that for which they are being blamed—rather than a judgment that we make about the individual after she has acted. Both assumptions, as we shall see, are part of a metaphysical understanding of moral responsibility that locates the source of blameworthiness in an individual's own free will. But we nevertheless incorporate each into our practical judgments of responsibility, even in cases that we ourselves think of as social and political.

Take again the case of apartheid. Presumably most of us are aware that our judgments of responsibility in this case are shaped in part by our more general beliefs about the proper role of U.S. businesses in the world. Likewise, when we make our judgments known, we do so presumably with some hope that they will have positive effects on both current and future investors. Nevertheless, we do not dwell on these effects in our arguments. Nor do we dwell on the fact that we ourselves may play a role in the act of blaming itself. Instead, we assume that we have discovered the real causes of harm and that U.S. capitalists are, or are not, blameworthy for the suffering of South African blacks.

By presenting our judgments of responsibility to others as purely objective, we invariably endow them with a moral authority that they would otherwise not have, an authority that I suggest in chapter 9 has its source in both a religious conception of moral objectivity and the present valuation of scientific inquiry. In the apartheid case, we rely heavily not only on the facts of the situation, but on the status that scientific argument now has in Western society. Likewise, we manage to appropriate such status for ourselves by obscuring the extent to which our causal analyses are themselves mediated by our own social and political norms.

But we inevitably create a great deal of confusion in the process. I argue throughout what follows that if we want to argue openly with one another about our responsibility for the suffering of others and explain the differences that arise among us, we will have to stop thinking about responsibility as a purely factual discovery and begin thinking about it as part of two more purely practical judgments that we ourselves make on the basis of our own social and political points of view. One of these judgments is that harm was the consequence of a particular individual's action. The other is that the individual herself is worthy of our blame.

I place both of these judgments at the center of my analysis of moral responsibility and explore the various social and political considerations that ground them in practice. I also challenge the particular understanding of moral responsibility that we bring to bear on these judgments, an understanding that leads us to view causal responsibility and blameworthiness not only as interchangeable terms of moral discourse, but as factual discoveries that we make about individuals supposedly without reference to our own interests and purposes. I argue that such an understanding of moral responsibility rests on a variety of metaphysical assumptions that are incoherent on their own terms and particularly ill suited to a discussion of moral responsibility in practice.

While scholars who write about moral responsibility do not always make their acceptance of the particular understanding of responsibility sketched above explicit, they do treat it as if it were the only one that ever existed. But it is, as we shall see, distinctly modern in two important respects. First of all, unlike its Classical Greek counterpart, it locates the source of blameworthiness outside the realm of social and political practice and draws a sharp line between moral responsibility, on the one hand, and social blameworthiness and legal accountability, on the other. Second, it views moral responsibility not only as independent of our social practice of blaming, but as completely under an individual's own control.

Joel Feinberg captures both aspects of the concept by distinguishing it from its more worldly counterparts, social blameworthiness and legal responsibility. According to Feinberg,

A stubborn feeling persists even after legal responsibility has been decided that there is still a problem—albeit not a legal problem—left over: namely, is the defendant *really* responsible (as opposed to "responsible in law") for the harm? This conception of a "real" theoretical responsibility as distinct from a practical responsibility "relative" to the purposes and values of a particular legal system is expressed very commonly in the terminology of "morality"—*moral* obligation, *moral* guilt, *moral* responsibility.[4]

Unlike either social blameworthiness or legal accountability, moral responsibility is, according to Feinberg, a purely factual matter and as such not susceptible to discretionary judgment. "Like all matters of 'record,' moral responsibility must be read off the facts or deduced from them: there can be no irreducible element of discretion for the judge."[5] Likewise, it must be construed as independent not only of any purposes, policies, or goals that we may embrace, but of our own opin-

---

4. Joel Feinberg, *Doing and Deserving* (Princeton, 1970), 30.
5. Ibid., 31.

ions about whether or not a particular individual is blameworthy. For unlike its worldly counterparts, it is

liability to charges on some ideal record, liability to credit or blame (in the sense that implies no action). Just as it is "forever to the credit" of a hero or a saint that he performed some noble act, so a man can be "forever to blame" for his faults.[6]

While the nature of "ideal liability" is never made clear, its supposed source is discussed at length. According to the perspective provided by our modern concept of moral responsibility, individuals are blameworthy not in virtue of our social practice of blaming but in virtue of their having themselves caused—freely willed—either their own actions or an external state of affairs. In other words, blameworthiness is ostensibly an aspect of moral agency itself: "an absolute responsibility within the power of the agent."[7]

Since we associate moral responsibility with a notion of blameworthiness that is ostensibly independent of all worldly considerations, we often refer to it as *moral* blameworthiness and distinguish it from other sorts of blameworthiness that we recognize as relative to our social practice of blaming or our legal institutions of punishment. But we are not always so careful in practice to distinguish between the two. Indeed, we often assume that while our judgments of moral responsibility may not be perfect, they have the same structure as "ideal liability" in that they are based on purely factual discoveries of blameworthiness rather than on our own subjective or communal judgments.

Take, for instance, the judgments of blameworthiness that we make in the case of South African apartheid. Here we are surely aware that those among us who consider U.S. capitalists responsible for apartheid in South Africa share a general political perspective on the role that U.S. businesses should play in our community. But we do not generally treat our own judgments of responsibility as politically biased unless we self-consciously fudge the facts of the situation to suit our own practical purposes, and even then, we often assume that there is a "correct" judgment of moral blameworthiness out there to be found.

How can we possibly assume the existence of a correct judgment of moral blameworthiness in a secular context? Since our modern concept of moral responsibility requires that we view correctness itself as a matter of both absoluteness and truth, we are obliged to construe moral blameworthiness as independent not only of our social practice of

6. Ibid., 30–31.
7. Ibid., 30.

blaming, but of all worldly considerations. Likewise, since moral blameworthiness is ostensibly independent of any relationship between individuals and external authority, we are obliged to construe it as an aspect of moral agency itself, or in other words, as a moral quality inherent in the causal connection between individuals and that for which they are being held responsible.

Since moral blameworthiness is ostensibly under an individual's own control, the causal connection that we focus on most often is that between an individual and her own actions. But we do not refrain from holding individuals morally responsible for external states of affairs as well. Indeed, we often assume that if an individual herself caused—freely willed—an action which was causally responsible for harm, she is morally blameworthy not only for her own actions, but for the harm itself. The question becomes what kind of causation or free will could possibly support such a notion of moral blameworthiness.

Until recently, philosophers concerned about moral responsibility have insisted that both free will and moral agency be considered independent of any judgments that we ourselves might make about a particular individual's state of mind. Similarly, they have made clear that if individuals are to be considered morally, as opposed to socially, blameworthy, they will have to be shown to exercise a will that is determined by the individual herself, rather then by her genetic inheritance or her social environment. In other words, they have insisted that we be able to construe free will as the antithesis of external determination: contra-causal freedom.[8]

While we ourselves may not, as social and political actors, be schooled in the complexities of contra-causal freedom, we do assume something very much like it whenever we refer to individuals as the authors of their own actions. Likewise, while we may not ourselves, as social and political actors, be attuned to the various sorts of determinism that philosophers talk about as running counter to free will, we do implicitly deny these sorts of determinism whenever we refuse to accept a socially or physically deterministic account of why a particular individual has failed to live up to our expectations of her. In these cases, we may recognize that an individual's environment or her family history

8. As I suggest in the next section, contemporary philosophers are now much less willing to talk about contra-causal freedom than they once were. Moreover, they often substitute for contra-causal freedom a "softer" notion of free will that is compatible with determinism. But they do not show how their softer notion of free will can be used to support the modern concept of moral responsibility which many of them continue to embrace.

influenced her in significant ways, but we are not willing to give up the belief that she could have transcended such influences and acted otherwise than she actually did.

Not surprisingly, we rarely, if ever, live up to the ideal standards that our modern concept of moral responsibility places on us. Nor has anyone yet discovered an actual instance of contra-causal freedom. But our shortcomings in this context have not generally stopped us from incorporating aspects of our modern concept of moral responsibility into our practical judgments. Even though we may not always talk about our judgments of responsibility as absolutely correct or rational, we do tend to assume that there is a right answer to the question, "Is individual X responsible for the suffering of others?" Likewise, even though we may not go as far as to assume that we ourselves have discovered the criteria of ideal liability, we do tend to attribute blameworthiness to an individual's moral agency rather than to our own purposes or policies.[9]

In my efforts to challenge our modern concept of moral responsibility, I focus on what is wrong with both its idealized conception of liability and the metaphysical notion of free will on which it is grounded. I also ask why it is that we now appear able to discover in practice that particular individuals are morally responsible for both their own actions and the suffering of others. I argue not only that we invoke our social criteria of blameworthiness to discover moral responsibility in practice, but that we fall back on the conditions provided by two other concepts of moral responsibility—the Classical and the Christian—to do so.

Why, one might ask, do we find it necessary to fall back on these two other concepts of moral responsibility to discover moral responsibility in practice? I argue that we do so not only because of inadequacies in our own concept of moral responsibility, but because the modern notion of moral blameworthiness makes no sense outside the context of both our social practice of blaming and a relationship between individuals and an ideal blamer—neither of which our modern concept of moral responsibility is supposed to take into consideration and both of which are supplied by the Classical and Christian concepts of moral responsibility respectively.

Both of these arguments require that I make explicit exactly what distinguishes our modern concept of moral responsibility from its

9. Jonathan Bennett asks in "Accountability," *Philosophical Subjects*, ed. Z. Van Straaten (Oxford, 1980), how widely accepted the modern (what he calls the Christian Kantian) concept of moral responsibility is in contemporary Western society. He responds that it is pervasive, although not completely dominant, and in any case, it is "not replaced by any coherent alternative to it" (27).

Classical and Christian counterparts. As things now stand, we do not generally identify ourselves as part of any one historical tradition. Hence we do not often think about our concept of moral responsibility as distinctly modern. Nor do we distinguish between it and other concepts of moral responsibility. Instead, we assume that we know roughly what moral responsibility entails and that the concept itself is logically coherent.[10]

But surely there are major differences between the modern concept of moral responsibility and those of, say, Aristotle or Aquinas. Likewise, our modern notions of free will and blameworthiness cannot possibly be as unproblematic as we generally assume them to be. How, we have to ask ourselves, can we possibly talk about an individual's free will as inherently good or bad? How, moreover, can we possibly talk about blameworthiness—ideal or not—outside the context of our social practice of blaming?

Both questions would seem to be absolutely crucial to any understanding of our modern concept of moral responsibility. But philosophers and political theorists who write about moral responsibility do not generally place them at the center of their analyses. Nor do they ask how a notion of blameworthiness that was originally construed as part of a relationship between individuals and an ideal blamer can now be construed as a moral fact about individuals themselves. Instead, they simply appropriate the form of such a relationship and assume that it makes sense in a secular context.[11]

I argue in my own analysis of moral responsibility that moral blameworthiness as now construed is essentially the Christian concept of sin minus the authority of God, and that if we want to develop a secu-

10. There are of course many among us—primarily philosophers—who doubt the existence of free will. But as we shall see, they do not generally question the coherence of our modern concept of moral responsibility itself.

11. Two major exceptions here are Elizabeth Anscombe and Judith Shklar. Anscombe points out in her analysis of modern moral philosophy that the language of morality associated with our claims of responsibility, obligations, and rights has its source in the "domination of Christianity for many centuries." "Concepts of *moral* obligation, *moral* duty . . . of what is *morally* right and wrong should be jettisoned if this is psychologically possible; because they are survivals from an earlier conception of ethics which no longer generally survives, and are only harmful without it" ("Modern Moral Philosophy," *Philosophy* 33 [1958], 1).

Shklar argues that the internal-external distinction underlying the modern concept of moral responsibility is "perfectly meaningless unless one believes in sin," and complains (rightly, I argue in chapter 4) that the trouble with internalist ethics (which she calls the "ethics of sin") is that "their origins and purposes, theological, philosophical and social, are rarely remembered by those who still adhere to them" (*Legalism* [Cambridge, Mass., 1964], 45–53).

lar concept of moral responsibility, we will have to focus on our own judgments of causal responsibility and blameworthiness in practice. Likewise, I suggest that if in doing so we want to fall back on the sorts of excuses that Aristotle explored in his efforts to articulate our judgments of social blameworthiness, we will have to recognize that the absence of such an excuse does not register contra-causal freedom, but rather the criteria that we ourselves invoke for deciding whether or not a particular individual is worthy of our blame.

I concentrate in part 1 of this study on showing why we cannot rely on the conditions of moral responsibility established by Aristotle and the Christian philosophers to discover moral responsibility as we now construe it. I do so not only by examining the modern concept of moral responsibility itself, but by demonstrating that all three concepts of moral responsibility rest on mutually exclusive notions of moral blameworthiness. The Classical and Christian concepts of moral responsibility differ in significant respects, but they both posit a relationship between individuals and an external blamer—the community and God, respectively. The modern concept of moral responsibility, on the other hand, denies the relevance of such a relationship and locates the source of moral blameworthiness in an individual's own free will.

I concentrate in chapters 2 and 3 on defending the Classical and Christian concepts of moral responsibility against those who wrongly dismiss them as naive or backward. I argue that once we grasp the particular notions of moral blameworthiness inherent in each concept, we are forced to acknowledge two things. One is that neither concept requires our modern notion of free will, as commentators often suggest. Hence we cannot justifiably characterize either concept as naive or backward on the grounds that it does not refer to contra-causal freedom. The other is that while each concept rests on premises that we might not ourselves want to accept, both concepts are coherent on their own terms.

I concentrate in chapter 4 on showing why the modern concept of moral responsibility is *not* coherent on its own terms. I do so by distinguishing between it and its Classical and Christian counterparts and by questioning the coherence of its notion of free will and the distinction that it posits between moral and social blameworthiness. I argue that the notion of causation inherent in moral responsibility is not the sort of thing in virtue of which individuals can be considered morally blameworthy and that moral blameworthiness itself makes no sense outside the context of a relationship between individuals and an external blamer (a relationship which, as we have seen, the modern concept of moral responsibility itself explicitly denies).

I go on in part 2 to show why we cannot—without contradicting ourselves—use the modern concept of moral responsibility to talk about the moral responsibility of particular individuals for external harm. I do so in chapters 5, 6, and 7 by examining three of the best efforts of contemporary philosophers and political theorists to establish the conditions under which individuals are in a factual sense morally responsible for the suffering of others.[12] I argue that while each of these efforts provides us with important insights into the nature of our practical judgments of moral responsibility, they all fail to establish the conditions in question as a result of their reliance on our modern concept of moral responsibility unreconstructed.

I suggest that their failure to establish these conditions registers a more general contradiction inherent in any attempt to apply our modern concept of moral responsibility, as it is now construed, to social and political practice. On the one hand, as these efforts themselves make clear, the causal responsibility of an individual for external harm is relative to a variety of social and political considerations over which individuals themselves have no control. On the other hand, the modern concept of moral responsibility insists that individuals be in total control over their own moral blameworthiness (or, in other words, that an individual herself have caused that for which she is being held morally responsible).

Not surprisingly, such an insistence frustrates the efforts of contemporary philosophers and political theorists to talk about the moral responsibility of individuals for external harm. As we shall see, they find themselves in the absurd position of having to show that such harm is the product of an individual's own moral agency. (While Harris and Casey talk about individuals as having themselves caused harm in the sense relevant to moral blameworthiness, Thompson goes as far as to talk about external harm as the product of an individual's own free will.)[13]

How, if at all, might we avoid finding ourselves in the same position that these three theorists find themselves in? How, in other words, might we make it possible for us to talk about the moral responsibility of individuals for the suffering of others without having to squeeze our causal judgments into the language of contra-causal freedom? Two options come to mind here. One requires us to develop a whole new ideal of moral responsibility. (I discuss this option in chapter 8.) The other

12. These are the efforts of John Harris, John Casey, and Dennis Thompson, respectively.
13. I point out the self-defeating nature of these efforts below.

requires us to reconstruct our judgments of causal responsibility and blameworthiness as part of social and political practice.

I pursue the latter of these two options throughout part 3 by exploring the social and political considerations that ground our judgments of causal responsibility and blameworthiness in a variety of contemporary political controversies. Two of these controversies are those surrounding the My Lai massacre and apartheid in South Africa. Another focuses on the responsibility of the entertainment industry for both drug addiction in the inner cities and the violence of teenage males. Two others take as their subject matter industrial pollution and the employment gains made by women and persons of color in recent years. (The first asks: "Can factory owners who dump chemicals in a town's water supply be held responsible for the illnesses that result?" the second: "Can women and persons of color be held responsible for the current divorce rate or the underemployment of American males?")

I focus in chapter 8 on the conditions under which we consider harm to be the consequence of a particular individual's actions in each of these controversies. I argue that while our judgments of causal responsibility are clearly based on the recognition of a causal connection between an individual and external harm, they also depend, among other things, on both our configuration of social roles and our conception of communal boundaries. If, for instance, we view those suffering as members of the individual's community, which is of course a relative matter, we are more likely to see a direct connection between the suffering and the individual's own actions. If, on the other hand, we do not include them in the individual's community, we are more likely to consider the causal connection indirect and to refrain from holding the individual herself responsible for the harm in question.

I argue that while our conception of communal boundaries plays a role in all of our judgments of causal responsibility, it plays an especially important role in the particular cases upon which I focus here. In these cases we generally agree on the causal connection between the individual and others' suffering. But we do not agree on whether or not the individual could have been expected to take the suffering into consideration when she formulated her own actions. Nor do we agree on whether or not the individual can be considered causally responsible for the harm or be described as bringing it about.

While the result of such disagreement is often simply chaos, there are situations in which we manage to change each other's minds about the causal responsibility of particular individuals for the suffering of others. In these situations, one of two things generally happens: either we become aware of causal connections between particular individuals and harm which we did not know about before, or else we manage to muster more power than those who disagree with us or more support among the population at large. I explore several of these situations throughout chapter 8 in an effort to underscore the dependence of our judgments of responsibility on both the publicity of causal discoveries and the wielding of political power among those with competing expectations of a particular individual or group.

Since we generally view our judgments of responsibility as purely factual, we might, understandably, be taken aback by any insinuation that these judgments are shaped by the exercise of political power. But once we explore them in detail, we are forced to acknowledge two things. One is that our judgments of causal responsibility often depend not only on our configuration of social roles and the boundaries of our community, but on the distribution of power between those suffering and those being held responsible. The other is that when our judgments of causal responsibility change over time, they do so not only because of new causal discoveries, but because we as a community have come to alter our expectations of particular individuals on the basis of shifts in social and political power.

While competing expectations and the wielding of power make such changes possible, they would not be effective if we were not also able to incorporate our judgments of causal responsibility into our social practice of blaming. In chapter 9 I explore our social practice of blaming in detail and suggest how it functions not only to reinforce our judgments of causal responsibility, but to maintain the configuration of social roles and the conception of communal boundaries on which our judgments of causal responsibility are based. I also challenge the distinction that we now posit between moral and social blameworthiness, and view the latter not as an aspect of free will, but as a conceptual mechanism for internalizing judgments of social blameworthiness in the absence of external authority.

What would happen if we incorporated such a view of moral blameworthiness into our practical discourse? I suggest in chapter 10 that if we were to construe moral blameworthiness as part of social and political practice, rather than as an aspect of free will, we would inevitably drain it of much of its existing moral authority. Moreover, we would take away from ourselves a conceptual mechanism for viewing our judgments of causal responsibility and blameworthiness as part of one factual discovery rather than as judgments that we ourselves make on the basis of our own social and political points of view. But we would gain in return a framework for arguing openly and honestly about our moral responsibility for external harm in cases where we are now unable to communicate with one another.

While the arguments that we might make within this framework could never be characterized as objective, they might in the end be more well thought out than the so-called factual claims that we now make about moral responsibility in practice. Likewise, while these arguments could never be expected to carry the moral weight that their metaphysical counterparts at one time did, they might in the end be able to attain a more worldly legitimacy if we elaborated them as part of an openly democratic debate about who is morally responsible for various sorts of suffering around the world. This, at least, is what I suggest in the study's conclusion.

Beyond Free Will and Determinism

This study differs from other works on moral responsibility in three general respects. First of all, it focuses on moral responsibility itself rather than on the notions of free will and determinism that engage most other scholars now writing on moral responsibility. Second, it views the modern concept of moral responsibility as part of social and political practice rather than as an ideal that supposedly exists outside of and superior to our social and political concerns. Third, it takes our practical judgments of moral responsibility seriously and uses them to open up channels of communication with regard to the moral responsibility of particular individuals for the suffering of others.

Most other scholars now writing on moral responsibility do not take our practical judgments of moral responsibility seriously, either because they are not interested in them or because they consider these judgments to be less than fully rational. While philosophers and political theorists who apply our concept of moral responsibility to social and political practice may end up borrowing from our practical judgments, they do not set out to do so. Instead, they take as their collective goal the articulation of those conditions under which individuals can be understood to have themselves caused harm in the sense relevant to moral blameworthiness.[14]

14. Among the best of these efforts are Jonathan Bennett, "Whatever the Consequences," *Analysis* 26 (1965), 83–102; John Casey, "Actions and Consequences," *Morality and Moral Reasoning* (London, 1971); Eric D'Arcy, *Human Acts* (Oxford, 1963); P. J. Fitzgerald, "Acting and Refraining," *Analysis* 4 (1967); John Harris, *Violence and Responsibility* (London, 1980); Eric Mack, "Bad Samaritanism and the Causation of Harm," *Philosophy and Public Affairs* 10 (1980); Carolyn Morillo, "Doing, Refraining, and the Strenuousness of Morality," *American Philosophical Quarterly* 14 (1977), 29–39; Elliot Sober, "Apportioning Causal Responsibility," *Journal of Philosophy* 85 (1988), 308–19; Dennis Thompson, *Political Ethics and Public Office* (Cambridge, Mass., 1987); Michael Tooley, "Abortion and Infanticide," *Philosophy and Public Affairs* 2 (1972–73), 37–65; J. Trammell, "Saving Life and Taking Life," *Journal of Philosophy* 72 (1975), 131–41; and Michael Walzer, *Just and Unjust Wars* (New York, 1977).

By doing so, they make clear not only that they have accepted our modern concept of moral responsibility unreconstructed, but that they have joined ranks with almost everyone else now writing on moral responsibility with regard to their starting point. While not everyone accepts the modern concept of moral responsibility—scholars such as P. F. Strawson view moral responsibility as part of social and political practice,[15] and utilitarians such as Richard Brandt have tried to develop their own concept of moral responsibility[16]—most others appropriate our modern concept of moral responsibility without question, even if they explicitly reject the notion of free will that grounds it.[17] Likewise, while these individuals might in other contexts scoff at the metaphysical notion of blameworthiness underlying our modern concept of moral responsibility, they nevertheless reinforce it in their writings by assuming both that moral responsibility has its source in free will and that it is independent of our social practice of blaming.[18]

My own assumption here is not only that we need to abandon the metaphysical baggage associated with our modern concept of moral responsibility, but that we cannot do so without reconstructing the con-

---

15. P. F. Strawson, *Freedom and Resentment and Other Essays* (London, 1974), 1–25. Strawson views moral responsibility as part of the process through which we express resentment against others for not following the rules of acceptable behavior. For an extremely interesting discussion of the value of Strawson's perspective, see Bennett, "Accountability," especially 21–48.

16. Richard Brandt, "A Utilitarian Theory of Excuses," *Philosophical Review* 78 (1969), 337–61. Interestingly enough, not all utilitarians are willing to ground moral responsibility in utility. Indeed, many assume, along with their Kantian counterparts, that individuals are morally blameworthy in virtue of their having themselves caused—freely willed—harm to others. I discuss the utilitarian concept of moral responsibility in chapter 8.

17. Not surprisingly, those who reject contra-causal freedom while holding onto the modern concept of moral responsibility find themselves faced with the possibility that moral responsibility does not exist. Two major groups emerge here: those who reject the possibility of moral responsibility altogether and those who try to replace contra-causal freedom with a "softer" notion of free will that is compatible with the modern concept of moral responsibility. I argue in chapter 4 that the softer notion of free will that the latter group comes up with is not strong enough to support the modern concept of moral responsibility, and that instead of rejecting moral responsibility altogether, we should reconstruct the concept of moral responsibility as part of social and political practice. In doing so, I implicitly side with P. F. Strawson, as well as with scholars such as Gerald Dworkin, Harry Frankfurt, Gary Watson, and Susan Wolf, who in very different ways are concerned to view the concept of freedom in a nonmetaphysical context.

18. Jonathan Bennett complains, in "Accountability" (27), about the absence of a "coherent alternative" to the modern concept of moral responsibility. I argue in my own analysis that it is because of this absence of a "coherent alternative" that even skeptics frequently fall back on what is essentially a metaphysical concept of moral responsibility.

cept of moral responsibility itself. As things now stand, there are plenty of philosophers and political theorists who are willing to concede not only that contra-causal freedom does not exist, but that it is totally irrelevant to moral responsibility.[19] Yet these same philosophers and political theorists continue to talk about moral responsibility not only as distinct from our social practice of blaming, but as a factual discovery that we ourselves make about an individual's moral agency.

I argue in my own analysis of moral responsibility that if we want to leave the metaphysical baggage now associated with moral responsibility behind, we will have to think about the nature of our modern concept of moral responsibility itself and the notions of free will and blameworthiness inherent in it. Likewise, we will have to ask what moral responsibility might look like if we were to replace contra-causal freedom with a "softer" notion of free will. Very few contemporary philosophers ever attempt to do either of these two things. (The exceptions are all utilitarians.) Nor, for that matter, do they explore the nature of moral responsibility itself.[20] Instead they concentrate on what is essentially a second-order question: "Is the notion of free will entailed by moral responsibility compatible with modern theories of determinism?"

The answers that they give to this question are many and varied. I examine them more fully in chapter 4. Suffice it to point out here that while those participating in the free will/determinism controversy view themselves as developing arguments in opposition to each other, they nevertheless make two assumptions that bring them much closer together than is often assumed to be the case. One is that the possibility of moral responsibility rests primarily, if not exclusively, on the logical coherence of free will—or in other words, that if free will is not possi-

---

19. For one of the most aggressive expressions of this position, see Daniel Dennett, "I Could Not Have Done Otherwise—So What?" *Journal of Philosophy* 84 (1981), 553–65. Dennett asserts that "it simply does not matter at all to moral responsibility whether the agent in question could have done otherwise in the circumstances" (553). While I agree with Dennett that our practical judgments of moral responsibility do not require contra-causal freedom, I disagree with his assumption that contra-causal freedom "does not matter" to moral responsibility. I try to show not only that our modern concept of moral responsibility entails contra-causal freedom, but that we often assume contra-causal freedom in our practical judgments. Likewise, I try to make clear that while we would be well-advised to leave the concept of contra-causal freedom behind, we cannot do so without first rethinking the nature of moral responsibility itself (a process which skeptics such as Dennett often ignore).

20. This was not always the case with earlier scholars. See, for example, Paul Fauconnet, *La Responsabilité* (Paris, 1920); John Dewey, *Ethics* (New York, 1908); and Richard McKeon, "The Development and Significance of the Concept of Responsibility," *Revue Internationale de Philosophie* 2 (First Trimester, 1957), 3–32.

ble, moral responsibility does not exist.[21] The other is that if we want to show that free will is possible, we will have to demonstrate its compatibility with modern theories of determinism.

By making both assumptions at the outset and then zeroing in on the compatibility of free will and determinism, libertarians and determinists alike manage to provide us with several very important insights into the nature of both free will and determinism. But they do not contribute to our understanding of moral responsibility itself. Indeed, they may do just the opposite by associating moral responsibility so closely with free will that we no longer remember what else moral responsibility entails.[22]

I try to remedy this situation in my own discussions of moral responsibility by shifting our attention back from the free will/determinism controversy to the nature of moral responsibility itself. I argue that by focusing on moral blameworthiness as well as on free will, we gain two advantages over contemporary participants in the free will/determinism debate. First of all, we are able to view the concept of moral responsibility not only in its entirety, but in relation to its sister concepts, such as social blameworthiness and legal punishment. Second, we are able to talk about the possibility of moral responsibility at a much more fundamental level than participants in the free will/determinism controversy are able to do.

While participants in the free will/determinism debate start out by saying that they are concerned about the possibility of moral responsibility, they rarely return to it in their discussions of free will and determinism. Nor, for that matter, do they ever air the possibility that the modern notion of moral blameworthiness may itself be incoherent (even if the notion of free will that we associate with it is not). Hence we are left with the impression that determinism is the only threat to our

21. Among the most eloquent formulations of this warning is that offered by Isaiah Berlin: "If social determinism is true, and we begin to take it seriously, then the changes in the whole of our language, our moral terminology, our attitudes toward one another, our views of history, of society, and of everything else will be too profound to be adumbrated. The concepts of praise and blame, innocence and guilt, and responsibility from which we started are but a small element in the structure, which would collapse or disappear" ("Historical Inevitability," in *Four Essays On Liberty* [London, 1969]).

22. Robert Audi makes a similar point in "Responsible Action and Virtuous Character," *Ethics* 101 (1991), 304–21, when he complains that "much of the literature is dominated by the question whether moral responsibility is compatible with determinism. Indeed, sometimes philosophers assume that actions for which we bear moral responsibility are equivalent to free actions, and they often say little about moral responsibility beyond illustrating the equivalence claim and discussing the relation between free will and determinism" (304).

modern concept of moral responsibility (or in other words, that the possibility of moral responsibility rests solely on the compatibility of free will and determinism).[23]

But such an impression is clearly false. While determinism is unquestionably a very serious threat to moral responsibility as we now know it, it is not the only threat. Nor is moral responsibility itself simply a matter of free will. If participants in the free will/determinism controversy were to focus on the concept of moral responsibility itself before going on to examine the relationship between free will and determinism, they would have to acknowledge not only that moral responsibility is as much a matter of moral blameworthiness as of free will, but that its possibility rests as much on our ability to make sense of our modern notion of moral blameworthiness as on the compatibility of free will and determinism.

Since so much of recent scholarly attention has been devoted to the compatibility of free will and determinism, I do not spend much time on it. Instead, I place at the center of my analysis of moral responsibility three equally important questions. First of all, how can we make sense of the distinction that we now posit between moral and social blameworthiness? Second, what would it mean to talk about moral responsibility in a determined context? Third, under what conditions can we hold individuals morally responsible for the suffering of others?

I argue with regard to the first question that while our modern notion of moral blameworthiness makes no sense on its own terms, it does make sense as a conceptual mechanism for internalizing judgments of social blameworthiness in the absence of external authority, whether that authority be the political community or God. Likewise, I suggest that while the modern notion of contra-causal freedom does not actually have an empirical referent, it does provide us with the conceptual means of obscuring the social and political considerations that ground our judgments of causal responsibility and blameworthiness in practice.

I argue with regard to the second question that moral responsibility makes sense in a determined context and that if we want to understand how our judgments of moral responsibility are determined, we will have to explore not only the biological aspects of willing, but two more purely social and political phenomena. One is the cluster of expectations that we bring to bear on our judgments of causal responsibility for

23. Jonathon Glover illustrates this attitude when he writes in the introduction to his study on responsibility: "In this book, questions concerning determinism will be taken as fundamental. This is because, if determinism were true, all other questions would be redundant" (*Responsibility* [London, 1970], 2).

external harm. The other is the group of conventions that we use to distinguish free actions from actions that are encumbered (and hence not blameworthy).

I argue with regard to the third question that if we want to articulate the conditions under which individuals can now be considered morally responsible for the suffering of others, we will have to focus not only on the above-mentioned expectations and conventions, but on the processes through which we are able to change the status quo concerning moral responsibility. While the latter project requires us to move outside of our particular judgments of moral responsibility, it does not require that we impose ideals from outside of social practice, since, as I try to show throughout this study, we can, and now do, alter our judgments of moral responsibility within the social practice of blaming by virtue of the different expectations that we bring to bear on each others' actions.

Not surprisingly, the third question is the most immediately important to the practical controversies with which I began. But very few contemporary philosophers and political theorists either ask it or explore the conditions under which individuals are morally responsible for external harm.[24] Instead, they restrict their attention to the moral responsibility of individuals for their own actions or character and in doing so concentrate their energies on articulating the conditions under which both can be understood as the product of free will.

Why are contemporary philosophers and political theorists reluctant to explore the conditions under which individuals are morally responsible for external harm? Many of them, as we shall see, assume that we do not need to articulate these conditions, since individuals are morally responsible for harm by virtue of their moral responsibility for actions of the form "X brought about harm." Others are more skeptical and argue that moral responsibility for external harm makes no sense, since the causal connection between an individual and external harm, unlike that between the individual and her own actions, is susceptible to moral luck and is hence not something which the individual can herself control.[25]

24. For a list of the most important exceptions, see n. 10.

25. "Moral Luck" has become a popular topic among contemporary moral and political philosophers in recent years. See, for example, Judith Andre, "Nagel, Williams, and Moral Luck," *Analysis* 43 (1983), 202–7); Henning Jensen, "Morality and Luck," *Philosophy* 59 (1984), 323–30; Thomas Nagel, "Moral Luck," in *Mortal Questions* (Cambridge, England, 1979); Norvin Richards, "Luck and Desert," *Mind* 95 (1986), 198–209; Bernard Williams, "Moral Luck," *Moral Luck* (Cambridge, England, 1981); and Michael Zimmerman, "Luck and Moral Responsibility," *Ethics* 96 (1987), 374–86. For an excellent discussion of moral luck outside the modern tradition, see Martha Nussbaum, *The Fragility of Goodness: Luck and Ethics in Greek Tragedy and Philosophy* (Cambridge, England, 1986).

VERNON REGIONAL
JUNIOR COLLEGE LIBRARY

Although the term "moral luck" may be somewhat deceptive in that it collapses together all sorts of physical and social determinism, it does capture the precariousness that often confronts us when we are trying to hold individuals morally responsible for external harm. The example often referred to here is that of a revolutionary who hopes to overthrow an authoritarian regime.[26] If the individual can keep her plans secret, then she may be able to overthrow the regime without violence. But if she cannot keep her plans secret—if, for instance, someone else steals them—then violence will assuredly reign. Since she cannot control others' actions, the situation is clearly precarious. How, then, can we possibly hold her morally responsible for either outcome?

Thomas Nagel argues that we cannot possibly do so and that "from the point of view which makes responsibility dependent on control," responsibility for external harm is "absurd."[27] Joel Feinberg goes one step further and asserts that while the precariousness inherent in these cases does not mean that we will have to give up talking about moral responsibility altogether, it does mean that we will have to give up talking about our moral responsibility for external harm. If we are "rational," Feinberg argues, we will

acknowledge that moral responsibility for external harm makes no sense and argue that moral responsibility is restricted to the inner world of the mind, where the agent rules supreme and luck has no place.[28]

Feinberg is correct to point out here that moral responsibility for external harm makes no sense according to our modern concept of moral responsibility. But he is somewhat premature in suggesting that we restrict our discussions of moral responsibility to the "inner world of the mind." For the fact is that we hold each other morally responsible for external harm all the time in practice and are unlikely to stop doing so simply because such a practice contradicts our concept of moral responsibility.

What, then, are we to do? I choose not to abandon our practical judgments of causal responsibility and blameworthiness or to develop a utilitarian concept of moral responsibility. Instead, I use our practical judgments of causal responsibility and blameworthiness to carve out a concept of moral responsibility that both enables us to talk about the moral responsibility of particular individuals for external harm and that is compatible with moral luck. I do so both by exploring the actual judgments of responsibility that we make in practice and by articulating

26. Thomas Nagel first uses the example in "Moral Luck," 30–31.
27. Nagel, "Moral Luck," 31.
28. Feinberg, *Doing and Deserving,* 32.

the concept of moral responsibility that we bring to bear on these judgments.

While both tasks take me into the realm of social practice, they do so in distinctly different ways. I use as my source material for our practical judgments of responsibility a series of popular arguments that have been made in recent years about our responsibility for various sorts of suffering in the world. I use as my source material for our concept of moral responsibility more purely philosophical and religious tracts, tracts which, I argue, register the efforts of particular communities to both shape and justify various developments in their respective practices of blaming.

Philosophical Pragmatism and Social Practice

Throughout this study I rely on what has come to be known as philosophical pragmatism to reconstruct one moral concept—moral responsibility—as part of social and political practice. In doing so I make two very broad methodological assumptions. One is that moral concepts evolve out of social practice in response to the actual tensions, problems, and crises that characterize our collective life. The other is that if we want to understand our moral concepts, we will have to grasp not only the social and political contexts in which they originally evolved, but also the conditions under which they are now applied in practice.

Both of these assumptions lead me to embrace fully the point of view—developed most eloquently by Richard Rorty—that philosophical inquiry is not by itself equipped either to understand the real nature of our moral concepts or to provide us with solutions to our moral problems.[29] In the context of this study, such skepticism leads me to make two more particular claims. One is that no matter how sophisticated their logical analysis of free will and determinism is philosophers are never going to be able to teach us anything about the real nature of moral responsibility. The other is that regardless of how carefully they analyze the idea of either causation or blame, they are not going to be able to establish the conditions under which individuals are in a factual sense morally responsible for external harm.

What do these two claims mean for our ability to develop a general understanding of moral responsibility? Critics of pragmatism suggest that once we give up on our philosophical foundations, we will no

---

29. Richard Rorty develops this point of view primarily in *Philosophy and the Mirror of Nature* (Princeton, 1979) and *Consequences of Pragmatism* (Minneapolis, 1982).

longer be able to structure our arguments on the basis of general principles, but will instead be thrown back into a world of particulars. I challenge this perspective throughout my analysis by showing that while we
may not be able to locate a universally correct understanding of moral
responsibility, we can locate general rules according to which our practices of causal responsibility and blaming are now governed—rules
which we inevitably apply according to our own particular interests and
purposes.

Since I concentrate on these rules, rather than, say, on the idea of a
social practice, I am led to develop a mode of pragmatic analysis that is
considerably less abstract than much of contemporary pragmatism.
While philosophical pragmatism has become increasingly popular in
recent years among both philosophers and political theorists, it is primarily as a theory of meaning, rather than as a mode of social or political inquiry, that it has gained its following. Likewise, while political
theorists such as Richard Flathman[30] and Hanna Pitkin[31] have relied
with great success on pragmatic method to help us understand our social and political concepts, most others who now call themselves pragmatists have focused on more abstract questions about how we convey
meaning to one another as members of an interpretive community.

In doing so, they have taken pragmatism in a surprisingly wide variety of directions. Analytically trained philosophers such as Hilary
Putnam have concentrated their energies on developing a pragmatic
theory of truth.[32] Wittgensteinians have set out to articulate the process
of rule following that grounds both our verbal and nonverbal exchanges.[33] Followers of Pierce have taken it upon themselves to develop
a pragmatic theory of signs,[34] and postmodernists such as Jean-

30. Richard Flathman, *Concepts in Social and Political Philosophy* (New York, 1973),
The Philosophy and Politics of Freedom (Chicago, 1987), *Political Obligation* (New York, 1972),
The Practice of Political Authority (Chicago, 1980) and *The Practice of Rights* (Cambridge,
England, 1976).

31. Hanna Pitkin, *The Concept of Representation* (Berkeley, 1967), and *Wittgenstein and
Justice* (Berkeley, 1972).

32. Hilary Putnam, *Reason, Truth, and History* (Cambridge, England, 1981).

33. See, for example, G. P. Baker and P. M. S. Hacker, *Wittgenstein: Rules, Grammar,
and Necessity* (Oxford, 1985), and *Skepticism, Rules, and Language* (Oxford, 1984); Colin
McGinn, *Wittgenstein on Meaning: An Interpretation and Evaluation* (Oxford, 1984); and
Fred Schauer's *Playing By the Rules: A Philosophical Examination of Rule-Based Decisionmaking in Law and in Life* (Oxford, 1991).

34. See, for example, Karl-Otto Apel, *Charles S. Pierce: From Pragmatism to Pragmaticism* (Amherst, Mass., 1981), and "Transcendental Semiotics and the Paradigms of First
Philosophy," *Philosophical Exchanges* 2 (1978), 3–22.

François Lyotard[35] have reduced pragmatism to a form of literary criticism.

The latter trend, not surprisingly, has been followed by a barrage of criticism from those who want to retain both the empirical and critical aspects of pragmatism. Richard Bernstein has developed a very persuasive set of arguments for bringing pragmatism back into the realm of praxis.[36] Eugene Rochberg Halton has underscored the importance of the phenomenal world to our generation of signs,[37] and a wide variety of contemporary pragmatists have argued for the re-introduction of the "practical" back into our discussions of pragmatism.[38] (Not surprisingly, they have frequently chosen to rely on the works of earlier pragmatists—Pierce, Dewey, and James—to make their points.)

While I do not address these trends directly in the study, I do implicitly side with those contemporary pragmatists who want to retain the concept of the practical as a guiding principle of pragmatism. But I do not, like Ronald Dworkin and others,[39] view pragmatism as a mere form of instrumental rationality or policy science. Nor do I confuse it with purely practical questions, such as, "What do we do now?" or "How do we solve problem X?" Instead, I view pragmatism as a mode of interpretation that takes "the practical" seriously in its efforts both to uncover the meanings of particular concepts and to convey those meanings to others.

The nature of "the practical" is of course of utmost importance here. I use it to convey a variety of different but closely related things. The first has to do with the importance of social practice in general to pragmatic inquiry. Like all pragmatists, I eschew essentialist theories of meaning and the criteria of truth on which they are based. But I do not go so far as to view the meanings that we associate with a particular concept as susceptible to rational control in the way, say, that instrumental pragmatists now do. Instead, I view the meanings that we associate with

35. Jean-François Lyotard, *The Postmodern Condition* (Minneapolis, 1984), and *Just Gaming* (Minneapolis, 1985).

36. See, for example, his arguments in Richard Bernstein, *Philosophical Profiles: Essays in a Pragmatic Mode* (Philadelphia, 1986); *Praxis and Action: Contemporary Philosophies of Human Action* (Philadelphia, 1971); *The Restructuring of Social and Political Theory* (New York, 1976), and "One Step Forward, Two Steps Backward," *Political Theory* 15 (1987), 538–63.

37. Eugene Rochberg Halton, *Meaning and Modernity: Social Theory in the Pragmatic Attitude* (Chicago, 1986).

38. See, for example, R. P. Sleeper's arguments in *The Necessity of Pragmatism* (New Haven, 1986).

39. Ronald Dworkin, *Law's Empire* (Cambridge, Mass., 1986), especially 151–75.

a particular concept as dependent on the complex web of symbols that we develop as a community and continuously reinterpret from our own perspectives. Likewise, I locate the source of such meaning not in rational discourse or in nature per se, but in the realm of social practice where rules of behavior are institutionalized and linguistic conventions are shared among members of a particular community.

While all contemporary pragmatists refer to social practice, they frequently mean different things by the term. Some use it merely to distance themselves from essentialist theories of truth. Others use it to refer to rule-governed behavior in general. I use the term in both ways myself, but I do so in the context of a more specific focus on those features of our communal life that enable us to exercise moral judgments, features that include the customs, habits, and beliefs shared by members of a particular community, the reactive attitudes and norms of behavior that govern the relations among us, the rules of discourse that tell us when it is appropriate to invoke a particular concept, and the evaluative criteria (both normative and logical) that guide us in our efforts to change or preserve our way of life.

I assume, and then try to show in one particular case, that the meanings that we associate with concepts such as moral responsibility depend on all of these features of social practice together. In the case of moral responsibility, we need to focus not only on the conceptual apparatus that has evolved to support it, namely, free will, but on the set of reactive attitudes and norms of behavior that it originally evolved out of and now shapes, namely, those associated with blame. Likewise, we cannot suppose that the concept is universally accepted or that it has remained constant in structure through time. Instead, we have to focus on the particular communities that embrace it and ask how it has evolved over the years.

While the latter two tasks are not impossible to meet, they do place obligations on us that contemporary pragmatists do not always recognize as such. One of these obligations is to take the historical source of our concepts seriously. Another is to become more sensitive to the various differences that exist among members of our community, differences that require us to ask who "we" are and what particular traditions and beliefs are relevant to the moral judgments that "we" make. Yet another is to acknowledge the extent to which both our social practices and our conception of "we" change over time.

Presumably if pragmatists such as Jean-François Lyotard were to take the historical source of our concepts more seriously, they could not treat meaning as a matter of "just gaming." Nor could they put forth as a means of deciphering meaning the self-contained forms of literary criticism that Lyotard himself describes. Instead, they, like all other pragmatists, would have to view meaning as something that evolves in response to what John Dewey talks about as the "actual tensions, needs, troubles" that confront the members of a particular community who are themselves constituted by a set of shared beliefs and practices.[40]

While very few contemporary pragmatists go as far as Lyotard does in flattening out social and political reality, they do not always recognize the extent to which our practices change over time as the result of concrete changes in the world. Nor, for that matter, do they always recognize the differences that exist in our own community with respect to both identity and values. Clearly this is the case with the recent work of Richard Rorty.[41] Rorty professes to take communities of belief seriously, but he continues to talk about an overarching "we," "our" values and beliefs, and what "we" deem to be acceptable behavior. Hence, even though he is sensitive to the importance of culture in general, he ends up leaving many particular cultures out of his analysis, including those of the least powerful.[42]

Presumably the assumption of a unified community of meaning is for Rorty theoretically useful. But it is neither empirically accurate nor necessary to pragmatism itself, since pragmatism is committed to locating the source of our values wherever they may be found. Moreover, such an assumption may actually *violate* the spirit of pragmatism both by distorting the identities of those whose interpretations go unrecorded and by underplaying the extent to which individuals apply the rules of a shared practice according to their own interests and purposes.

Pragmatists such as Rorty often focus their attention on the rules of a shared practice rather than on the ways individuals actually apply these

40. John Dewey, *Logic of Inquiry* (New York, 1938), 499. While I agree with much of Dewey's pragmatism, I argue that it needs to be reconstructed by both shifting the focus of attention from his scientism to his principles of interpretation and by recognizing the overlapping and conflicting *wes* that constitute our community. I attempt to show what such a reconstruction might look like in my "Pragmatic Inquiry and Social Conflict: A Critical Reconstruction of Dewey's Model of Democracy," *Praxis* 9 (1990), 365–80.

41. See, for example, the works cited above, as well as Richard Rorty, "Postmodernist Bourgeois Liberalism," *Journal of Philosophy* 80 (1983), 583–89; "Habermas and Lyotard on Postmodernity," *Praxis International* 4 (April 1984), 32–44; "Solidarity and Objectivity," *Nanzen Review of American Studies* 6 (1984), 1–19; "The Priority of Democracy to Philosophy," in *The Virginia Statute For Religious Freedom*, ed. Merrill D. Peterson and Robert C. Vaughan (Cambridge, England, 1988), 257–81; and *Contingency, Irony, and Solidarity* (Cambridge, England, 1989).

42. I develop this criticism of Rorty more fully in "A More Political Theory of Pragmatism," my response to Rorty's 1990 *Tanner Lecture* at the University of Michigan, to be published in the *Michigan Quarterly* in 1991.

rules. Hence, while they may be totally aware of the importance of individual interpretation to social norms in general, they do not ask how particular individuals stamp their own interests or identities on common practices and develop their own judgments. Nor do they take into consideration the fact that these judgments might themselves reflect interests and purposes that are shared by larger cultural groups or groups based, for example, on class, gender or race.

In my study of moral responsibility, I attempt to reverse this trend by zeroing in on the different judgments that we make on the basis of rules of a shared practice. I try to demonstrate that individuals necessarily apply the rules of a shared practice to situations which they themselves construct either as individuals or as members of a particular group. Likewise, I try to demonstrate that while individuals may agree on the rules of a particular practice, they will not arrive at the same judgment in any one situation, especially if, as in the case of moral responsibility, these judgments rest not only on social rules, but on the expression of particular interests.

Since the particular interests that I locate in this study have their source in, and in turn reinforce, structures of power in our community, they are in at least one important respect not only practical, but political. Likewise, by focusing on them in conjunction with the moral judgments that particular individuals make, we can go farther than many contemporary political theorists now go in talking about the political structures that ground our interpretation of particular concepts. As things now stand, political theorists of many stripes talk loosely about the "politics of meaning," but they rarely specify exactly what they have in mind. I try to show in my own analysis of moral responsibility how, by exploring the relationships between the particular perspectives that we incorporate into our moral judgments, on the one hand, and the structures of power in our community, on the other, we can provide at least a few concrete examples of the "politics of meaning."

But I do not try to provide a deterministic account of our moral judgments as purely political. Indeed, by showing how our moral judgments can themselves lead to structural changes in our community, I try to underscore the dialectical nature of the relationship between morality and politics in general. Likewise, by demonstrating how many of these structural changes involve the creation of a new "we," I try to show how the "we" that Rorty himself assumes as stable over time is constantly in the process of rebirth as a result of our overlapping and often conflicting moral judgments.

By doing both things together, I hope not only to underscore the dynamic nature of our social practices in general, but to develop a mode of pragmatic analysis that is both sensitive to group interpretations and more politically informed than other versions of pragmatism. But it might still be said of my own analysis that I do not take differences seriously enough in that I am willing to talk about both concepts of moral responsibility which, while applied differently, are relatively unified, and general rules of a practice that are less rough at the edges than they might be in practice. I do not dismiss such a challenge out of hand, but I do try to show throughout the study why pragmatists are not obliged to talk about "endless difference"[43] and how they might as pragmatists generalize about our concepts and the practices of which they are a part on the basis of both the shared assumptions of historical actors and the practical concerns and goals that they as inquirers bring to their own analysis of particular social practices.

Since my own analysis begins with the stated goal of establishing channels of communication among us with regard to our moral responsibility for external harm, I am necessarily led to zero in on both the assumptions that many (if not all) of us share about the nature of moral responsibility and the conventions and expectations that best help to explain many (if not all) of our major differences concerning the moral responsibility of particular individuals for the suffering of others. Not surprisingly, the picture that I paint leaves out much detail and necessarily imposes a level of generality upon us that does not necessarily reflect the particularities of our respective lives. But such an imposition is not necessarily "wrong"—as long as the pragmatist both takes responsibility for it and acknowledges that in recording the rules of a particular practice, she has not only imposed on them her own purposes of inquiry, but has intervened into them by virtue of the picture that she has painted of them.

Pragmatists such as Lyotard and Rorty contend that they can "read off" of or "embellish" the practices which they study without altering them. But such a contention becomes problematic when we acknowledge that social practices are not the distinct, naturally bounded entities that philosophers often assume they are. They are configurations of rules and actions that extend out into the world in ways that make it difficult for us to distinguish between them.

While we might be able to distinguish between our various social practices and even locate a cultural "we," we cannot do so without imposing our own boundaries on them. In my analysis of moral responsi-

43. Postmodernists are frequently accused of taking "endless difference" as their starting point. For an excellent discussion of this possibility, see Susan Bordo, "Feminism, Postmodernism, and Gender Skepticism," in *Feminism/Postmodernism,* ed. Linda Nicholson (London, 1990), 133–56.

bility, I expand the boundaries of what is conventionally understood as our practice of moral responsibility in order to establish a basis upon which we can argue openly about our moral responsibility for the suffering of others. I also focus on controversies that are themselves socially and politically charged. Hence, I am bound to emphasize the political aspects of our practice of moral responsibility more than I might do if, say, I had begun with a question of aesthetics. Likewise, I am bound to take a particular view of it that is more clearly political than other views that we might take.

By taking this view, I am also led both to shape the practice according to my own purposes and goals and to emphasize one cultural tradition over others, a cultural tradition that I can characterize at this point only as one that takes the modern, distinctly secular, notion of moral blameworthiness seriously. Rorty and his followers assume that they can identify a homogeneous "we." Hence, they feel free to talk about "our" traditions and beliefs. But "we" are many different communities, and "our" traditions and beliefs do not form one seamless web. Thus, it is inevitable that in describing a particular social practice, we will not only emphasize one set of traditions over another, but in doing so shape that practice according to who "we" are.

Moreover, we will inevitably become participants in the practices that we explore to the extent that we highlight particular aspects of them over others. But we will not have to consider ourselves mere "conversationalists." For pragmatism, as I present it throughout what follows, requires us to explore both the historical evolution of our social and political concepts and the function that these concepts now serve in our community. If pragmatists such as Rorty were to acknowledge in practice what they obviously recognize in theory, namely, the importance of discerning the practical context in which our concepts developed, they would be led to take a more openly historical approach to the concepts which they purport to be embellishing. Likewise, they would be forced to explore how those concepts, along with the social practices of which they are a part, function in our larger community.

But they would not, as pragmatists, have to discover *the* historical source or function of our social and political concepts. Nor would they have to go outside of our social and political practices to argue for change within the practices themselves. As Rorty himself makes clear, any change in the governance of a practice will have to come from within, as a result of either contradictions inherent in the practice itself or of difficulties encountered by individuals in trying to apply the practice to new situations. I argue below that in their efforts to argue about moral responsibility in politically controversial cases, contemporary social actors have not only begun to expose the contradictions inherent in our modern conception of moral responsibility, but have done so in such a way that we are able to get beyond these contradictions and develop a more practical way of talking about our moral responsibility for the suffering of others.

PART ONE

2

Communal Blame and the
Classical Worldview

Why We Cannot All Be Kantians

Throughout chapters 2, 3, and 4, I explore the nature of, and distinctions between, the Classical, Christian and modern concepts of moral responsibility. I do so both to understand the evolution of our own concept of moral responsibility and to challenge the assumption that the Classical and Christian concepts are inadequate because they do not recognize the importance of contra-causal freedom. I argue not only that the concept of moral responsibility has changed in significant ways over the years, but that it has done so in response to changes in our social practice of blaming.

Most scholars who talk about moral responsibility assume that there are no significant differences between the three concepts, or in other words, that the notion of blameworthiness associated with each has remained constant over time. Likewise, they assume that the notion of blameworthiness in question is our own and that it requires contra-causal freedom. Hence, they feel free to chastise those who do not recognize the importance of contra-causal freedom to moral responsibility.

While Christian philosophers are labeled naive, Classical philosophers, and especially Aristotle, are contrasted unfavorably to those modern moral philosophers who recognize the importance of contra-causal freedom. A. W. Adkins argues that because Aristotle does not impute moral agency to individuals, he is unable to develop the "enlightened" concept of moral responsibility that we ourselves possess.[1]

---

1. A. W. H. Adkins, *Merit and Responsibility: A Study in Greek Values* (Chicago, 1959), 334. Adkins's remarks here come out of a careful study of Greek philosophy and tragedy. Hence, we cannot help but be surprised at their arrogance—until we recall his earlier comments on the "moral deficiency of those who are so unfortunate as not to be Kantians" (3).

W. D. Ross argues that although Aristotle's concept of moral responsibility is clearly superior to that of Plato, it is deficient in a number of respects, including both its failure to develop an adequate notion of free will and its contention that moral responsibility is a kind of desire (which, according to Ross, "it plainly is not").[2]

Adkins and Ross not only assume that the modern notion of moral blameworthiness associated with Kant and others is the only one worth pursuing, but go on to chastise Aristotle for not developing the notion of free will that it entails. Adkins is totally open about his Kantian biases; he writes that Aristotle's concept of moral responsibility is an "indication of the moral deficiency of those who are so unfortunate as not to be Kantians."[3] Ross, unlike Adkins, does not posit Kantianism as an absolute standard for judging the value of all moral theories. But like so many other of Aristotle's commentators, he assumes that Aristotle should be able to account for our modern notion of moral blameworthiness by developing a modern notion of free will.[4]

I challenge this assumption below by presenting both the Classical and the Christian concepts of moral responsibility as coherent on their own terms and by showing that neither concept entails contra-causal freedom. I argue that while we may not ourselves want to accept the premises on which these two concepts of moral responsibility are based, we have to acknowledge that they are coherent in that the notion of free will that they develop is consistent with their respective notions of blameworthiness. I argue that the modern concept of moral responsibility, on the other hand, is *not* coherent, in that it assumes a notion of moral blameworthiness that is not supportable in a secular context (even if contra-causal freedom does exist).

How, if the modern concept of moral responsibility is not theoretically supportable, can we as modern individuals manage to discover moral responsibility in the world? I suggest that we do so by relying on both the Christian notion of sinfulness and our own social practice of blaming (via the volitional excuses that we invoke to discover free will). While our reliance on the Christian notion of sinfulness is generally not self-conscious, our reliance on volitional excuses is often quite open, and if we are philosophers, coupled with a reference to Aristotle.

The interesting thing is how often contemporary philosophers use the association between volitional excuses and Aristotle's theory of

2. W. D. Ross, *Aristotle* (London, 1960), 200–201.

3. Adkins, *Merit and Responsibility*, 3. On page 2 of the same work Adkins proclaims that with regard to moral responsibility, "we are all Kantians now."

4. Ross, *Aristotle*, 199.

blameworthiness to bolster their own distinctly modern concept of moral responsibility.[5] Dennis Thompson, for instance, develops a theory of Aristotelian excuses to support what is clearly a modern or Kantian understanding of moral blameworthiness.[6] Jonathan Glover turns to Aristotelian excuses without giving up the modern distinction between moral and social blameworthiness.[7] And Bernard Williams, who is clearly far more sensitive than most others to Aristotle's general worldview, uses Aristotle's volitional excuses in *Ethics and the Limits of Philosophy* to bolster his own more purely modern notion of moral agency.[8]

I suggest that we cannot rely on either the Christian or the Classical concepts of moral responsibility to bolster our own. For all three concepts rest on mutually exclusive notions of moral blameworthiness. While the Christian notion of sinfulness requires an all-powerful God to blame individuals, the modern concept of moral responsibility denies the relevance of such an authority. Likewise, while the notion of voluntariness registered in the absence of an Aristotelian excuse depends on our own standards of social blameworthiness, the modern concept of moral responsibility views such standards as irrelevant to moral blameworthiness.

In my efforts to articulate the three concepts of moral responsibility I try to avoid viewing the Classical and Christian understandings through Kantian eyes. But I cannot hope to provide an objective description of each concept, since the most that any conceptual analyst can do is bring together common strands of thought which inevitably differ in particular respects and which in any case are always open to interpretation. Moreover, the term "moral responsibility" has been in use for only two centuries.[9]

---

5. Two notable exceptions are Martha Nussbaum and Jean Roberts. In *The Fragility of Goodness: Luck and Ethics in Greek Tragedy and Philosophy* (Cambridge, England, 1986), Nussbaum provides us with an excellent discussion of why the classical and modern concepts of moral responsibility cannot be invoked together. See especially 282–89. In "Aristotle on Responsibility for Action and Character, *Ancient Philosophy* 9 (1989), 23–36, Roberts makes it crystal clear that "Aristotle's notion of voluntariness does not coincide with any later notion of moral responsibility" (25).

6. Dennis Thompson, *Political Ethics and Public Office* (Cambridge, Mass., 1987), 40–65.

7. Jonathon Glover, *Responsibility* (London, 1970), 49–61.

8. Bernard Williams, *Ethics and the Limits of Philosophy* (Cambridge, England, 1985).

9. The first use of the term recorded in Murray's *Oxford English Dictionary* was by Alexander Hamilton in 1789 in *The Federalist Papers*. Albert Jonsen writes in *Responsibility in Modern Religious Ethics* (Washington, 1968) that the term appeared somewhat earlier in French, most notably in Pascal's *Lettres Provinciales* (1656), although Jonsen fails to point out that Pascal's own words are "responsibility and blame," rather than "moral responsi-

How, if the term has been in use for only two centuries, can contemporary interpreters talk about Classical and Christian thinkers as having a concept of moral responsibility? Presumably, they notice that both Classical and Christian thinkers posit causation as a condition of blameworthiness. Hence they feel free to assume that both groups share our own concern for moral responsibility, since moral responsibility as we now construe it is a matter of both causation and blameworthiness together.

But we have to be careful here. For while both Classical and Christian philosophers may have expressed concern for both causation and blameworthiness together, they did not attach the same meanings that we do to each. Nor did they view the two terms as related in the same way that we do. (While we employ one term to cover both causation and blameworthiness together, they talked about causation as one among several conditions of blameworthiness.) Hence, if we want to carve out of their writings a concept of moral responsibility, we will have to ask not only what each group meant by causation and blameworthiness but exactly how they construed the two terms as related.

My assumption here is that by taking each of the three concepts of moral responsibility on their own terms, we can both avoid writing Kantian assumptions back into others' works and discern what is special about our own concept of moral responsibility. Likewise, by tracing the evolution of our own concept of moral responsibility out of earlier concepts, we can both understand its nature more fully and explain the contradictions inherent in it. But we cannot do either of these two things without reorienting our attention away from the conventional focus on free will to the nature of blameworthiness associated with each concept.

As things now stand, those who talk about moral responsibility generally focus on free will rather than on blameworthiness. Moreover, when they do recognize the importance of blameworthiness, they assume that it has remained constant over time. But clearly moral responsibility is a matter of both free will and blameworthiness together. Moreover, as I suggest below, the notion of free will has evolved over time in the context of changes in our social practice of blaming. Hence we might want to begin with blameworthiness, and not free will, in our discussions of moral responsibility.

By doing so, we will be able not only to fill out the concept of moral

---

bility." For an extremely interesting discussion of the term's evolution, see Richard McKeon, "The Development and Significance of the Concept of Responsibility," *Revue Internationale de Philosophie* II (1957), 3–32.

responsibility, but to underscore the extent to which the concept of free will has evolved in part as a way of supporting particular understandings of blameworthiness. I argue not only that our social practice of blaming has changed in important ways over the years, but that particular communities have endeavored to rework the notion of free will associated with moral responsibility in light of these changes. Likewise, I suggest that if we want to understand how the modern concept of moral responsibility has evolved out of its Classical and Christian counterparts, we will have to pay special attention to both the evolving nature of blameworthiness and the different notions of free will that have been associated with it.

I suggest that the best way to do both things is to go back through various philosophical and religious texts that were written in defense of particular understandings of blameworthiness. For these texts enable us not only to explore the nature of blameworthiness assumed during each period, but to grasp the notion of free will required by it. I argue that while the philosophical debates about free will and determinism that we find in these texts may appear to be distinct from the practice of blaming, they are ultimately part of that practice in ways that I try to demonstrate.

How, one might ask, can we talk about unified notions of blameworthiness? In the case of Aristotle, we can assume that he has articulated in at least a somewhat accurate fashion the notion of blameworthiness embraced by his community. (I defend this assumption in my discussion of Aristotle's general moral theory.) In the case of both Christian and modern thinkers, we can look for assumptions about blameworthiness held in common and shared by other members of their respective communities.

But we cannot assume, in sketching the concepts of moral responsibility found in these texts, that we have captured *the* concept of moral responsibility developed in any one period. Instead, we can only hope to capture a general set of shared assumptions about blameworthiness and the notion of free will required by it. I attempt to capture both in this chapter by reconstructing what I take to be Aristotle's concept of moral responsibility.

Aristotle and the Conditions of Voluntariness

Aristotle develops most of his ideas about causation and blameworthiness in book 3, chapter 1, of the *Nicomachean Ethics,* where he explores the two primary conditions under which we blame individuals for their bad actions. The first condition is that the individual's actions were indeed bad, a condition that Aristotle thinks can easily be met with reference to our communal standards of acceptable behavior. The second condition is that the individual's actions were voluntary, or at least not involuntary. "When our actions are voluntary, we receive praise and blame, when involuntary, we are pardoned and sometimes even pitied."[10]

Aristotle's overall task in book 3, chapter 1, is to articulate the latter of these two conditions and to show how it can be used to ground a coherent view of praise and blame. Although he focuses primarily on our social acts of blaming rather than on our legal institutions of punishment, he does not completely ignore the institutions of punishment or treat them as separate from our social judgments. Indeed, he makes clear that both forms of accountability rest on very similar standards of voluntariness, standards which are "indispensable" to students of virtue and "useful" to lawgivers when they mete out legal punishments.[11]

Three methodological points are worth making at the outset. The first is that while Aristotle refers to his approach to the study of moral responsibility as scientific, he does not set out to discover the conditions under which individuals are, in a purely factual sense, morally blameworthy for having brought about harm. Instead, he tries to distill out of our social practice of blaming the conditions under which we conceive of individuals as acting in a blameworthy fashion. These conditions are, as we shall see, based not on an ideal assessment of moral responsibility, but on the systematization of what is "generally recognized" by all of us, that involuntary actions are not appropriate grounds for blaming individuals.[12]

The second methodological point is that while Aristotle is clearly a teleological thinker in many respects, he does not develop a teleological understanding of blameworthiness as he does when talking about, say, justice or the good life. In other words, he does not talk about blameworthiness as related to the ends of human action. Instead, he views blameworthiness as part of the social practice of blaming, a practice which he explicitly articulates throughout his writings.[13]

The third methodological point is that while Aristotle concentrates

10. Aristotle, *Nicomachean Ethics,* trans. Martin Ostwald (Indianapolis, 1962), 52. I use this translation throughout my discussion of Aristotle's concept of moral responsibility.

11. Ibid.

12. Ibid.

13. For an excellent discussion of the relevance of Aristotle's teleological outlook to his moral and political thought, see Bernard Yack, *The Problems of a Political Animal: Community, Conflict, and Justice in Aristotelian Political Thought* (forthcoming, Berkeley, 1992).

primarily on involuntariness rather than on voluntariness, he does not, as J. L. Austin and others suggest, develop a wholly negative approach to moral responsibility.[14] Instead, he assumes that once he has explored the boundaries of involuntary actions, he will have shown us what it means for an action to be voluntary. Likewise, he assumes that once he has articulated the conditions under which we consider volitional excuses to be acceptable or unacceptable, he will have provided us with the basis for taking actions which are our own.[15]

Aristotle focuses his attention in book 3, chapter 1, on two sorts of volitional excuses in particular: those based on constraint and those based on ignorance. He argues that if an individual who acted badly can justifiably fall back on either sort of volitional excuse, his actions can be considered involuntary and he can be excused from blame. Likewise, if the individual cannot justifiably fall back on an excuse such as ignorance or constraint, his actions can be considered voluntary and he can be considered worthy of our blame.

Since Aristotle's overall task is to break down and reassemble the conditions under which we blame individuals in general, he finds it necessary to ask two questions about the excuses that he invokes. First of all, what do the notions of constraint and ignorance inherent in them mean about an individual's actions? Second, under what conditions can an individual justifiably fall back on such excuses? (In other words, under what conditions can we consider the excuses valid?)

Critics of Aristotle often focus on the first of these two questions and give short shrift to the second. In other words, they tend to concentrate on what Aristotle means by ignorance and constraint per se, rather than on the conditions under which ignorance and constraint can be considered valid excuses. Hence, they find it relatively easy to view Aristotle as striving to develop a notion of free will rather than as establishing the conditions of social blameworthiness.

But Aristotle was not, I suggest below, concerned primarily with free will or an individual's own state of mind in the way that modern thinkers are when they talk about moral responsibility. Instead he was concerned primarily with the conditions under which we as social and political blamers consider an individual's actions to have been voluntary or involuntary. Hence, he concentrated the bulk of his energies in book 3, chapter 1, not on the nature of voluntariness per se, but on the conditions under which members of a particular community consider volitional excuses such as constraint and ignorance to be acceptable.

14. See, for example, Austin's discussion of responsibility in "A Plea For Excuses," *Proceedings of the Aristotelian Society* 57 (1956–57), 1–30.
15. Aristotle, *Nicomachean Ethics,* 57.

Aristotle begins by providing two very general definitions of actions which are constrained and actions which are the result of ignorance. Constrained actions are characterized by the fact that the "initiative or source of motion comes from without."[16] They are actions "in which the agent or person acted upon contributes nothing."[17] What does it mean for an individual to "contribute nothing" to his actions? Aristotle addresses this question by providing us with two examples.

The first example is that of an individual who is carried away by a strong wind to a place where he did not want to go. Since the individual in this case is unable to control his situation in even the most basic physical sense, he can, according to Aristotle, be understood as contributing nothing to it. The second example is that of a bad action, e.g., theft, which is motivated by a noble purpose, e.g., the saving of others' lives. According to Aristotle, this action is mixed in nature, although it comes closer to being voluntary than involuntary.

In cases such as these, the agent acts voluntarily, because the initiative in moving the parts of the body which act as instruments rests with the agent himself: and where the source of motion is within oneself, it is in one's power to act or not to act.[18]

The upshot of both examples is that the involuntariness or voluntariness of an individual's action rests on the amount of control that he can exert over both external harm and his own physical and mental capacities. In the first example, such control was taken away from the individual by the physical circumstances of his action. In the second example, the individual did not have as many choices open to him as he might have had if he had been placed in another situation. But he was still able to control not only his own bodily movements and mental faculties, but, to a lesser extent, the events that resulted from them.

While Aristotle claims that the individual's actions in this second example are mostly voluntary, he acknowledges that they are involuntary to the extent that the individual did not choose them for their own sake. Likewise, he makes clear that in general the end for which an action is performed depends partly on when it was chosen. If the end in question was chosen at the outset rather than, say, as a last resort, then it is more likely to be voluntary than involuntary. In this sense, Aristotle writes, "the terms 'voluntary' and 'involuntary' are to be used with reference to the moment of action."[19]

16. Ibid., 52.
17. Ibid., 54.
18. Ibid., 53.
19. Ibid.

Aristotle's concern here is largely with the amount of control that an individual has over both himself and his circumstances. But control cannot be everything, or rather it cannot be a purely physical matter. For Aristotle is unwilling to accept pleas of constraint in two cases where individuals would seem to have very little control. The first case is one in which an individual is faced with death if he does not perform a very cruel action. The second is one in which an individual is compelled to act wrongly by virtue of his drunkenness.

Aristotle argues with regard to the first case that the individual cannot validly plea constraint on the grounds that he was forced by his circumstances to do so. For there are "acts which no man can possibly be compelled to do, but rather than do them he should accept the most terrible suffering and death."[20] Aristotle's point here is that whether we consider an act voluntary or involuntary depends not only on the individual's state of mind, but on our own sense of what sorts of actions an individual can be expected to resist. In the case that Aristotle cites, it is because we expect individuals not to perform very cruel acts in order to save themselves that we reject the characterization of the individual's actions as involuntary.

Not surprisingly, such expectations also enter into Aristotle's rejection of drunkenness as a valid plea of compulsion. Individuals who are drunk are clearly out of control, especially if they are very drunk. But Aristotle rejects drunkenness as a form of involuntariness on the grounds that individuals can be expected not to get drunk. While Aristotle does not explore the source of such expectations, he does make clear both that there are sorts of compulsion that individuals can be expected to resist and that "praise or blame depends on whether or not a man successfully resists compulsion."[21]

Aristotle acknowledges that he has not shown that voluntary actions are totally free from external determination. Indeed, he goes so far as to state that all actions are to some extent determined by external forces. But such determinism does not bother him in the way that it bothers modern philosophers. Nor need it do so. For Aristotle, as we shall see, is not concerned to articulate an absolute notion of voluntariness. Nor is he concerned to justify a notion of blameworthiness that is free from the contingencies of the phenomenal world. Instead, he is concerned only to systematize the criteria of voluntariness that we invoke in our social practice of blaming.

Aristotle underscores the relationship between these criteria of vol-

20. Ibid.
21. Ibid.

untariness and our social practice of blaming in his refutation of those who would view all actions as both constrained and involuntary. Aristotle's concern here is that if all acts were considered constrained and involuntary, we would have to conclude that noble acts are performed under constraint because the pleasant and the noble are external to us and have compelling power. Aristotle does not choose to refute such a conclusion on the basis of an analysis of constraint or involuntariness per se. Instead, he chooses to refute it by pointing out the "absurd" consequences it would have for our social practice of blaming.[22]

Aristotle proceeds in a similar fashion when he talks about pleas of ignorance. He begins by acknowledging that individuals never act with complete knowledge of their situation. But he points out that we cannot characterize all of their acts as involuntary. Where, then, do we draw the line? Aristotle does not answer this question by analyzing the nature of ignorance per se. Instead, he proceeds to explore a set of distinctions that we invoke in practice for separating voluntary actions from actions that are involuntary.

The primary distinction that he invokes is that between ignorance of particular circumstances, on the one hand, and moral ignorance, on the other. According to Aristotle, we cannot consider an act involuntary because the agent in question is ignorant of right and wrong. "Ignorance in moral choice does not make an act involuntary—it makes it wicked."[23] But we can consider an act involuntary if it is based on ignorance of either the particular issues or the circumstances associated with the action itself. "It is on these acts that pity and pardon depend, for a person who acts in ignorance of a particular circumstance acts involuntarily."[24]

By "ignorance of particular circumstances" Aristotle has several things in mind, including ignorance of the act that one is performing, ignorance of the results of one's actions, and ignorance of the manner in which these actions are performed. Aristotle points out that while no one except a madman could be ignorant of all these factors, a person might easily not realize what he is doing, say, if he divulges a secret without knowing that it is a secret. Likewise, he might easily mistake the object of his actions if his friends and enemies look alike or if he mistakenly gives his friend poison instead of water.

Why can such actions as these be considered involuntary and not those based on moral ignorance? Aristotle does not respond to this

22. Ibid., 54.
23. Ibid.
24. Ibid., 56. Aristotle amends his views somewhat in the *Eudemian Ethics* (book 2, chap. 9) by distinguishing between the possession and use of knowledge.

question directly. But he does make clear in another context that individuals can be expected to know certain things, and that if they do not, they cannot use their ignorance to plea involuntariness.[25] Hence, we might want to invoke such expectations and the standards of acceptable behavior on which they are based as a way of showing how Aristotle fills in the content of involuntariness (or in other words, draws a line between acceptable and unacceptable pleas of ignorance).

Aristotle does not explore the nature of voluntariness as thoroughly as the nature of involuntariness. But we can assume that since actions are involuntary when they are either constrained or based on ignorance, they are voluntary when they are not constrained or when they are based on a specific level of knowledge. Aristotle appears to have something like this in mind when he defines a voluntary act as one in which the "initiative lies with the agent who knows the particular circumstances in which the action is performed."[26] But he does not make totally clear what he means by initiative in this context. Hence, there is considerable confusion about the meaning that he attaches to voluntariness.

Four interpretations stand out from the others. The first views Aristotle's notion of voluntariness as interchangeable with moral responsibility itself. While adherents of this interpretation do not spell out what they mean by moral responsibility, they do assume that it entails both causation/voluntariness and blameworthiness. Likewise, while they do not go back to Aristotle's own text to justify such an assumption, they do make clear that both causation/voluntariness and blameworthiness are registered together in the absence of an Aristotelian excuse.

The problem with this interpretation is that it is not really an interpretation of Aristotle at all, but is a misinformed reference to Aristotle as if he were a modern moral philosopher. Aristotle does not, as we shall see, merge voluntariness and blameworthiness into one factual discovery of moral responsibility. Nor does he treat voluntary acts as inherently blameworthy or praiseworthy in the way, say, that Kant treats an individual's will as inherently good or bad. Instead, he views voluntariness as one among several criteria that we invoke in blaming individuals in practice.

The other three interpretations are much more faithful to Aristotle's own meaning in that they do not ascribe to voluntariness the sort of moral value found in Christian or modern discussions of moral respon-

25. In book 2, chapter 9, of the *Eudemian Ethics,* Aristotle argues that an individual who does not possess knowledge can still be blamed if the knowledge which he lacks could easily have been obtained.
26. Ibid., 57.

sibility. The first among them views Aristotle's notion of voluntariness as purely negative or defeasible. The second tries to construct out of Aristotle's writings a modern notion of free will. The third—to which I adhere—views Aristotle's notion of voluntariness as part of our social practice of blaming.

J. L. Austin is perhaps the best-known proponent of the negative interpretation of Aristotelian voluntariness. While he recognizes that it is conventional to present freedom as a positive term, he argues that there is "little doubt that to say that we acted 'freely' is to say that we acted *not* unfreely. . . . Like 'real,' 'free' is only used to rule out the suggestion of its antithesis."[27] H. L. A. Hart, like Austin, attributes to Aristotle a negative interpretation of voluntariness and argues—again, ostensibly with Aristotle—that while words like "voluntary" are generally treated as having a positive force, they do not, as we often assume, serve to designate a particular state of mind. Instead, they serve to exclude a particular range of external forces, such as compulsion and ignorance, from our understanding of human agency.[28]

Austin and Hart are correct to point out that the particular actions that we consider voluntary are often chosen on the basis of what we do not consider to be *in*voluntary actions. But this does not mean that we can do without a positive concept of voluntariness. Indeed, it suggests that such a positive concept exists, if only on a formal level, to be filled in substantively by the very process of elimination that Austin, Hart, and others explore.

Aristotle appears to have such a concept in mind when he describes the nature of a voluntary act.

Since an action is involuntary when it is performed under constraint or through ignorance, a voluntary act would seem to be one in which the initiative lies with the agent who knows the particular circumstances in which the action is performed.[29]

This passage suggests both that Aristotle wants to be able to talk about voluntariness as a positive construct and that what counts as a voluntary action is relative to our own volitional excuses. The question becomes what Aristotle means by the "moving principle" that is "in the agent himself."

While commentators answer this question in a variety of ways, two

27. J. L. Austin, "A Plea for Excuses," *Proceedings of the Aristotelian Society* 57 (1956–57), 6.

28. H. L. A. Hart, "Ascription of Responsibility and Rights," *Proceedings of the Aristotelian Society* 49 (1948–49), 171–94.

29. Aristotle, *Nicomachean Ethics*, 57.

general interpretations have come to the forefront. The most widely accepted among them attributes to Aristotle a theory of free will on the basis of Aristotle's own claim in book 3, chapter 5 that we "cannot trace back our actions to starting points other than those within ourselves."[30] Aristotle does not use a term similar to our own "free will." But according to these scholars, we can assume that he had something very close to free will in mind.

David Furley attributes to Aristotle a theory of "fresh starts."[31] W. F. R. Hardie argues that we can interpret Aristotle as stating here that individuals are the uncaused cause of their actions.[32] John Burnet asserts straightforwardly that "prohairesis is really what we call the will."[33] And while Ross translates *prohairesis* as "choice" in most places, he also claims that "sometimes 'intention' or 'will' would bring out the meaning better" and that Aristotle's doctrine of free choice is "clearly an attempt to formulate a conception of free will."[34]

Not surprisingly, those who attribute to Aristotle a theory of free will are more critical of him than those who do not. Ross argues that "on the whole, we must say that Aristotle shared the plain man's belief in free will but that he did not examine the problem thoroughly."[35] While other commentators may not condescend to Aristotle in the way that Ross does, they do criticize him for not taking into consideration the threat that determinism poses to free will. "How," Jeffrey Silberberg asks, "can we accept Aristotle's theory of free will when we know that he did not take the threat of determinism seriously?"

The interpretation of voluntariness as free will offered here is based on Aristotle's own comments that there is an internal origin of our voluntary conduct. But Ross and others go too far in assuming that "origins" implies "first cause." For as Richard Sorabji makes clear in his excellent discussion of Aristotle's concept of causation, an internal origin may be a member of a chain which stretches back ultimately to external factors.[36] Aristotle needs to be able to exclude necessity from the origins of an individual's action in order to describe an individual as having more than one choice open to him. But he does not need to exclude external cooperating influences. Nor, for that matter, does Aristotle ever try to do

30. Ibid.

31. David Furley, "Self-Movers," in G. E. R. Lloyd and G. E. L. Owen, eds., *Aristotle On Mind and the Senses* (Cambridge, England, 1978), 193–94.

32. W. F. R. Hardie, *Aristotle's Ethical Theory* (Oxford, 1968), 178.

33. John Burnet, *Nicomachean Ethics: Text and Commentary*, (London, 1900), 131.

34. Ross, *Aristotle*, 199.

35. Ibid., 201.

36. Richard Sorabji, *Necessity, Cause, and Blame*, (Ithaca, N.Y., 1981), 231–33.

so. Instead, he argues that if our actions are *necessary*, we cannot be blamed for them.[37]

I suggest later in this chapter that Aristotle's notion of blameworthiness, unlike our own, is completely compatible with determinism. I also suggest that Aristotle's lack of concern for either free will or determinism is due not to ignorance, as Ross and others suggest, but to his particular notion of blameworthiness. Suffice it to point out here that although Aristotle is not obliged to develop a concept of free will or to argue against determinism, he is obliged to explain how he can describe our actions as "up to us"[38] in the sense relevant to his own understanding of moral responsibility.

Aristotle, as it turns out, does not provide us with a full explanation of how actions can be "up to us." But he does provide us with the makings of such an explanation. Recall his definition of involuntariness in book 3, chapter 1 of the *Nicomachean Ethics*, where he argues that an action is involuntary when the individual does not contribute anything to it. Since he defines "voluntary" on the basis of what is involuntary, we might define the voluntary action as one to which an individual contributes something. But curiously, Aristotle does not draw such a conclusion himself. Instead, when he moves from a discussion of involuntariness to a discussion of voluntariness, he simply describes the origin of an individual's act as internal. Hence, it is not surprising that commentators automatically assume that Aristotle is insisting on the *complete* freedom of the individual from external circumstance.

But we need not jump to such a conclusion ourselves. For there are places where Aristotle claims only that we contribute "in a way" to our dispositions and actions.[39] And in any case, he never denies the contributions that external circumstances can make. Indeed, he openly recognizes the influence of external factors such as heritage and family socialization on an individual's choice of actions.[40] Hence, despite the fact that he talks about internal origins, we do not have to assume that these origins are exclusive or are not part of a chain which stretches back ultimately to external factors.

What, then, in a positive way, can Aristotle mean by an action's "being up to us"? What is the "something" which, according to Aristotle, we

37. Ibid., 235.

38. Aristotle, *Nicomachean Ethics, The Complete Works of Aristotle,* ed. Jonathan Barnes (Princeton, 1984), 1954. Aristotle makes a similar claim in book 2 of the *Eudemian Ethics,* where he adds "up to him to refrain" from acting.

39. Sorabji makes this claim in *Necessity, Cause, and Blame,* 227–42, by reconstructing passages from Aristotle.

40. Aristotle, *Nicomachean Ethics,* 295–97.

contribute to our voluntary actions? Aristotle provides us with two clues here. The first is his reference to punishment as proof that our conduct is up to us. (Aristotle claims not only that "all actions in which the initiative lies in ourselves are in our power and are voluntary actions," but that such a claim is "corroborated by the judgment of private individuals and by the practice of lawgivers who chastise and punish evil doers, except those who have acted under constraint or due to some ignorance.")[41] The second is the set of criteria that he uses to specify when the volitional excuses that he has already cited are valid.

Interestingly enough, Aristotle cites the effectiveness of punishment, not as a threat to voluntariness, but as a way of showing that voluntariness exists. Similarly, he explores our criteria of punishment, not to defeat the possibility of voluntariness, but to make explicit the conditions under which individuals are considered to have the "power to act" in practice.[42] Here he makes three observations. First of all, we do not blame or punish individuals if they acted under constraint or out of ignorance. Second, when we praise and blame individuals, we do so partly with a practical purpose in mind: to encourage individuals to perform good actions and avoid bad ones in the future.[43] Third, we are never encouraged to perform actions which we cannot perform.

Nobody encourages us to perform what is not within our power and what is not voluntary: there would be no point in trying to stop by persuasion a man from feeling hot, in pain, or hungry.[44]

Aristotle clearly does not treat voluntariness as an absolute power in the way modern thinkers treat free will. Indeed, he recognizes that voluntariness is a relative phenomenon whose contours rest on both an individual's powers to perform a particular action and the individual's malleability vis-à-vis our social practice of blaming. If the individual could have been motivated by our social practice of blaming to take control of his own situation and to act in a salutary fashion, then we can say that he has met the minimal conditions of voluntariness.[45]

41. Ibid.
42. Ibid.
43. Ibid. In line with this observation, Aristotle writes in book 1 of the *Nicomachean Ethics* that in "morally weak men we praise the reason that guides them and the rational element of the soul, because it exhorts them to follow the right path and do what is best" (31).
44. Ibid., 65.
45. Jean Roberts, in "Aristotle on Responsibility" (25), uses these and other of Aristotle's observations to argue that according to Aristotle, "voluntary actions are the sorts of actions that, in principle, one can be trained or become habituated or be educated to do or not to do."

But these conditions are not sufficient in themselves. If we are going to consider an individual's bad actions voluntary, we will have to be able to view the sort of control that he did not exert as the sort that he could have been expected to exert. Aristotle does not expect individuals to exert complete control over themselves in the way, say, that seventeenth-century Puritans did. But he does expect them not to act negligently or to get drunk. Hence, he concludes in the case of negligence that "it was in the offender's power not to be ignorant."[46] The same sort of argument holds true for compulsion. Aristotle points out that the penalty is twice as high if an individual acted in a state of drunkenness, "because the initiative was his own: he had the power not to get drunk."[47]

But he does not have the power not to get drunk in any absolute sense, say, involving contra-causal freedom. His power comes instead from both his ability to abstain from drinking if he chooses to do so and our own sense that individuals can be expected to resist, i.e., not indulge in, the sort of compulsion associated with heavy drinking. Such an expectation, like Aristotle's refusal to accept pleas of ignorance based on laziness or negligence, may appear to be a matter of universal principle. But it is clearly relative to the cultural standards of Aristotle's own community. (Presumably, Aristotle's community did not go as far as our own in allowing for excuses such as junk-food depression, but it at least allowed for excuses based on mental illness—which was more than many seventeenth-century Puritan communities were willing to do.)

The "ability to do otherwise" that emerges from Aristotle's treatment of volitional excuses is thus very much related not only to the individual's own abilities, but to our largely conventional expectations of him. Likewise, the sense of "power" that Aristotle associates with voluntariness is something that must be understood as resting not only on an individual's malleability and personal preferences, but on our own standards of acceptable behavior. Since Aristotle develops these standards in the context of his discussion of blameworthiness, we should not be surprised at their lack of precision. Nor should we be dismayed that they make voluntariness a murky category. For voluntariness may simply be a murky category when properly understood as part of our social practice of blaming.

Aristotle makes this point himself in book 2, chapter 9, of the *Nicomachean Ethics,* where he writes that "it is not easy to determine by a formula at what point and for how great a divergence a man deserves blame, but this difficulty is, after all, true of all objects of sense percep-

---

46. Ibid., 66.
47. Ibid., 65.

tions."[48] Aristotle had already laid the foundations of this point in book 1 by arguing that in matters of action we can never be precise; nor should we try to be. For the subject matter is itself fluid. "Any discussion on matters of action cannot be more than an outline and is bound to lack precision; for . . . one can demand of a discussion only what the subject matter permits and there are no fixed data in matters concerning action."[49]

I should point out here that in focusing on the fluid communal standards that we use to evaluate particular pleas of ignorance and compulsion, I have provided one possible interpretation of Aristotle's notion of voluntariness. I think that it is the appropriate interpretation of voluntariness in the context of Aristotle's arguments about blameworthiness. But it is not the only appropriate interpretation that might fit Aristotle's general works. Indeed, I suspect that it is because Aristotle meant something slightly different by voluntariness in other contexts, e.g., in his writings about deliberation, that we are now confronted with so many different interpretations of his concept of voluntariness.

I do think, though, that if our concern is with Aristotle's concept of moral responsibility rather than, say, with his theory of deliberation, we should explore what voluntariness means to him in his discussions of blameworthiness. I have suggested on the basis of such an exploration that voluntariness does not mean for Aristotle anything like our modern notion of free will. Instead, it means both that in acting, the individual, rather than something or someone else, did that for which he is being blamed, not out of ignorance or compulsion (unless either was intentionally brought about by the individual himself), and that in doing so, he registered something about his character or desires which, if bad, are alterable through blame.[50]

The interpretation of voluntariness that I have provided here jibes, I have suggested, with several aspects of Aristotle's' thought, including his discussion of voluntariness and his claim that punishment is a proof that our conduct is up to us. It also jibes, I suggest below, with three other aspects of Aristotle's thought. One is his treatment of adults, chil-

48. Ibid., 51.

49. Ibid., 35.

50. Jean Roberts, in "Aristotle on Responsibility" (25), offers a similar interpretation of Aristotle's concept of voluntariness when she writes that "an action is voluntary only if it reveals something about the particular agent. . . . Voluntary actions are the sorts of actions that, in principle, one can be educated to do or not to do." Roberts makes it a point in her discussion of responsibility to underscore that "this notion of voluntariness, which isolates one particular kind of cause or explanation, does not coincide, as far as I can see, with any later notion of moral responsibility" (25).

dren, and animals together in his discussion of responsibility. The other two are the particular conception of blameworthiness that he associates with voluntariness and his choice to talk about voluntariness in the context of a discussion of volitional excuses.

The Responsibility of Children

Aristotle is, as his readers have frequently pointed out, content to assume that his notion of voluntariness can be shared by children, animals, and adults. He argues in book 3 of the *Nicomachean Ethics*, for example, that those who deny "that even animals or even children are capable of acting voluntarily" are wrong and "that even children and animals have a share in the voluntary."[51] How can Aristotle make such a claim without distorting the nature of responsibility itself? Aristotle's critics argue that he cannot make such a claim without distorting the nature of both responsibility and voluntariness, as well as morality in general. But they do so only by attributing to Aristotle a concept of moral responsibility—the Kantian—which, I have tried to show, Aristotle did not share.

T. H. Irwin, for example, makes his criticism of Aristotle rest on the need for a theory of responsibility that is more adult and exclusive, one that insists that only creatures who engage in rational deliberation about, and have control over, their actions and states of affairs should be held morally responsible for their actions. According to Irwin, "a person is responsible for her actions and states of affairs in so far as she proceeds from states of character that are in her control as a rational agent." "A rational person will choose the states of character that involve rational control and, if she does not, she fails to realize her nature as a rational agent."[52]

If Irwin's characterization of Aristotle's concept of responsibility were accurate, then he would be correct to find fault with Aristotle's ascription of responsibility to children and animals. But Irwin's characterization of Aristotle's concept of moral responsibility is inaccurate to the extent that he confuses it with Kant's. Aristotle does not view moral responsibility as having its source in the "rational control" or free will of adult human beings. Nor does he view voluntariness as transcendent. Voluntariness is, for Aristotle, something mediated by social and political norms and dependent on criteria of malleability. Since Aristotle views voluntariness as something mediated by social and political norms and dependent on criteria of malleability, he is justified in claiming that the actions of chil-

51. Ibid., 57.
52. T. H. Irwin, *Aristotle's First Principles* (Oxford, 1988), 373–74.

dren and animals are sometimes voluntary. Likewise, since he makes clear that individuals are deserving of blame, not because their noumenal selves have violated the moral law, but because there is something wrong with them that can be corrected, he is justified in holding adults and children responsible for their actions on the same basis, even though the forms of blame are somewhat different. (In the case of animals and small children, blame is a matter of directing irrational desires. In the case of adults, it is a matter of changing rational desires as well.)

Once we take Aristotle on his own terms rather than on those of Kant, we see that Aristotle does not distort either blame or voluntariness in his discussion of children and animals. Indeed, he may do just the opposite by shedding light on both. Moreover, if we ourselves were to begin with Aristotle's terms rather than with Kant's in our discussions of responsibility, we might be able to understand our own practice of blaming better than we now do. How so?

First of all, like Aristotle, we would be able to talk about the blaming of both children and the mentally impaired in terms of voluntariness. Likewise, we would be able to draw distinctions between different sorts of voluntariness and ask what sorts of blameworthiness are appropriate to them. As things now stand, we tend to construe voluntariness as an all-or-nothing thing. Hence, we find it difficult not only to talk about the voluntary actions of children and the mentally impaired, but to draw distinctions between different levels of voluntariness and ask what each means for blameworthiness.

If we were to view voluntariness as something mediated by social and political norms and dependent on criteria of malleability, we might be able to distinguish between different levels of voluntariness and discuss openly what sorts of blameworthiness are appropriate to each. Moreover, we might, like Aristotle, be able to avoid positing what Martha Nussbaum refers to as a "mysterious shift" in human nature that takes place as we move from childhood to maturity, a shift that, Nussbaum rightly points out, Aristotle himself avoids by virtue of his particular concept of voluntariness.[53] While we would still have to talk about children as different from adults in many respects relevant to moral judgment, we would not, contrary to Irwin's insistence, have to explain a cutting-off point between childhood and adulthood. Instead, we could talk about a gradual transition from one point to the other which brings with it new forms of voluntary action and blame.[54]

53. Nussbaum, *Fragility of Goodness*, 285.
54. For a series of excellent (and more detailed) discussions of Aristotle on the responsibility of children and adults, see Nussbaum, *Fragility of Goodness*, 285–87; Sorabji, *Necessity, Cause, and Blame*, 227–33; Yack, *Political Animal;* and Roberts, "Aristotle on

Blameworthiness, Communal Standards, and the Primacy of Moral Luck

Scholars who set out to articulate Aristotle's concept of moral responsibility often forget about blameworthiness in their efforts to discover what Aristotle means by voluntariness. Likewise, when they do refer to blameworthiness, they often confuse Aristotle's notion with our own or else ask a more contemporary question: Does Aristotle provide us with the conditions of blameworthiness as we ourselves understand it?[55] But certainly we need to know what Aristotle himself means by blameworthiness if we want to understand both his general concept of responsibility and his particular understanding of voluntariness (which, recall, he develops in the context of a discussion of praise and blame).

Aristotle talks about praise and blame throughout the *Nicomachean Ethics*. But unlike, say, the early Christian philosophers, he does not fully spell out what he means by blameworthiness. Nor does he distinguish between blameworthiness and other sorts of accountability. Hence, it is up to us to piece together a concept by exploring his own use of the term and by asking what blameworthiness signified more generally during the Classical period.

First of all, Aristotle cannot possibly have a notion of blameworthiness in mind that transcends social and political practices. For he makes clear at the outset of book 3 of the *Nicomachean Ethics* that his discussion of volitional excuses is useful not only for those who want to clarify our social practice of blaming, but "useful also for lawgivers, to help them in meting out honors and punishments."[56] Likewise, he stresses that in articulating the conditions of blameworthiness, he is perfectly comfortable in referring to what is "generally recognized" by us all:[57] that we do not blame individuals for bad actions that are involuntary.

Responsibility," 25–27. Roberts's defense of Aristotle on this question includes the very interesting observation that Aristotle's lack of concern for distinguishing between adults and children with regard to responsibility has its source in Aristotle's belief that adults frequently behave like children.

55. T. H. Irwin states outright that we can "expect Aristotle's concept of voluntariness to clarify and justify our own judgments of responsibility" (T. H. Irwin, "Reason and Responsibility in Aristotle," in A. Rorty, ed., *Essays on Aristotle's Ethics*, 137). The interesting thing is that Irwin, unlike many others who talk about Aristotle's concept of moral responsibility, is aware that Aristotle does not articulate our own notion of blameworthiness in book 3 of the *Nicomachean Ethics*. But since he (Irwin) is disdainful of the notion of blameworthiness that Aristotle develops, he feels free to reconstruct out of Aristotle's writings what he calls a "complex theory" of responsibility, a theory that is more conducive to modern forms of accountability.

56. Aristotle, *Nicomachean Ethics*, 52.

57. Ibid.

Blameworthiness for Aristotle, then, is not distinct from more purely social or political forms of accountability. Nor is it in any way supremely rational or absolutely correct. Aristotle himself points out that while our conventions can be rendered more systematic than they now are, they can never achieve the limits of an exact science.[58] Nor would such scientific exactitude be in line with the moral conventions that Aristotle is himself trying to articulate, since these conventions have to do with actions, which are, according to Aristotle, "bound to lack precision."[59]

Moreover, even if blameworthiness were for Aristotle not part of social practice, it could not be considered morally correct in the way that it is, say, for Kant. As K. J. Dover points out, the Greeks did not generally believe in a rational moral system. Nor did they expect their gods to be wholly just. Indeed, according to Dover, most Greeks were aware that propositions about divine justice were not conclusively demonstrable or refutable. Hence, they did not find it necessary to formulate a generalized ideal of either free will or moral blameworthiness.[60]

Nor did they find it necessary to take moral blameworthiness as seriously as we now do. For blameworthiness—moral or otherwise—did not entail the sort of guilt that we now associate with both the Christian and modern concepts of moral responsibility. As J. W. Jones points out in *Law and Legal Theory of the Greeks,* the Greeks did not in general think of themselves as qualified to delve into an individual's mental state for the purpose of distinguishing different degrees of guilt.[61] Naturally it mattered to them what other individuals thought about them. Hence, they did their best to avoid blame. But they did not do so under the impression that they were shunning guilt.

Aristotle, in his efforts to clarify and systematize the social conventions of his day, was not likely to go against these sentiments and develop an absolute notion of moral blameworthiness independent of social and political practice. Nor would doing so make any sense given two other points that he makes about the nature of blameworthiness. One is that our criteria for blameworthiness are relative to the interests of our particular community. The other is that moral luck has an important role in our ascriptions of blameworthiness.

Aristotle makes room for communal standards throughout his theory of moral responsibility. The two most important places are in his standards of good actions and in his standards of honorable character.

58. Ibid., 5.
59. Ibid., 35.
60. K. J. Dover, *Greek Popular Morality in the Time of Plato and Aristotle* (Oxford, 1974), 156–57.
61. J. W. Jones, *Law and Legal Theory of the Greeks* (Oxford, 1956), 261.

He writes about the former that standards of good actions are based on values already existing in society, values which developed out of the practical necessities of communal life. He writes about the latter that standards of honorable character are relative to the sorts of behavior that the community values in its citizens. As Adkins, among others, suggests, "to say 'this is *arete*' is [for Aristotle] to say 'this is the type of man which a state should have if it is to operate efficiently.'"[62]

Aristotle's critics often use the dependence of Aristotle's standards of behavior on communal values to dismiss Aristotle's understanding of moral responsibility as "backward." Adkins, for instance, writes that the "chief impediment in the way of the development of a satisfactory concept of moral responsibility in Greek has hitherto been the nature of *arete*."[63] Likewise, he makes clear that because Aristotle continually appeals to ordinary language in ethical matters, his concept of *arete* cannot help but be inimical to the concept of moral responsibility.[64] But this, of course, would be true only if Aristotle accepted our modern concept of moral responsibility, a concept which is ostensibly independent of worldly contingencies. Aristotle not only did not accept this concept, but made a place in his own concept of moral responsibility for both worldly contingencies and moral luck.

Aristotle talks about moral luck in conjunction with blameworthiness in three general contexts. The first has to do with the circumstances in which our actions are defined. While he does not go so far as to rule out the importance of intentionality to our descriptions of actions, he does concede that luck can cause our intentional descriptions not to be the relevant ones with regard to praiseworthiness and blameworthiness. Indeed, he makes clear in his discussion of Priam's predicament that we can be considered praiseworthy or blameworthy for actions which we do not even recognize as our own.[65]

The second context in which moral luck becomes relevant is that concerning our performance of good and bad actions. Aristotle writes here that while virtue is partly a matter of personal initiatives, it also requires external goods in many cases. "Many actions can be performed only with the help of instruments, as it were: friends, wealth and political power. And there are some external goods the absence of which spoils supreme virtue, e.g., good birth, good children and

62. Adkins, *Merit and Responsibility,* 335.

63. Ibid., 333, 346.

64. Ibid., 336.

65. For an excellent discussion of Priam's predicament as it sheds light on Aristotle's concept of responsibility, see Nussbaum, *Fragility of Goodness,* 333–35.

beauty."[66] While these external goods are sometimes earned, they are often the product of good luck. "Instances of good and likewise of bad luck . . . by their very nature . . . afford the opportunity for noble and good actions."[67]

The third context in which luck becomes relevant to moral responsibility is in Aristotle's discussion of the socialization process through which individuals achieve virtue. Here Aristotle makes clear that virtue requires the existence of both moral instruction and good laws. Moral instruction is necessary to "encourage and stimulate young men of generous mind" and lead them to become "enamored of what is noble and possessed by virtue."[68] Good laws are necessary because even "young men of generous mind" are not naturally inclined to the achievement of virtue; they need to be conditioned by a system of law which is itself the "rule of reason derived from some sort of practical wisdom and intelligence."[69]

The question of luck becomes a matter of birth in this context. "The common run of person," Aristotle writes, cannot be turned to goodness and virtue.[70] For they do not have a notion of what is noble. Nor can they obtain such a notion without moral education. Since moral education is afforded only to young men of the upper classes, poorer men and all women are, by the unfortunate facts of their birth, unable to develop the sort of *arete* that is considered most praiseworthy in Greek society.[71]

While the dependence of blameworthiness on luck would be disastrous for either Kant or the Christian philosophers to concede, it does not threaten Aristotle's concept of moral responsibility. For Aristotle, unlike these others, does not conceive of blameworthiness as a black spot on one's soul. Instead, he conceives of it as part of our social practice of blaming. The same holds true for Aristotle's notion of voluntariness. While the Kantian and Christian notions of free will could in no way tolerate the dependence of blameworthiness on luck, Aristotle's notion of voluntariness is not threatened. Indeed, it appears to be completely compatible with a notion of blameworthiness that is relative to

66. Aristotle, *Nicomachean Ethics*, 21.
67. Ibid., 25.
68. Ibid., 295.
69. Ibid., 297.
70. Ibid., 295.
71. For a more extensive discussion of the exclusion of women from Aristotle's concept of virtue, see Arlene Saxonhouse, "Aristotle: Defective Males, Hierarchy, and the Limits of Politics," in *Feminist Interpretations of Political Theory,* ed. Mary Lyndon Shanley and Carole Pateman (Cambridge, England, 1991), 32–52.

the various sorts of contingencies that characterize our worldly communities.

Volitional Excuses and the Criteria of Blameworthiness

What, though, if we did not know anything about the notion of blameworthiness that Aristotle assumed in his discussions of voluntariness? How could we be sure of our interpretation of it? One way, of course, would be to piece together the scattered comments that Aristotle makes about blameworthiness throughout his writings. Another— much more helpful to the general claims that I want to make in this study—would be to turn to the nature of volitional excuses themselves. I examine the nature of such excuses more thoroughly in chapter 9. But it is useful to note here the absurdity of trying to develop a notion of contra-causal freedom that could be registered in the absence of a volitional excuse of any kind.

First of all, volitional excuses are not factual accounts of our actions that we make in a vacuum. They are pleas or justifications that we make to others as a way of establishing our own innocence or lack of guilt. As such, they cannot be understood outside the context of a relationship between us and actual or potential blamers. Nor can they be considered independent of the communal standards that enable us to say "this is an acceptable excuse," or "this is not."

As I argue more fully in chapter 9, excuses such as ignorance and compulsion are acceptable not because they register something absolute about an individual's will, but because we as a community consider them to be relevant to our social practice of blaming or to our legal practice of punishment. The same holds true for our judgments about whether or not a particular plea of ignorance or compulsion is valid. While we may think about the validity of such a plea as inherent in the nature of the excuse itself, it is clearly dependent on more purely communal criteria.

Aristotle himself makes clear that the volitional excuses about which he is concerned depend for their validity on our own social expectations of individuals. Likewise, he makes clear that it is because we do not want to accept all excuses that individuals might possibly make on the basis of ignorance or compulsion that we find it necessary to develop criteria of validity in the first place. Aristotle's own criteria, as we have seen, rest on both our own standards of acceptable behavior and the effects that blaming could be expected to have on a particular individual. (Among other things, we are not as willing to excuse individuals for acting badly if we think that if we blamed them, they might alter their behavior in the future.)

Two implications follow from these criteria for any notion of voluntariness that rests on volitional excuses. One is that the absence of such an excuse cannot possibly register contracausal freedom. The other is that any notion of voluntariness that rests on volitional excuses will necessarily be shaped by the practice of blaming of which it is a part. In chapter 9, I try to show how our own notion of free will is shaped by the criteria of blameworthiness that we smuggle into our volitional excuses. In this chapter, I have tried to show, not that Aristotle has smuggled such criteria into his volitional excuses, but that he has self-consciously placed such criteria at the center of his theory of responsibility in such a way that he is able to develop a notion of voluntariness that is both coherent in its own terms and compatible with his particular understanding of blameworthiness.

Transcendental Authority and the Damnation of Christian Sinners

Transcendental Authority Threatened

The Christian concept of moral responsibility is difficult to articulate for two reasons. One is that while modern theologians use the term "moral responsibility," early Christian philosophers did not conflate their notions of causation and blameworthiness into one moral concept. Instead, they viewed causation—free will—as both a condition and a partial source of moral blameworthiness. The other is that while there exists a general consensus among Christians with regard to their acceptance of God as the supreme blamer, there does not exist such a consensus among them with regard to the nature and possibility of free will.

While the lack of such a consensus prevents us from locating a universally shared concept of moral responsibility in Christian writings, it does not prevent us from providing a series of generalizations about the Christian notion of moral blameworthiness. Nor does it prevent us from providing a series of generalizations about the relationship between causation/free will and moral blameworthiness inherent in Christian doctrine. I attempt to provide such a series of generalizations throughout what follows by focusing on the free will/determinism debate as it developed among Christian thinkers.

I assume, and then try to demonstrate, that the efforts of Christian thinkers to justify the possibility of free will are not motivated by the modern fear of determinism. Instead, they are motivated by the need to reconcile man's sinfulness with the omniscience of God. I argue that once we understand their efforts in this light, we are able to construct a coherent, if not "correct," concept of moral responsibility out of what is now often considered to be simply an antiquarian, and singularly unscientific, debate about free will and determinism.

The debate in question begins in the fifth century with the early Christians' concern about a possible conflict between God's omnipotence and the Christian concept of moral blameworthiness. How, Christian theologians asked, can we possibly blame individuals for acting badly if their actions are under God's control? Augustine, Aquinas, and others set out to answer this question by developing a notion of free will that, according to them, is perfectly compatible with, and indeed supports, the Christian concept of moral blameworthiness.

Augustine introduces the problem of free will in his debate with Evodius, who challenges the possibility of both free will and moral responsibility in general. "If free will is so given that it has the movement by nature," Evodius writes, "it turns of necessity to mutable goods, and no blame attaches where nature and necessity prevail." Likewise, "since God foreknew that man would sin, that for which God foreknew must necessarily come to pass. . . . How, then, is the will free when there is this unavoidable necessity?"[1]

In his response to Evodius, Augustine not only interprets necessity as God's foreknowledge, but goes on to claim that we can exercise our wills in the future only because God has foreknowledge that we shall do so.

God has foreknowledge of all things. . . . God has foreknowledge of our will, so that of which he has knowledge must come to pass. . . . Indeed, we shall exercise our wills in the future only because he has foreknowledge that we shall do so.[2]

Augustine avoids the problem of necessity as we now know it by denying that foreknowledge entails agency. Likewise, he manages to deflate the control normally associated with foreknowledge by blurring the distinction between it and memory.

Just as you apply no compulsion to past events by having them in your memory, so God by his foreknowledge does not use compulsion in the case of future events. Just as you remember your past actions, so God has foreknowledge, but is not the agent of all that he foreknows.[3]

Augustine's assumption here that foreknowledge does not entail compulsion, and that compulsion is the primary threat to free will, enables him to get around the logic of Evodius's challenge. But he is not able to demonstrate the compatibility of God's omnipotence and the Christian concept of moral blameworthiness without offering what ap-

1. Saint Augustine, *On Free Choice of the Will* (Indianapolis, 1964), 88.
2. Ibid., 93.
3. Ibid., 49.

pears to be a very peculiar demonstration of free will itself. According to Augustine:

Our will would not be a will if it were not in our power. Because it is in our power, it is free. We have nothing in our power which is not free. Hence it is not necessary to deny that God has foreknowledge of all things, while at the same time our wills are our own.[4]

Commentators have been quick to point out that instead of demonstrating the possibility of free will, Augustine has defined it in such a way that it is necessarily possible. But they have not made explicit exactly what is wrong with such a definition other than that it violates our modern understanding of scientific proof. I suggest later in this chapter why such a definition might be acceptable on nonscientific, i.e., religious, grounds. I merely point out here that Augustine offers a more straightforward definition of free will elsewhere. In *On Two Souls Against the Manichees,* he defines free will as a mental state: "will is an uncompelled movement of mind either to acquire or to avoid losing some object."[5]

The problem is that once Augustine moves away from his analytic and seemingly circular definition of free will as individual power and specifies the importance of noncompulsion to free will, he is forced once again to take into consideration the possibility that God is not omniscient. Augustine does not want to take such a possibility into consideration and in the *City of God* reverts back to his definition of free will as an individual's "own will."[6] Likewise, he makes clear that while God may be the creator of all things, he is not the bestower of all wills: "wicked wills are not from him."[7] They are from us, who have the "power" over our own actions.

But the power that Augustine has in mind in the *City of God* is not as strong as that adhered to in his earlier works. Indeed, Augustine now restricts free will to the first sin in the first human being. After the first sin, he argues, we sin involuntarily and are the moral agents of our bad actions only in the sense that we are the authors of the conditions in which we cannot help but sin. As William Babcock points out,[8] Augustine's shift here forces him to abandon a crucial element in his

4. Ibid., 93.
5. Augustine, "On Two Souls Against the Manichees," *The Works of St. Augustine,* ed. John E. Rotelle (New York, 1990), 54.
6. Augustine, *City of God* (New York, 1950), 153.
7. Ibid., 155.
8. William Babcock, "Augustine on Sin and Moral Agency," *Journal of Religious Ethics* 16 (1988), 28–55.

argument for human moral agency. He can no longer argue, as he did in earlier works, that we are always free to do otherwise than what we actually do. Instead, he can argue only that we once had such opportunities open to us.

While such an analysis posits mankind as a collective entity, it does not preclude the importance of free will to moral blameworthiness. Indeed, free will becomes central to both the Fall and the Redemption of mankind. Before the Fall, individuals had a good will given to them by God. The Fall itself represents the bad will's movement away from God. And Redemption is a matter of the individual's realization of true free will: the exercise of God's laws.

While various theologians since Augustine have appropriated both his discussion of the Fall and its implications for free will, not all theologians have wanted to do so. Thomas Aquinas, for instance, argues that we can demonstrate the compatibility of God's omniscience and moral blameworthiness without positing a sharp break in man's development of free will. Aquinas approaches the question of free will in a somewhat different manner than Augustine did, and in doing so, he adumbrates many of the philosophical difficulties that plague our own concept of moral responsibility.

Aquinas begins his discussion of free will in the *Summa Theologica* by pointing out why free will is necessary to both rationality and moral blameworthiness.

Man has free choice, or otherwise counsels, commands, exhortations, prohibitions and punishments, would be in vain. In order to make this evident, we must observe that . . . man is rational. And that man is rational, it is necessary that we have free choice.[9]

In an effort to justify the possibility of free choice, Aquinas distinguishes between the first cause of an individual's action (God) and voluntariness (which he equates with free choice). Likewise, he makes clear that an individual's own choice is no less free because God, and not the individual, caused it.

Free choice is the cause of its own movement, because by his free choice man moves himself to act. But it does not of necessity belong to liberty that what is free should be the first cause of itself, as neither for one thing to be the cause of another need it be the first cause.[10]

9. Thomas Aquinas, from *Summa Theologica*, part 1, question B, in *Basic Writings of Saint Thomas Aquinas*, ed. A. C. Pegis (New York, 1945), 247.
10. Ibid., 750.

Indeed, writes Aquinas, not only do individuals not have to be the first cause of their actions to exercise free will, they can recognize another as their actions' first cause without sacrificing their own freedom of choice.

God is the first cause, who moves causes both natural and voluntary. But just because he moves natural causes he does not prevent actions from being natural. Likewise, by moving voluntary causes he does not deprive their actions of being voluntary; but rather is He the cause of this very thing in them, for he operates in each thing according to its nature.[11]

But if an individual's will is not the "first cause of itself," how can the individual, as opposed to either God or the individual's environment, be considered morally blameworthy? Aquinas does not ask the modern philosopher's question here. Instead, he goes on to stress that while God is the creator of an individual's will, he does not render the individual's actions necessary.

Since the will is an active principle that is not determined to one thing, but having an indifferent relation to many things, God so moves it that He does not determine it of necessity to one thing, but its movement remains contingent and not necessary, except in those things to which it is moved naturally.[12]

The question becomes what Aquinas can mean by an individual's act not being necessary in this context. Like Aristotle, he clearly wants to distinguish between determinism and necessity, but he does not do so in a way that would satisfy modern philosophers of science. Instead, he redefines free will in terms of power and domination.

An act is imputed to an individual when it is in his power, so that he had domination over it; and this is the case in all voluntary acts, because it is through his will that man had domination over his acts.[13]

Since Aquinas, like Augustine, assumes, rather than demonstrates, the power of an individual over his or her actions, he has been criticized for not developing a strong enough concept of free will. But such a criticism may not be warranted. For while Aquinas's notion of free will is clearly not strong enough to support our own modern concept of moral blameworthiness, it may be strong enough to support the Christian concept of sinfulness that he embraces. At the very least, we should try to figure out what Aquinas and other Christians mean by moral blameworthiness before dismissing their notion of free will—and their concept of moral responsibility—as inadequate.

11. Ibid.   13. Ibid., 361.
12. Ibid., 264.

From Communal Accountability to Moral Sin

Here we might begin with the differences between the Christian conception of moral blameworthiness and its Aristotelian counterpart. Aristotle, as we have seen, viewed blameworthiness as part of our social practice of blaming, a practice that for him was very closely tied to legal punishment. Christian theologians like Augustine and Aquinas want to move beyond our social practice of blaming and talk about a more purely moral or religious form of accountability between individuals and God. Similarly, they want to view that form of accountability as independent not only of our own practical judgments of blameworthiness, but of the circumstances in which we define individuals' actions as good or bad. Hence, they find it necessary not only to replace Aristotle's discussion of volitional excuses with a stronger notion of willing, but to argue for the absolute goodness and badness of an individual's actions.

Aquinas is of course willing to acknowledge the important role that both circumstances and luck play in the makeup of an individual's action. But unlike Aristotle, he is not willing to give either sort of contingency a place in his discussion of sinfulness. Indeed, he makes perfectly clear that while the contingencies of a situation may determine the way in which we as bystanders describe an individual's action, they "add nothing" to the individual's moral worth.[14] Aquinas's moral theory is straightforwardly intentionalist: only intentions ("movements by which the will tends to a certain end")[15] can render individuals morally praiseworthy or blameworthy.

Aquinas, like all Christians, has to be able to assume not only that luck has no place in our ability to will a particular end, but that the standards according to which we judge actions good and bad are themselves absolute. He is able to make the first assumption by defining intentions as those "internal movements" through which we are able to control and "dominate over" our actions.[16] He is able to make the second by an elaborate schema of sins and virtues which are all absolute by virtue of God's authority.

Whether or not Aquinas can justify either of these two assumptions is a question long debated. Let me just point out here that by making both assumptions he is able to develop a notion of blameworthiness that is far removed from the very contingencies that Aristotle embraced. But his notion of blameworthiness is not yet our own secular notion of moral blameworthiness, for God still plays a pivotal role in it. While

14. Ibid., 335.
15. Ibid., 319.

16. Ibid., 361.

Christian theologians claim the independence of sinfulness from our social practice of blaming, they do not claim its independence from God's authority. Indeed, as Aquinas himself makes clear, "human acts acquire merit or demerit in relation to Him; or otherwise it would follow that God did not have care over human actions."[17]

Aquinas stresses that individuals do not have complete control over either the conditions under which they act or the moral value that is eventually attached to their actions.

All that man is, and can be, and has, must be referred to God; and therefore every act of man, whether good or bad, acquires merit or demerit in the sight of God from the fact of the act itself.[18]

But God cannot be blamed for the actions of individuals. For, Aquinas reminds us, we can—and need to—distinguish the first cause of action from a "created cause."

The defect of sin is from a created cause, viz., free choice, as falling away from the First Cause, viz., God. Consequently, their defect is not reduced to God as its cause, but to free choice.[19]

Aquinas, as a Christian, makes two things clear here. One is that individuals are responsible for their own bad actions. (These actions have their origins in a "created cause," i.e., free will.) The other is that individuals are sinful by virtue of both their own bad actions *and* their relationship to external authority (i.e., God). God defines sinfulness, and it is to God that Christians hold themselves accountable. "Human society," writes F. R. Tennant, "may punish us for *crimes*; human monitors may reprove us for *vices*; but God alone can charge upon us the *sin*, which he alone is able to forgive."[20]

Sinfulness is thus not, like our modern notion of moral blameworthiness, something which individuals themselves initiate. While individuals may act out their own personality in action, they always do so within a moral (or immoral) relationship to God.

Sinfulness is the estrangement from God, breach of that fellowship with God which is the end of human life. . . . Sinfulness is always characterized by blameworthiness or demerit, something punishable, something incurring the Divine displeasure or disfavor, something calling for repentance on the side of God.[21]

17. Ibid., 363.
18. Ibid., 365.
19. Ibid., 653.
20. F. R. Tennant, *The Concept of Sin* (Cambridge, England, 1912), 22.
21. Ibid., 33.

The concept of moral responsibility that has come to be associated with Christianity thus rests on a relationship between individuals and God, but that relationship has not always been interpreted in the same way. Here, at the risk of greatly oversimplifying important theological controversies, we can distinguish between two distinct views of sinfulness: one which leads to the development of a concept of moral responsibility, the other which does not. The first view focuses primarily on original sin and views all individuals as sinful by nature. The second view focuses primarily on individual actions and views sinfulness—or at least moral guilt—as ascribed differentially.

The first view, which is taken primarily, but not exclusively, by followers of Paul, advocates universal sinfulness. Individuals are sinful, not in light of particular actions as intentions, but in light of the sinfulness of humanity after the Fall. While advocates of this view differ with regard to the results of such universal sinfulness, they agree on two things. One is that the essential evil remains the same in every action and in the life of every person. The other is that this evil is a form of pride or selfishness by which personality as a whole is affected.

Since advocates of universal sin do not find it necessary to show how particular individuals have brought sinfulness upon themselves, they do not get caught up in the free will/determinism controversy. But they do open themselves up to criticism by contemporary philosophers of religion that they have sacrificed both morality in general and moral responsibility in particular. H. D. Lewis, for example, argues that "there are two corollaries of the belief in universal sin. One is that man is neither moral nor immoral. The other is that moral responsibility in the proper sense is an illusion."[22]

While Lewis's point of view is not shared by all contemporary philosophers of religion, it is shared by many. Tennant, for instance, concentrates an enormous amount of energy on demonstrating both that sinfulness is not the same thing as imperfection and that at least one aspect of sinfulness is correlative with moral responsibility and guilt. Moreover, in several places, he goes as far as to argue that sin is an activity for which the agent is accountable and that no human activity falls outside the sphere of individual accountability.

What kind of free will does such a conception of moral blameworthiness require? Tennant himself establishes four conditions of sinfulness. First, the individual must have violated a moral law. Second, he or she must have known, or have been capable of knowing, the law which he or she violated. Third, the individual must have had at least two

22. H. D. Lewis, *Morals and the New Theology,* (London, 1947), 60.

paths of action open to him or her. And finally, his or her actions must be the outcome of intention and of choice "characterized by the freedom which the subject's will possesses."[23]

Tennant makes clear that the "freedom which the subject's will possesses" is very close to what Aristotle and we have in mind by "voluntariness." Likewise, he makes clear that what is important about voluntariness is that it reflects the "individual's own self." But he does not go so far as to equate the Christian conception of free will with Aristotle's notion of voluntariness itself. Nor could he do so given the important differences between their respective understandings of moral blameworthiness.

These differences, as we have seen, are essentially two. First, the Christian conception of blameworthiness, unlike its Aristotelian counterpart, is ostensibly independent of social and political practice. Hence, it requires standards of action that are absolute, or at least not dependent on our own interests and policies. Second, the Christian conception of moral blameworthiness, unlike its Aristotelian counterpart, refers to the moral worth of an individual. Hence, it requires a notion of voluntariness that is, so to speak, attached to the individual's self and reflective of his or her moral being. In other words, it requires a notion of free will.

But it does not require that the will itself be free from all external determination. For unlike its secular counterpart, it does not view moral blameworthiness as totally within an individual's own control. Indeed, it makes clear that without God's authority, moral blameworthiness makes no sense. ("The responsibility for the possibility of sin—or for man's being a moral subject at all—lies with his maker.")[24] The difference that such authority makes is clear: while the notion of free will that grounds the Christian concept of moral blameworthiness is necessarily independent of our social practice of blaming, it is not necessarily independent of a Creator or a first cause. Indeed, as Aquinas makes clear, it may be considered a "creative cause" which follows in a long chain of other causes back to its Maker.

Religious Ascription vs. Scientific Discovery

But how can such a cause be equated with free will? How, moreover, can it be considered the cause relevant to moral blameworthiness? Modern philosophers, as we shall see, generally construe free will as undeter-

23. Tennant, *Concept of Sin*, 209.
24. Ibid.

mined by all forces external to itself. But that is only because they view moral blameworthiness as under an individual's own control. Neither Aristotle nor the Christian philosophers go this far. Both groups view moral blameworthiness as relative to external authority—the community and God, respectively. Hence, they do not have to construe free will as absolutely undetermined.

But they do have to distinguish between actions which are based on free will and those which are not. Aristotle distinguished between these two sorts of actions by developing empirical criteria of compulsion and ignorance out of the moral and political standards of his own comments. Christian theologians focus on a notion of moral blameworthiness that they do not themselves feel qualified to discover in practice. Hence, they are not obliged to specify criteria that will allow us to distinguish between free and unfree actions in particular cases.

But they are obliged to specify how they can talk about free will without invoking the absolute categories of contra-causal freedom. Aristotle was able to avoid locating absolute boundaries between the voluntary and the involuntary by viewing both categories as part of our social practice of blaming and by viewing that practice as itself open-ended. Christian theologians cannot follow in Aristotle's footsteps here because moral blameworthiness is for them not only independent of our social practice of blaming, but absolute. Yet they too may be able to rely on external criteria to locate the boundaries between free will and not-free will. Only in their case, the criteria would have to be religious rather than purely social.

The criteria that come to mind here are those associated with both moral sin and God's omniscience. Christian theologians are not, like Aristotle, concerned to distinguish empirically between actions which are based on free will and those which are not. Instead, they are concerned to show how, in a world where God exists, individuals can be blameworthy. The road they take, as we have seen, is to ascribe to individuals enough power over their own actions to sustain the Christian concept of moral blameworthiness, but not so much power over everything else that God's omnipotence is threatened.

While the demonstration of free will that these theologians provide amounts to mere religious ascription, it cannot simply be dismissed as unscientific. For Christian theologians do not set out to demonstrate the scientific possibility of free will in the way, say, that modern philosophers do. Instead, they set out to develop a notion of free will compatible with their religious beliefs about both moral sinfulness and God's omniscience. Whether or not they would be willing to concede that their distinction between free will and not-free will is based on these religious dogmas rather than, say, on scientific evidence, is not a question that I can answer here. But I can suggest that if they were willing to concede the former, they could justify their interpretation of free will as an individual's "own will," rather than, say, as contra-causal freedom, on purely religious grounds.

As things now stand, the notions of causation and power that Christian theologians associate with an individual's "own will" appear to be circumscribed by the relationship which they posit between individuals and God. Likewise, the differences that exist between these theologians with regard to both causation and power appear to follow from the concept of moral blameworthiness which they associate with that relationship. Hence, we might want to consider free will to be a religiously ascribed feature of human existence, i.e., a feature of human existence that is ascribed to individuals within a particular religious system.

The debate between Erasmus and Luther demonstrates not only how such an ascription might occur, but how steadfastly the Christian notion of free will, like its Classical and modern counterparts, is tied to a particular conception of moral blameworthiness. While both Erasmus and Luther debate the possibility of free will, they do not try to provide abstract arguments about the possibility of its existence. Instead, they set out to show how their particular conceptions of free will follow from their religiously based views of reality, or in other words, why, if we accept their religiously based views of reality, we have to accept their particular conceptions of free will as real.

Erasmus and Luther do not agree on the nature of either reality in general or the relationship between individuals and God. Hence, they develop radically different conceptions of free will, conceptions which they feel compelled to defend publicly. But contrary to modern expectations, they do not defend their particular conceptions of free will by developing what we would call rational arguments. Instead, they concentrate on articulating these conceptions as part of a larger worldview, a worldview that at least according to Luther, is not susceptible to, and indeed transcends, more worldly forms of proof.

Erasmus, who develops what has come to be known as a full-blown theory of moral responsibility, extends the individual's power much further than does Luther, who interprets moral blameworthiness almost exclusively in terms of the Fall and man's association with the Devil. Erasmus does not intend to disparage grace, but he does argue that individuals are by their own power able to perform good works and hence merit the grace which they receive. Likewise, he does not want to challenge God's omnipotence, but he does define free will very broadly as the "power of the human will by which man can apply himself to the things which lead to human salvation, or turn away from them."[25]

Erasmus's willingness to endow individuals with the sorts of powers necessary to do good works follows largely from his rejection of more pessimistic accounts of the Fall. He argues that individuals before the Fall were endowed with certain natural powers (reason and free will), along with a supernatural gift of grace. At the Fall, they chose to use their natural powers to disobey God and consequently lost all of their supernatural gifts and some of their natural powers. But they retained both a capacity for knowledge and obedience to God and the ability to participate actively in the securing of their own salvation.

Erasmus makes clear in this context that it is because individuals retained freedom of choice after the Fall that they are accountable for their actions. Likewise, he makes clear that it is because they can "do what in them lies" that they can respond to the divine grace. "Nature must cooperate with grace, the human will with the divine, and this is a matter of man's own choice."[26] Salvation thus turns out to be a cooperative enterprise in which both God and human beings contribute to the redemption of human beings.

Luther takes a significantly different approach to the relationship between individuals and God, an approach that views individuals after the Fall as necessarily corrupt and hence incapable of participating in their own salvation. He argues that individuals before the Fall were one with God. They acted necessarily (in that they "had no will of their own"), voluntarily (in that they were in no way coerced), and freely (in that they participated spontaneously in divine love). Then came the Fall. While individuals retained limited powers of reason and will, they exercised both in a radically corrupt fashion (being governed from the start by Satan). Likewise, while they were able to exercise freedom in respect to what Luther considers "those things beneath them" (i.e., temporal choice),[27] they were no longer free to cooperate with God as a precondition of their own salvation, since by this point they were totally under Satan's power.

The two theorists develop significantly different notions of free will in their efforts to bolster significantly different notions of moral sinfulness. While Erasmus considers individuals accountable for their own actions, Luther considers them to be sinful by nature. Likewise, while

25. Desiderius Erasmus, "Free Will," *Luther and Erasmus: Free Will and Salvation* (Philadelphia, 1969), 10.

26. Ibid., 15.

27. Martin Luther, "On Free Will," *Luther and Erasmus: Free Will and Salvation* (Philadelphia, 1969), 17.

Erasmus is led to talk about individuals as participating actively in their own salvation, Luther is bound not only to deny such power, but to relinquish the possibility of individual free choice in general.

Erasmus's notion of free choice is not nearly as strong as that required by our modern concept of moral responsibility. Nor is it as clearly defined or justified according to scientific evidence. But why should it be? Erasmus, like Augustine and Aquinas before him, did not begin with the question "How can we reconcile free will with scientific theories of determinism?" He began instead with a significantly different question: How can we reconcile moral sinfulness with God's omniscience?

Since Erasmus began with this question rather than with that of modern philosophers ("How can we reconcile free will with scientific theories of determinism?"), or with Aristotle's ("What are the conditions under which we blame individuals in practice?"), we should not be surprised to discover that his notion of free will is both abstract and religiously ascribed (i.e., ascribed according to a set of religious beliefs rather than discovered as part of empirical reality or social practice). If he had begun with the modern philosopher's question, then we would be right to consider his notion of free will too weak, in that it does not deny external causation. Likewise, if he had begun with Aristotle's question, then we would be right to find his notion of free will to be overly general, lacking in the specificity necessary to distinguish between particular instances of voluntary and involuntary actions.

But Christian thinkers such as Erasmus were not, like Aristotle, concerned to articulate the rules of our social practice of blaming. Nor did they think that ordinary beings could ever have any insight into the occurrence or nonoccurrence of moral sinfulness. Hence, they did not find it necessary to develop specific criteria for deciding when an individual's will is free or not free. Nor did they find it necessary to justify the wisdom or empirical validity of these criteria by invoking logical arguments or empirical data.

Instead, they found it necessary to ascribe to individuals the sort of power that would make them participants in their own actions. Augustine ascribes to individuals a "will of their own," Aquinas "voluntary causation." Both terms appear not only to be overly general, but to be justified in a circular fashion, according to the questions that modern philosophers ask about free will. But each is in fact appropriate to the tasks that Christian philosophers set out to accomplish.

Why, we might ask, do we have to take them on their own terms? Why can we not apply our own, more straightforwardly logical or empirical criteria to their respective notions of free will? Two responses come to mind here. First of all, there may be no such thing as a notion of free will that is not constructed within a particular theoretical context. Hence, while we may be very attached to our own notion of free will (for reasons I discuss in the next chapter), we cannot impose it on others without also imposing on them a host of other assumptions that they do not share—including our own conception of moral blameworthiness.

Second, while we may think that our own questions concerning free will are obviously the smart questions to ask, we do so only by obscuring the extent to which these questions are grounded in two very basic modern cultural assumptions that we rarely acknowledge. One is that moral blameworthiness is totally under our own control, an assumption which leads us to construe free will as contra-causal freedom rather than, say, mere voluntariness. The other is that phenomena such as free will can be demonstrated only through scientific, i.e., logical or empirical, truth.

Since neither assumption is true in any absolute sense, Christian philosophers are not obliged to incorporate them into their own worldviews. But they are obliged to clarify their own worldviews to show how we can talk about free will as part of them. Likewise, they are obliged to show how the notions of "power" and an "individual's own will" that they ascribe to individuals are not merely their own theoretical inventions, but the "truth" as dictated by God's reality. Such a demonstration would appear to be extremely difficult, if not impossible, since their conceptions of free will appear to follow in their arguments from a particular theoretical starting point rather than from religious experience.

Suffice it to point out here that in focusing on their ascriptions of free will, I have in no way tried to suggest that Christian philosophers are able to provide us with convincing arguments for the existence of God or the coherence of a religious view of reality. Instead, I have tried to show two other things. One is that the notion of free will that many of them develop appears to be compatible with their conceptions of moral blameworthiness. The other is that Christian philosophers are not in general obliged to counter determinism, since for them determinism is a matter of God's will and God's will is at least a partial source of moral blameworthiness.

Internalized Transcendence and the Modern Moral Conscience

Moral Guilt and the Internalization of Social Blame

In the following passage, Lars Hertzberg underscores what many contemporary thinkers now take to be the "problem of moral responsibility."

Many of us, from time to time, have been haunted by the following thought: "One day science will tell us about all the causes of human behavior. And when that day comes, we will no longer be able to hold people morally responsible for their actions."[1]

Isaiah Berlin's warning of several decades ago was even more dramatic in scope.

If social determinism is true, and we begin to take it seriously, then the changes in the whole of our language, our moral terminology, our attitudes toward one another, our views of history, of society, and of everything else will be too profound to be adumbrated. The concepts of praise and blame, innocence and guilt, and responsibility from which we started are but a small element in the structures which would collapse or disappear.[2]

Neither Classical nor Christian thinkers, as we saw in chapters 2 and 3, took determinism as such a threat. But many modern, i.e., secular, thinkers do so. Why is this the case? Sidney Hook, among others, has suggested that the fear of determinism experienced by so many modern thinkers has its source in the relative sophistication of modern individuals who have been educated in the natural and physical sciences.[3] While I agree with Hook that those with a scientific education have

1. Lars Hertzberg, "Blame and Causality," *Mind* 84 (1974), 500.
2. Isaiah Berlin, "Historical Inevitability," in *Four Essays on Liberty* (Oxford, 1969), 113.
3. Sidney Hook, *Determinism and Freedom in the Age of Modern Science* (New York, 1958).

VERNON REGIONAL
JUNIOR COLLEGE LIBRARY

made the tension between moral responsibility and determinism considerably clearer to us than it would otherwise be, I suggest below that the fear of determinism experienced by modern, secular individuals has its source not in scientific sophistication, but in the modern concept of moral responsibility itself, a concept which is often referred to as Kantian, but which is much more widely accepted than such a designation would lead us to believe.

Ironically, the very pervasiveness of the modern concept of moral responsibility makes it difficult to articulate. Like its Classical and Christian counterparts, it is not a logically airtight construction. Instead, it is a cluster of shared assumptions and beliefs that are held by a large percentage of the modern, secular individuals who talk about moral responsibility. But these shared assumptions and beliefs are not held in exactly the same way by everyone. Nor are they held with the same degree of commitment. Hence, they are difficult to present together as one overarching concept.

The task of presentation becomes even more difficult when we acknowledge two further characteristics of the modern concept of moral responsibility. One is that the modern concept of moral responsibility is not, like its Classical and Christian counterparts, internally coherent. (I concentrate most of my energies throughout this chapter on showing why this is so.) The other is that unlike its Classical and Christian counterparts, the modern concept of moral responsibility is most frequently presented negatively, i.e., in terms of what it is not, rather than in terms of what it is.[4]

Interestingly enough, what the modern concept of moral responsibility is frequently presented as *not* being is the other two concepts of moral responsibility that we have explored so far. Unlike its Classical and Christian counterparts, the modern concept of moral responsibility is not supposed to be a communal form of accountability or one based on religious authority. Nor is it supposed to compete with these other two sorts of accountability on equal terms. Instead, it is supposed to exist beyond them as *real* responsibility. According to Joel Feinberg:

A stubborn feeling persists even after legal responsibility has been decided that there is still a problem—albeit not a legal problem—left over: namely, is the defendant *really* responsible (as opposed to "responsible in law") for the harm? This conception of a "real" theoretical responsibility distinct from a practical

4. Not surprisingly, the fact that the modern concept of moral responsibility is presented negatively is not lost on those who want to show that it it is based partly on the denial of other forms of accountability. I offer such an interpretation in chapter 9, where I view the modern concept of moral responsibility as a secularized version of Christian sinfulness that internalizes the standards of social blameworthiness.

responsibility "relative" to the purposes and values of a particular community is expressed very commonly in the terminology of "morality"—*moral* obligation, *moral* guilt, *moral* responsibility.[5]

Moral responsibility is thus not only more real than its more worldly counterparts, but independent of the sorts of practical considerations upon which they are based. Moral responsibility is a matter of

Judgments which are in no way forced by practical considerations, which are superior in rationality and perfectly precise, imputing an absolute responsibility within the power of the agent.[6]

Since moral responsibility is ostensibly independent of all practical considerations, it must not only be absolute but precisely decidable. Likewise, it must be purely factual rather than dependent on the discretion of a worldly (or even otherworldly) judge. Like all matters of "record," moral responsibility must be "read off the facts or deduced from them: there can be no irreducible element of discretion for the judge, if his judgments are to have the stamp of superior rationality."[7]

What kind of factual judgment is moral responsibility? Since it requires that individuals have caused that for which they are being blamed, it is in some respects a scientific judgment. But it cannot be construed as value neutral, since it embraces within itself a moral judgment about the individual in question: that she is morally blameworthy for having brought about harm. Hence, we might want to talk about it as a morally charged sort of causation or judgment of moral agency.

William Frankena captures the conflation of causation and blameworthiness that is characteristic of our modern concept of moral responsibility when he writes:

Saying that X was responsible for Y seems, at first, to be a causal, not a moral, judgment; and one might, therefore, be inclined to say that "X was responsible for Y" simply means "x caused y," perhaps with the qualification that he did so voluntarily, intentionally, etc. But to say that X is responsible for Y is not merely to make a causal statement of a special kind. . . . It is to say that it would be right to blame or otherwise punish him.[8]

By conflating causation and blameworthiness into one moral fact about persons, modern moral thinkers such as Frankena are able to use a single term—moral responsibility—to cover both causation and blameworthiness together. Aristotle, as we saw, viewed causation/

---

5. Joel Feinberg, *Doing and Deserving* (Princeton, 1970), 30.
6. Ibid.
7. Ibid., 31.
8. William Frankena, *Ethics* (Englewood Cliffs, N.J., 1963), 56.

voluntariness as one of the two primary conditions of blameworthiness. Christian thinkers viewed free will as much more intimately connected to sinfulness. But even they did not conflate the two into one moral term similar to our own "moral responsibility." Modern individuals not only conflate causation and blameworthiness into a single moral term, but treat the two as part of one moral fact about an individual's moral agency.

What could moral blameworthiness possibly mean in this context? Since moral responsibility is itself ostensibly independent of all practical considerations, moral blameworthiness cannot be a judgment that *we* make about an individual after she has acted. Nor can it be relative to our social practice of blaming. Instead, it must be a moral judgment that is written, so to speak, into the individual's moral agency itself (unless, of course, we are willing to reintroduce God as an external judge).

Moreover, since it is a judgment of the individual's moral worth, it cannot refer simply to his actions, but must refer to him as a moral person. Moral blameworthiness, writes Jonathan Glover, is a moral fact about the worth of persons as moral agents. It is a "kind of moral accounting, where a person's actions are recorded on an individual balance sheet, with the object of assessing his moral worth."[9] To say that someone is morally blameworthy for some state of affairs "is to say that he is a bad person."[10]

But it is not only to say that he is a bad person. It is also to say that he is worthy of blame, or, in Frankena's words, that "it would be right to blame or otherwise punish him." Since blameworthiness is not supposed to be dependent on a relationship between individuals and those

9. Jonathon Glover, *Responsibility* (London, 1970), 96.

10. Ibid., 64. Just what the "person" is who is morally bad is not always clear. While many of those who talk about moral responsibility are willing to include an individual's character and personality in that which is morally bad, others are not, in large part as a result of their recognition that neither character nor personality is completely intrinsic to an individual (or in other words, free from the effects of external environment). Michael Zimmerman, for example, argues that when we hold an individual morally responsible for doing something bad, it is *him*, and not his character or personality, that we condemn. According to Zimmerman, "to appraise someone in the manner just indicated is to 'measure the man.' It is to evaluate *him* in a certain way; it is not to evaluate his character or his personality. . . . It is to make a judgment of his moral worth" (*An Essay on Moral Responsibility* [Totowa, N.J., 1988], 38). I suggest later on in the chapter that there may be nothing left of a person after you take away character and personality, and that without a transcendental God, moral, as distinct form social, blameworthiness, makes no sense. Suffice it to point out here that those who accept the modern concept of moral responsibility are obliged to come up with *some* concept of the person that enables us to talk about intrinsic moral worth.

who might want to blame them, it is necessarily an ideal state, one that is often referred to as "ideal liability":

Liability to charges and credits on some ideal record, liability to credit or blame (in the sense that implies no action). Just as it is, as we say, "forever to the credit" of a hero or saint that he performed some noble act, so a man can "forever be to blame" for his faults.[11]

What would it mean for an individual to "forever be to blame for his faults" in a secular context? Modern thinkers, with the notable exception of Kant, do not generally address this question in a great deal of depth. Nor do they elaborate what we might think of as a secular notion of moral blameworthiness. Instead, they generally associate moral blameworthiness with terms such as "moral guilt" and then assume that such guilt makes sense outside the context of a relationship between individuals and an external blamer.

Not surprisingly, the notion of moral blameworthiness that emerges from their discussions turns out to look very much like the Christian notion of sinfulness minus God.[12] Indeed, the only major difference between the two appears to be that while the Christian notion of sinfulness rests on the existence of an ideal blamer, God, the modern notion of moral blameworthiness rests on a notion of ideal liability per se: "liability to charges and credits on some ideal record, liability to credit or blame (in the sense that implies no action)."

Not all contemporary thinkers, of course, go as far as to use terms such as "ideal liability" or "credits on some ideal record" in their discussions of responsibility. But many do use the language of intrinsic moral worth and insist on a distinction between moral and social blameworthiness.[13] Moreover, even those who steer away from the language of ideal liability may, as I suggest below, be obliged to accept it if they want to continue viewing moral blameworthiness as distinct from social blameworthiness in a secular context.

Interestingly enough, many of those philosophers now writing on moral responsibility hedge their bets by using as their working definition of moral blameworthiness the one sketched above while treating it as a metaphor, even though they never say what, as a metaphor, it rep-

11. Feinberg, *Doing and Deserving*, 30–31.
12. Such a likeness is clearly not coincidental. As Elizabeth Anscombe points out in "Modern Moral Philosophy" (1), our modern concepts of moral responsibility and moral obligation have their source in Christian doctrine and may not make sense without it. Judith Shklar goes as far, in *Legalism* (45), as to characterize "internalism" or "conscience morality" as the "ethics of sin."
13. See, for example, Jonathon Glover's discussion of the differences between moral and social blame in *Responsibility* (London, 1970).

resents or how they can go on to justify it in purely philosophical, as distinct from metaphorical, terms. Michael Zimmerman is a perfect case in point. According to Zimmerman,

Moral responsibility has to do with the type of *inward* moral praising and blaming that constitutes making a private judgment about a person. . . . It is "credit" on his "ledger of life," a "positive mark" on his "report card," or a "blemish" or "stain" on his "record"; that his record has been "tarnished"; that his "moral standing has been diminished." . . . Someone is blameworthy if he is deserving of such blame; that is, if it is correct, or true to the facts, to judge that there is a "debit" on his "ledger."[14]

Zimmerman is quick to stand back from his notion of moral blameworthiness and point out that "it is metaphorical" and "of course, the metaphor is only a metaphor."[15] But he defends it as traditionally presented, i.e., not as a metaphor, and concludes by pointing out that "even if there were no moral ledgers, it remains a fact that certain events occur and that a person's moral worth is a function of these events."[16] Hence, he is obliged to acknowledge that he has accepted the modern notion of moral blameworthiness in its most raw form.

Not all of those who accept the modern notion of moral blameworthiness are as disingenuous as Zimmerman appears to be in these passages. Nor are they generally as willing to go as far as to talk about "credits" on the "ledger of life" or "blemishes" or "stains" on one's "record" or "positive marks" on one's "report card" or even "intrinsic moral worth." But even those who resist metaphysical language in general frequently insist that moral responsibility is distinct from mere social blameworthiness and has its source in an individual's own moral agency.[17] Hence, they are obliged, at the very least, to come to terms

14. Zimmerman, *Moral Responsibility,* 38.

15. Ibid.

16. Ibid., 39.

17. H. Offstead documents the great extent to which contemporary philosophers still retain an understanding of moral responsibility as both causation and moral blameworthiness together, in "Recent Work on the Free Will Problem," *American Philosophical Quarterly* 4 (1967), 179–207. There are of course exceptions. See, for example, H. L. A. Hart, "The Ascription of Responsibility and Rights," *Proceedings of the Aristotelian Society* 49 (1948–49), 171–94; J. J. C. Smart, "Free Will, Praise, and Blame," *Mind* 70 (1961), 291–306; and P. F. Strawson, "Freedom and Resentment," *Proceedings of the British Academy* 48 (1962), 187–211. Hart argues that moral responsibility is something that we ascribe to individuals within locutions such as "A did X" or "A brought about Y." Smart views moral responsibility as a form of social blameworthiness, although, as we shall see, he does not make it clear why he continues to use the term moral responsibility, as opposed to mere blameworthiness or accountability. Strawson conceptualizes our judgments of moral responsibility as relative to both our sense of resentment and our principles of fairness.

with what distinguishes moral from social blameworthiness—and in doing so make clear how they can talk about *moral* obligation, *moral* guilt, and *moral* responsibility without referring to either God or a more worldly community of blamers.

Likewise, if they cannot distinguish between moral responsibility and social blameworthiness in a secular context without resorting to the language of "ideal liability," they are obliged to recognize that they too have accepted the modern notion of moral blameworthiness and along with it two very stiff requirements. The first is to make sense of "ideal liability" outside the context of a relationship between individuals and actual or potential blamers. The second is explain how moral blameworthiness can have its source in an individual's own free will (or at the very least in something over which individuals have "total control.")

In the next section, I suggest why the notions of ideal liability and free will associated with the modern concept of moral responsibility make no sense in a secular context. Let me stress here that both requirements are obviously stringent and—contrary to conventional wisdom—ones that only modern, secular thinkers are forced to meet. Classical and Christian thinkers, as we saw, were willing to recognize external authority and hence did not have to locate moral blameworthiness in an individual's own free will. Moreover, Christian thinkers were able to talk about moral blameworthiness as independent of our social practice of blaming because they assumed the existence of both transcendental souls that could be blackened by the performance of bad acts and an all-powerful and omniscient blamer, God. Secular thinkers deny that moral blameworthiness has anything to do with a relationship between individuals and God. Hence, they are obliged to view moral blameworthiness not only as "ideal liability," but as a moral fact about individuals over which they themselves have total control— "an absolute responsibility within the power of the agent."[18]

Since modern thinkers view individuals as having total control over their own moral blameworthiness, they cannot accept determinism of any kind, and it is here that they differ the most from their Classical and Christian counterparts. Aristotle, as we saw, was comfortable with social determinism, since moral blameworthiness for him was a social construct. Christian thinkers were comfortable with God as a determining force, since moral blameworthiness for them was part of a relationship between the individuals to be blamed and God. But modern thinkers cannot accept either social practice or God as a source of moral blameworthiness. Hence, they must deny the deterministic force of

18. Feinberg, *Doing and Deserving*, 30.

each with respect to moral responsibility and locate the source of moral blameworthiness not only in an individual's own will, but in a will that is free from all external determination.

Why—given the extreme difficulty of such a project—not simply get rid of the modern concept of moral responsibility altogether? As I suggested in chapter 1, there are a handful of modern philosophers who have attempted to do so, including both utilitarians and those who, like P. F. Strawson, are willing to view moral blameworthiness as part of our social practice of blaming. But as Jonathan Bennett points out in his discussion of the modern notion of moral blameworthiness, the number of philosophers who have tried to come up with an alternative concept of moral responsibility is extremely small. Moreover, those utilitarians who have tried to do so have met with a great deal of resistance, even from other utilitarians, who note that once blame is justified on the basis of utility, it loses much of its moral force and may even violate personal integrity.

If the difficulties associated with the modern concept of moral responsibility and its utilitarian counterpart were purely academic, they might not be crucial to a study of our actual judgments of moral responsibility. But these difficulties are not purely academic. Nor are modern philosophers the only ones who accept the modern concept of moral responsibility or reject its utilitarian counterpart. As we shall see in later chapters, even those of us who have not pursued the philosophy of free will generally interpret moral responsibility as a matter of both causation and blameworthiness and contrast it with either legal punishment or social blameworthiness. Likewise, even though many of us may not feel comfortable talking about intrinsic moral worth, very few of us are willing to acknowledge that the moral blameworthiness of any one individual has anything to do with either social expectations or policy considerations. Hence, even the most skeptical among us often attributes to individual moral agency the moral badness that we associate with our moral responsibility for external harm—unless, of course, we are willing to invoke the will of God.[19]

But we do not always keep our judgments of moral responsibility— or even the idea of moral responsibility itself—separate from our more worldly judgments. Indeed, we often use the possibility of moral re-

19. Contemporary Western societies are clearly not as secular as the term "secular society" would lead us to believe. As things now stand, there are are many more adherents to the Christian concept of moral responsibility in Western society than is usually acknowledged. Moreover, many individuals go back and forth between the two concepts with ease. It is perhaps for this reason that Jonathan Bennett chooses to talk about the "Christian-Kantian concept of moral responsibility" in "Accountability," 24–29.

sponsibility to justify our social practices of blaming and punishment.[20] Likewise, we often assume that even though others' judgments of blameworthiness are mere reflections of their personal interests, our own judgments come close to being the real thing.

By "real thing" here we may mean only that our judgments of moral blameworthiness are independent of our own purposes and interests. In other words, we may not think of ourselves as incorporating a metaphysical understanding of blameworthiness into our practical judgments. But we nevertheless do just that whenever we assume that individuals are blameworthy, not in virtue of a judgment on our part, but in virtue of their having themselves caused that for which they are being held morally responsible.

The metaphysical assumptions that we make here become especially stark when we are pushed to express what it is about individuals that enables us to impute moral blameworthiness to them: free will. While we may not as social and political actors think a great deal about the notion of free will that we invoke, we do assume that if individuals are mentally sound, they have the ability to do otherwise than they actually did, an assumption that often leads us to reject pleas of social determinism as unacceptable in many cases. Likewise, while we may not as social and political actors often stop and think about the source of moral blameworthiness, we do often assume that individuals are morally blameworthy because they have freely willed a bad action.

J. J. C. Smart views these assumptions as caught up with a "pharisaical attitude to sinners and an almost equally unhealthy attitude to saints."

The appropriateness of praise and blame is bound up, in the eyes of the ordinary man, with a notion of free will which is quite metaphysical. Admittedly, this metaphysics is incoherent and unformulated (as indeed it has to be, for when formulated, it becomes self-contradictory). Nevertheless, we can see that a rather pharisaical attitude to sinners and an almost equally unhealthy attitude to saints is bound up with this metaphysics in the thinking of the ordinary man if we look at the way in which very often his whole outlook and tendency to *judge* (and not just grade) other men changes when he is convinced by an analysis of free will.[21]

20. Lars Hertzberg suggests, in "Blame and Causality," what might happen to our practice of punishment if we were no longer able to believe in moral responsibility: "One striking consequence is that our present penal system would have to be altered. It seems nothing could make the penal system of modern society tolerable to us—except the thought that, to some degree, most convicts deserve their punishment. But if no one is responsible for his actions, there can be no just punishment" (501).

21. Smart, "Free Will, Praise, and Blame," 212.

Smart's claims here may be somewhat exaggerated with regard to the "ordinary man." (Or perhaps we simply cannot generalize to the extent that Smart wants us to do.) But surely he is on the mark to point out that when we hold an individual morally responsible in practice, we often think of ourselves as judging the moral worthiness of the individual herself rather than the quality of her actions. Likewise, he is surely correct to associate such a stance with the metaphysical claims about free will associated with our modern concept of moral responsibility.

But we do not need to go as far as Smart does in locating metaphysical claims about moral blameworthiness and free will in our everyday discourse in order to talk about how we incorporate a metaphysical concept of moral responsibility into our practical judgments. Indeed, it would not be at all difficult to show that even those among us who would never take a "pharisaical attitude to sinners or an even almost equally unhealthy attitude to saints," i.e., even those of us who were not reared in the Christian religion, nevertheless fall back on our modern concept of moral responsibility in practice.

Presumably, we could do so by pointing out that even those among us who would never admit to embracing metaphysical assumptions such as those associated with moral guilt nevertheless embrace the structure, if not the full content, of our modern concept of moral responsibility. In other words, we could show that even those who would never use terms such as "ideal liability" or "moral report card" assume both the independence of moral responsibility from our social practice of blaming and the notion that moral blameworthiness is a fact about individuals rather than a judgment that we ourselves make about individuals on the basis of our own social and political points of view.

My sense is that while there are now more individuals than ever before who would, if asked, reject the metaphysical claims associated with ideal liability, such individuals nevertheless continue to view moral responsibility as distinct from more purely social or political sorts of accountability. Likewise, while these same individuals might balk at the notion of an abstract will that is itself morally charged, i.e., morally good or bad, they nevertheless continue to locate the source of moral blameworthiness in an individual's own free will, rather than in our social practice of blaming. Hence, we are fully justified in assuming that the possibilities of both ideal liability and free will are still crucial to their judgments of moral responsibility and that if either turns out not to exist, they will have to rethink their concept of moral responsibility instead of simply pretending that they as sophisticated individuals would never accept its fuzzier features.

The Burdens of Free Will

What would have to be true of free will if it were really something in virtue of which individuals could be considered morally blameworthy? First of all, it would have to be free from all physical and social determinism, i.e., it would have to be undetermined by any forces external to itself. For otherwise, as we have seen, it could not be construed as under an individual's own control. Second, it would have to be intrinsically good or bad, since according to our modern concept of moral responsibility, free will is no longer a mere condition of moral responsibility but its very source.

Contemporary philosophers are completely aware of the first requirement that our modern concept of moral responsibility places on free will. Indeed, they devote their discussions of moral responsibility almost exclusively to the possibility of contra-causal freedom.[22] But they do not as a rule acknowledge the importance of being able to consider an individual's will as intrinsically good or bad. Nor do they generally acknowledge the historically specific nature of either the modern notion of free will or the concept of moral responsibility of which it is a part. Instead, they zero in on what is essentially a second-order question: "Is free will compatible with determinism?"

I suggest throughout what follows that even though the modern notion of free will may now be treated in abstraction from its original moral context, it is still historically and morally shaped by the controversies over moral blameworthiness out of which it evolved. Likewise, even though it may now be thought of as a requirement of moral responsibility in general, it is necessary only to our modern concept of moral responsibility by virtue of the fact that it construes moral blameworthiness as totally under an individual's own control. Both points—as well as the limitations of our modern concept of moral responsibility—become especially clear when we return to the original debates out of which our modern notion of free will developed.

Like their Classical and Christian counterparts, these debates have frequently been understood to be about the compatibility of free will and determinism. But they are in fact about the possibility of moral blameworthiness as construed by a modern, i.e., self-consciously secular, community. Hume, an instigator of the modern debate, was totally open about the normative thrust of his determinist account of human actions. So too was Kant in his efforts to develop a notion of free will compatible

---

22. Note in this context the number of volumes entitled *Moral Responsibility and . . .* which are in fact about free will and determinism.

with determinism. Both philosophers made clear that determinism is a threat to moral responsibility largely, if not solely, because of the particular notion of moral blameworthiness that it assumes.

Hume challenged Kant to show how we could continue talking about the modern notion of blameworthiness if human actions were determined. According to Hume, since actions are produced by motives, and motives can only be understood as part of a chain linking physical phenomena, the "liberty which is opposed to necessity" cannot possibly characterize human actions. Moreover, even if such a liberty *could* characterize human actions, it would not, according to Hume, be a very good way of grounding morality. For the "liberty which is opposed to necessity" exists only in the realm of pure chance.[23]

Kant, in response to Hume's arguments, concentrates on developing a notion of free will that is not only totally within an individual's own control, i.e., completely outside the realm of chance, but is itself intrinsically moral. Likewise, he sets out to defend this notion of free will, not by demonstrating its physical existence, but by making two further claims about the nature of modern morality in general. One is that modern morality in general presupposes the existence of a will that is both free and intrinsically moral. ("In order for something to be good, it must be absolutely good; and the only thing that is absolutely good is a good will.")[24] The other is that if we want to defend the modern notion of moral blameworthiness, we will have to think about the world in such a way that a free and absolutely good will is possible.

According to Kant, modern thinkers are obliged to construct a morality that embraces both a good will and the limitations and obstacles of human existence, i.e., phenomenal determinism. In this context, Kant attempts to construct a morality based on duty, which for him amounts to the self-imposition of the laws of morality. As Kant argues in the *Groundwork,* such a morality necessitates the existence of free will, a notion that he conceives of initially in negative terms.

As will is a kind of causality of living beings as far as they are rational, freedom is the property of this causality by which it can be effective independently of foreign causes determining it.[25]

From this negative conception of free will, Kant derives a more positive one. According to Kant, since the concept of causality entails law-

23. David Hume, "Of Liberty and Necessity," in *An Inquiry Concerning Human Understanding* (New York, 1907), 100.
24. Immanuel Kant, *Groundwork of the Metaphysics of Morals,* trans. H. J. Paton (New York, 1964).
25. Ibid., 100.

abidingness, free will can be construed as "autonomy, the property of the will to be a law unto itself."[26] Moreover, since laws are by nature universal, autonomy can be understood as the property of the will to conform to the law of morality. And finally, since law-abidingness is, according to Kant, an absolute good, it can be conceived of as rendering absolutely good those wills that conform to it.

By deriving moral autonomy from contra-causal freedom, Kant enables himself to talk about a will that is both free and morally good. But he does not do so without placing two further requirements on himself. One is to show how we can talk about the absolute goodness of law-abidingness on which his derivation rests. The other is to show how we can talk about contra-causal freedom in a world that is itself physically determined.

Kant does not address the first challenge directly, but instead simply assumes that law-abidingness is an absolute good—an assumption that I question below. Suffice it to point out here that if Kant were unable to justify such an assumption, he might have to concede that the value of law-abidingness has its source in modern Protestant culture rather than in free will per se. Likewise, he might have to abandon his positive notion of free will or else find another way of establishing its absolute goodness.

Kant does address the second challenge—physical determinism—directly, by positing two realms of reality: the phenomenal realm of necessity and the noumenal realm of freedom. According to Kant:

Man puts himself into another order of things . . . when he conceives of himself as intelligence endowed with a will and consequently with causality, than he does when he perceives himself as a phenomenon in the sensible world (which he actually is as well) and subjects his causality to external determination in accordance with the laws of nature.[27]

By separating out a noumenal realm from the phenomenal realm of nature, Kant appears able to preserve a realm of moral autonomy for individuals. But as philosophers since Hegel have been quick to point out, the noumenal realm may be dependent on the phenomenal realm in ways which would seem to preclude the possibility of contra-causal freedom.[28] Kant may be able to show how our assumption of a split between the two realms enables us to think about ourselves as rational

---

26. Ibid., 108.
27. Ibid., 120.
28. G. W. F. Hegel, *The Philosophy of Right* (Oxford, 1952), 75–104.

moral actors, but he cannot rely on such an assumed (as opposed to real) split to justify the possibility of moral blameworthiness.[29]

Moreover, the ideal concept of free will that Kant develops in the *Groundwork* may not be the appropriate one with regard to the concept of moral responsibility. For the notion of free will that he develops there is absolutely good, and moral responsibility in most cases entails moral blameworthiness. (Interestingly enough, while philosophers and political theorists often talk about moral responsibility as a matter of both blameworthiness and praiseworthiness, they almost always focus exclusively on blameworthiness in their examples, a hangover, one might argue, from the concept's Christian origins.)

Can Kant provide us with a notion of free will that embodies both causation and *moral disvalue*? As Kant scholars have been increasingly willing to point out, Kant's discussion of free will in the *Groundwork* may rule out any further discussion of guilt, which of course was not Kant's intention. In other words, by talking about free will and the moral law together in the way that Kant does, Kant may find himself in the position of having to acknowledge that if an individual does not embrace the moral law, he is not free and hence cannot be considered morally guilty.

In their efforts to show why Kant does not need to find himself in this position, Lewis White Beck, J. J. Paton, and other Kant scholars have in recent years suggested that we refocus our attention on Kant's discussions of free will in the *Critique of Practical Reason* and *Religion Within the Limits of Reason Alone*.[30] The difference between Kant's treatment of freedom in these two works and in the *Groundwork* is that in these two works he not only distinguishes between two sorts of will, *Wille* and *Willkür*, but allows for the latter sort of will (hitherto considered heteronomous) to exercise the sort of freedom required by moral blameworthiness.

While the two sorts of will that Kant has in mind come together in the good will, they are conceptually distinct. *Wille* is pure practical reason, the moral law. *Willkür* is what we might call a human or an empirical will. While *Wille* is the principle of moral agency, *Willkür* is the human

29. It is for this reason, presumably, that contemporary Kantians feel more at home incorporating Kant's epistemological split into their hypothetical notions of political deliberation than in incorporating the split into their discussions of moral responsibility.

30. Louis White Beck, *A Commentary on Kant's Critique of Practical Reason* (Chicago, 1960); H. J. Paton, *The Categorical Imperative* (London, 1967); John Silber, "The Ethical Significance of Kant's Religion," in Kant's *Religion within the Limits of Reason Alone* (New York, 1960).

faculty that enables individuals to act freely, a faculty which for Kant amounts to the initiation of a new causal series in nature. The *Willkür*, unlike the *Wille*, is influenced, but not wholly determined, by human impulses. As John Silber points out, its actions are always determined by the strongest among an individual's impulses, but only after the *Willkür* itself has made the decision by which the strongest impulse is determined.[31] In this sense, the *Willkür* determines itself and is free.

The freedom of the Willkür is of a wholly unique nature in that an incentive can determine the Willkür to an action only so far as the individual has incorporated it into his maxim (has made it the general rule in accordance with which he will conduct himself).[32]

Since the *Willkür* is that which enables individuals to choose among various options, it is the *Willkür* to which Kant turns when he wants to evaluate the moral worth of particular individuals. Kant argues that although *Wille* is a good in and of itself, *Willkür* may be good, prudent, or evil. When the *Willkür* takes the *Wille* (moral law) unto itself, it is autonomous and good. When it takes upon itself maxims not opposed to the law of reason, it is prudent (or morally indifferent). When it self-consciously opposes the moral law, it is evil. "The proposition 'Man is evil' can only mean 'He is conscious of the moral law but has nevertheless adopted into his maxim the deviation therefrom.'"[33]

In this sense, individuals can be both free and morally responsible even though they do not do what is morally right, i.e., even when they do not follow the dictates of their own *Wille*. Likewise, they can be considered inherently guilty in virtue of their free will, *Willkür*, even though their *Wille* is always good.

Inherent guilt is so denominated because it may be discovered in man as early as the first manifestations of the exercise of freedom.[34]

This guilt is not a mere social judgment, but registers a "certain insidiousness of the heart."[35] Unlike the Christian conception of guilt from which it is derived, it does not entail a relationship between individuals and God. Indeed, Kant makes clear that "morality does not need religion at all. . . . It is self-sufficient by virtue of pure practical reason."[36] Likewise, he makes clear that there is no original sin and no original goodness in persons except in the sense that sins and virtues originate in free *Willkür*. Individuals create themselves and hence are

---

31. Silber, "Ethical Signifcance," xcv.   34. Ibid., 33.
32. Kant, *Religion*, 19.   35. Ibid.
33. Ibid., 27.   36. Ibid., 3.

obliged to take full responsibility for their actions. The "disposition to evil (or good) is something fully chosen."[37]

Man *himself* must make or have made himself into whatever, in a moral sense, whether good or evil, he is or is to become. Either condition must be an effect of his free choice; for otherwise he could not be held responsible for it and could therefore be *morally* neither good nor evil.[38]

Kant makes clear in this passage not only the nature of moral blame-worthiness itself but the conditions under which it is possible. According to Kant, moral blameworthiness is a matter of both free causation and a moral disposition. It is possible only if individuals' actions can be considered the product of their own free wills and if their wills can be considered either intrinsically good or intrinsically bad. Kant thinks that both conditions can be met and suggests why this is so throughout the *Groundwork*.

Kant concedes in the *Groundwork* that we are not able to show that free will actually exists, since the laws of nature are themselves necessary. Nevertheless, he argues, once we separate the noumenal from the phenomenal realm, we are able to show that free will and determinism are compatible.

Man puts himself into another order of things . . . when he conceives of himself with a will and consequently with causality, rather than when he perceives himself as a phenomenon in the sensible world (which he actually is as well) and subjects his causality to external determination in accordance with the laws of nature.[39]

By separating the world into distinct noumenal and phenomenal realms, Kant is able not only to endow individuals with contra-causal freedom, but to demonstrate the compatibility of free will and determinism. But what happens when, in discussions of moral blameworthiness, Kant is forced to distinguish between *Willkür* and *Wille* in order to talk about individuals' actual wills? As we have seen, Kant is led in these discussions to bring the noumenal and phenomenal realms together. As a result, he can no longer assume contra-causal freedom to be an aspect of free will, or at least he cannot assume that it is an aspect of the free will relevant to moral responsibility. Nor can he talk about free will as inherently moral in the way that he did in the *Groundwork*.

Kant's dilemma runs very deep here. He is able to talk about an indi-

---

37. Kant, *Critique of Practical Reason*; Beck, *Kant's Critique*, 205.
38. Kant, *Religion*, 40.
39. Kant, *Groundwork*, 120.

vidual's will as inherently moral in the *Groundwork* only because he associates free will with the categorical imperative. But in the *Critique of Practical Reason* and in the *Religion,* where he is concerned with moral evil, as well as with moral goodness, he is forced not only to distinguish between *Wille* and *Willkür,* but to give up his identification of free will with absolute goodness. By doing so, he cannot help but sacrifice his ability to assume that individuals are morally good when they act according to the moral law and morally bad when they act against it.

Kant's dilemma here is not isolated to his own moral theory, either. Indeed, by moving back and forth between his two understandings of free will, Kant may have underscored better than anyone else the two conflicting requirements that our modern notion of blameworthiness places on us: that an individual's will be undetermined by forces external to itself and that it be intrinsically morally good or bad. Kant was able to meet the first requirement only by splitting the world into two separate realities—the noumenal and the phenomenal. He was able to meet the second requirement only by returning to the realm of phenomena where contra-causal freedom is not possible and by smuggling into free will a relationship between individuals and external authority (or at least the form of such a relationship).

Kant of course never acknowledged that he was invoking a relationship between individuals and external authority, but we cannot help but be suspicious of both his ideal conception of law-abidingness and his very Christian-sounding conception of an evil will. Recall that Kant was able to talk about an absolutely good will only by assuming that both law-abidingness and the notion of universality embodied in it are themselves absolutely good. Since Kant never provides us with a convincing argument for the absolute goodness of either law-abidingness or universality, and since the language that he uses to describe an absolutely good will is clearly derived from Christian dogma, we cannot help but wonder if the structure of Kant's arguments do not require an external authority to sustain his notion of moral goodness and badness.

Kant wants to stay as far away as possible from such an authority in his moral theory. But his notion of intrinsic moral worth may require it nevertheless, since without such an authority, it is not clear how individuals become good or bad. While Kant never resorts to talking about goodness or badness as substances floating around in an individual's soul, he refers in both the *Critique* and *Religion* to an individual's will as evil, a characterization that comes very close to the Christian notion of sinfulness and which would as such seem to require a relationship between individuals and an external being with the authority to pass moral judgments.

Since Kant denies the relevance of such an authority to moral blameworthiness, he is at the very least obliged to explain how individuals can be considered evil in a secular context. Likewise, he is obliged to explore the relationship between moral badness, on the one hand, and moral blameworthiness, on the other. Christian philosophers were able to conflate these two terms by assuming that God, the supreme judge of good and bad, was also the supreme judge of moral blameworthiness. Secular philosophers are not only unable to make such an assumption, but are obliged to justify how, if at all, individuals can be considered morally blameworthy outside the context of a relationship between them and an ideal blamer.

How, we have to ask, can individuals be considered morally blameworthy simply in virtue of their having freely willed a bad action? Modern thinkers choose to characterize individuals as in complete control over their own moral states of being. Hence, they cannot invoke a relationship between individuals and external authority to explain moral blameworthiness. Nor can they fall back on the conventional standards of our more worldly communities. Instead, they are obliged to show how an individual's will could possibly be considered intrinsically praiseworthy or intrinsically blameworthy.

How could they possibly manage to develop such a demonstration? Presumably they would have to demonstrate two things. One is that individuals' wills are either intrinsically good or intrinsically bad. The other is that intrinsic goodness and intrinsic badness are equivalent to moral praiseworthiness and moral blameworthiness (or in other words, that individuals are morally praiseworthy and blameworthy in virtue of the moral goodness and badness of their wills rather than in virtue of a relationship between the individuals and someone who might want to blame them).

The intrinsic goodness or badness of an individual's free will is hard enough to show, since, among other things, we would have to demonstrate not only that there exist absolute standards of goodness and badness, but that goodness and badness are themselves attributes of an individual's own free will. While the former demonstration would entail defending either moral realism or a form of moral objectivity, the latter demonstration would entail conceiving of moral goodness and badness, not as moral judgments, but as attributes or qualities that we can locate in an individual's own will. I do not think that demonstrations of either sort are possible. But they do not need to be refuted in this context if we can show that an individual's own free will, construed as contra-causal freedom, cannot possibly sustain moral attributes of any sort.

A variety of contemporary philosophers come to our aid in pointing out the potentially amoral nature of contra-causal freedom. A. J. Ayer argues that contra-causal freedom does not give the moralist what he wants to the extent that contra-causal freedom entails indeterminism and as such leaves no room for a self which can be considered blame-worthy.[40] P. H. Nowell-Smith goes further and argues that contra-causal freedom removes the possibility of calling a particular individual's action *his* action and hence makes it difficult to talk about blameworthiness in conjunction with the individual himself.[41] Both theorists assume, I think correctly, that the modern notion of moral blameworthiness entails a personality which is both constant over time and undetermined by the social forces normally associated with personality formation.[42]

But even if we could talk about a personality that was not associated with these social forces, we would not necessarily be able to talk about individuals themselves as morally blameworthy in virtue of their hav-ing freely willed a bad action. For moral badness and moral blamewor-thiness are not one and the same thing. While moral badness is ostensibly a quality inherent in individuals, moral blameworthiness sig-nifies that an individual is worthy of being blamed. The difference be-tween the two terms in this context is that while moral badness is ostensibly independent of any reaction we (or an ideal blamer) have to an individual who acted badly, moral blameworthiness is clearly depen-dent on the rules according to which such reactions are governed.

How could individuals be worthy of being blamed simply in virtue of their having freely willed a bad action? Presumably blameworthiness itself would have to be independent of our social practice of blaming. But such independence does not appear to be possible, since the notion of blame itself does not make any sense outside the context of either a relationship between individuals and actual blamers or social criteria for deciding whether or not a particular individual is worthy of our blame.

Defenders of our modern concept of moral responsibility might want to point out here that moral blameworthiness does not rest on ac-tual blame, or in other words that individuals can be considered mor-ally blameworthy even though we do not ourselves choose to blame

40. A. J. Ayer, *Philosophical Essays,* 275.

41. P. H. Nowell-Smith, *Ethics* (London, 1954), 281–82.

42. Hume made this assumption the cornerstone of his own arguments against the moral viability of contra-causal freedom in his *Treatise of Human Nature* (Oxford, 1956). Hume writes in book 2, part 3, that "an undetermined action would be one for which it would be impossible to blame or praise, punish or reward a man, because it would be connected with nothing permanent in his nature."

them. But they could not use such a point to isolate moral blameworthiness from our social practice of blaming. For even though moral blameworthiness may not require us to blame individuals, it does require that we acknowledge the existence of standards of blameworthiness, standards that have to come from somewhere, if not from God, then from our own social conventions and communal practices.

Why, if we want to avoid mention of such conventions and practices, do we not simply consider individuals morally blameworthy in virtue of the fact that they are morally bad? Those who invoke our modern concept of moral responsibility often take this step and as such appear to be able to talk about moral blameworthiness as under an individual's own control. But they appear able to do so only by blurring the distinction between moral blameworthiness, on the one hand, and moral badness, on the other—or in other words, by assuming that since moral badness is a condition of moral blameworthiness, moral blameworthiness can be considered independent of our social practice of blaming.

Moral blameworthiness, though, requires more than that a particular individual be morally bad. It requires that the individual be able to meet either ideal standards of blame (which themselves require an ideal blamer) or a set of communal standards according to which blame is fairly distributed in society. Since these standards are part of a practice—blaming—that is itself composed largely of reactive attitudes, it is not clear how they could be discussed together with free will. Nor is it clear how they could be considered independent of our social practice of blaming.

Since defenders of our modern concept of moral responsibility are obliged to sustain the independence of these standards from our social practice of blaming, they invoke terms such as "abstract blame" and "ideal liability." But they cannot invoke either term without arguing circles around themselves. For, both terms—"blame" and "liability"—rely for their meaning on concrete relationships of authority between individuals who have the power to hold each other accountable in practice. Hence, they make no sense outside of a relationship between individual members of a blaming community.[43]

Neither Aristotle nor the Christian philosophers were at all bothered by the importance of such relationships. Aristotle fully recognized the importance of communal opinion to our standards of blameworthi-

43. For an excellent discussion of the necessity of talking about liability *relations*, see Nicholas Haines, "Responsibility and Accountability," *Journal of Philosophy* 30 (1955), 141–46. Haines argues that "liability is essentially social, and, one might add, institutional; for one could not think of liability if society had not in some way organized its liability relations." (144).

ness, and Aquinas located the source of all moral standards in the authority of God. But modern philosophers can do neither of these things. Hence, they are forced to tack words such as "abstract" and "ideal" onto liability relationships that are clearly social and/or religious in both form and content.

In chapter 9 I suggest that while constructs such as abstract blame and ideal liability are logically incoherent, they nevertheless function in modern society not only to internalize the standards of social blameworthiness, but to obscure the practical nature of our moral judgments of responsibility. Likewise, I suggest that while the distinction between moral and social blameworthiness ultimately breaks down under logical scrutiny, it nevertheless enables us to sustain our view of morality in general as free from the contingencies that characterize our social and political life. Suffice it to point out here, or rather below, that even if our modern concept of moral responsibility were coherent, it would not help us discover who is morally responsible for various sorts of suffering in the world.

Determinism, Moral Luck, and Insufficient Control

I suggested in the last section that our modern notion of moral blameworthiness is incoherent on its own terms. I concentrate here on sketching several further difficulties associated with our modern concept of moral responsibility that render it inappropriate to a discussion about our moral responsibility for external harm. I do so not in a thorough fashion, but simply to suggest the range of difficulties that one might expect to encounter in applying our modern concept of moral responsibility to social and political affairs. The first of these difficulties is one that philosophers have argued about endlessly. I refer here to the possibility that the notion of free will required by moral blameworthiness does not exist.

The two major defenses of contra-causal freedom among secular philosophers are libertarianism and "two-domainism." Libertarians, who assert the existence, and not just the possibility, of free will, tend to make two general claims. One is that an individual's decision to act is made by a self that is not determined by either heredity or environment. The other is that the individual can always decide otherwise than she actually does, in the contra-causal sense of "can."

Neither of these claims is counterintuitive. Indeed both claims play an important role in our modern practices of individualism. But they are difficult, if not impossible, to demonstrate. Those who attempt such a demonstration usually do so on the basis of our moral conscious-

ness. C. A. Campbell, one of the most intelligent defenders of libertarianism, maintains that we are free in the sense indicated because our
"moral consciousness" shows that it is impossible for us *not* to believe
that we are free in this sense. According to Campbell, once we

place ourselves imaginatively at the standpoint of the agent engaged in the typi-
cal moral situation in which free will is claimed, we cannot possibly believe,
while in this state, that we must act on our strongest desire, but rather that we
are free to choose between desire and dutyfree in the sense of being the arbiter
between genuinely open possibilities.[44]

As many of Campbell's critics have pointed out, the major drawback
to relying on moral consciousness in this context is that we cannot possibly know that our sense of freedom is not merely an illusion. And unless we can know this much, we can never be sure that our choice has not
been determined for us. Moreover, in order for moral consciousness to
confirm the existence of free will, it would have to precede our decision
to act. Such precedence would not seem possible. For as J. S. Mill
pointed out over a hundred years ago,

to be conscious of free will must mean to be conscious, before I have decided,
that I am able to decide either way. . . . Consciousness tells me what I do feel.
But what I am able to do is not subject to consciousness. Consciousness is not
prophetic.[45]

One way of getting around the problems posed by libertarianism is
to follow Kant's example and separate actions from mere behavior.
This is essentially what two-domainists such as A. I. Melden do. Melden
claims that what distinguishes actions from behavior is that actions involve intention and are as such not, like behavior, susceptible to causal
analysis. According to Melden, "an individual's action, although involving bodily movements, is not identical with a bodily movement, and neither caused nor uncaused."[46]

By separating the two spheres out from one another in this way,
Melden and others are able to carve out a place for contra-causal freedom. But they are not able to do so without placing a great deal of strain
on their own arguments. First of all, contrary to Melden's analysis, we
do not usually explain actions with reference to intentions alone. (We
usually refer also to bodily movements.) Second, even if we did explain
actions with reference to intentions alone, we could not do so without
reference also to the rules of social behavior, rules that enable us to rec-

44. C. A. Campbell, "Is Free Will a Pseudo-Problem?" *Mind* 10 (1951), 441.
45. J. S. Mill, *An Examination of Sir William Hamilton's Philosophy* (London, 1967), 448.
46. A. I. Melden, *Free Action* (London, 1961), 31.

ognize, for instance, the waving of a hand as the act of signaling. While such rules do not replace a subjective notion of willing, they do render actions at least partially susceptible to causal analysis.

Third, Melden never explains why actions, even if they could be distinguished from mere behavior on the basis on intention, are not susceptible to the sort of causal analysis which he cites. Instead, he, like other two-domainists, falls back on the "fact" that our normal explanations of an individual's actions are of a noncausal nature. Likewise, in his reliance on such a "fact," he assumes what he says he is trying to establish: that intentions are not socially or physically determined. We see Melden, for example, writing that to explain an action by saying that an individual intended to bring about harm is not a causal statement—for the individual's intention is "intelligible only as an intention and as such not susceptible to causal analysis."[47] Melden may be right about how we construe an individual's action as noncausal. But he clearly leaves open the possibility that our activity of intending is itself caused by forces external to the individual's will.

Critics of contra-causal freedom often pick up on the latter point and place it at the center of their analyses. Determinists in general claim not only that intentions are caused, but that they must be caused, given the truth of determinism. While the arguments which they develop to back up these two claims are many and varied, the best among them concentrate on showing that even if determinism were not true, contra-causal freedom would not be possible. For there is no middle ground between determinism, on the one hand, and pure randomness, on the other. Hence, the opposite of determinism cannot, as libertarians assume, be conceived of contra-causal freedom. Instead, it must be conceived of as the sort of randomness that stands as the antithesis of individual control.[48]

Defenders of free will at this point do not appear to be as willing as they were twenty years ago to demonstrate the existence of free will. Instead, they question the truth of determinism itself—pointing out, among other things, that determinism is merely a way of looking at the world and hence is not susceptible to the sorts of truth claims often associated with it. Here they are supported to a certain extent by discoveries in modern physics. But they cannot use these discoveries to justify the existence of free will. Nor can they escape the fact that even if determinism were only a theoretical construct through which we as human

47. Ibid., 32.
48. For an example of this sort of argument, see Smart, "Free Will, Praise, and Blame."

beings appropriate the world, it would still get in the way of our ever discovering free will in practice.

The point here is that regardless of the basis of our moral judgments, we as human beings can only appropriate the world through deterministic categories. Kant himself made this point very clearly in the *Groundwork*, where he argued that even if we could keep the noumenal and phenomenal realms separate, contra-causal freedom could not be grasped by human beings. For human beings can only grasp things when they have an object given to them in some possible experience, and such experience necessarily requires the application of deterministic categories.

While the inability of human beings to grasp contra-causal freedom in the world does not pose a threat to moral responsibility itself, it does pose a problem for those who are concerned to establish the conditions under which individuals are morally responsible in practice. As things now stand, very few scholars concerned about moral responsibility are willing to defend the notion of contra-causal freedom required by the modern concept of moral responsibility. Libertarians, who defend the possibility of contra-causal freedom on the basis of either our moral intuitions or God, are still in force.[49] But the vast majority of scholars now writing about moral responsibility argue either that determinism rules out the possibility of contra-causal freedom or that there is no logical middle ground between determinism, on the one hand, and pure randomness, on the other.[50]

Since moral responsibility as now construed requires contra-causal freedom, one might expect such arguments to create a crisis among those intent on retaining our modern concept of moral responsibility itself. But such a crisis has not occurred. Indeed, it appears that only hard determinists, of which there are now relatively few, have chosen to leave our modern concept of moral responsibility behind altogether.[51] The rest have generally chosen to pursue what has come to be known as soft determinism.

"Soft determinism" is itself somewhat of a misnomer. While those

49. The most famous libertarian is, I suppose, Jean-Paul Sartre. See his *Being and Nothingness* (New York, 1956). For one of the most vehement defences by an analytic philosopher of the possibility of contra-causal freedom, see the works of C. A. Campbell listed in the bibliography.

50. The number of works on determinism is extremely large. For one of the most straightforward and broadly argued defenses of determinism, see Smart, "Free Will, Praise, and Blame."

51. For one of the most influential sets of arguments along these lines by a hard determinist, see Peter Van Inwagon, "The Incompatibility of Responsibility and Determinism," in *Moral Responsibility*, ed. John Fischer (Ithaca, 1986), 241–49.

who adhere to it may be soft on free will, they are not generally soft on determinism. Indeed, they often build on the analyses of hard determinists in their efforts to show that contra-causal freedom is both logically incoherent and empirically impossible. But unlike their "harder" colleagues, they do not give up on the concept of moral responsibility. Instead, they try to develop an alternative notion of free will, or sense of "X could have done otherwise," that is compatible with determinism in that it requires only that an individual have had the "power" to do otherwise.

The power referred to here entails that an individual normally be capable of doing that which he did not do—or in other words, that he possess certain talents or capacities for action. According to John Canfield, for example:

Because we know that Jones is a normal, healthy person, we know that he has the physical ability to raise his arm. We also know that he has the ability to keep still. Thus, it is true that he can raise it, and it is true that he can keep it still. If, on the contrary, a person Smith is paralyzed, we say, referring to his physical disability, that he cannot raise his arm.[52]

The situation is similar with respect to psychological abilities. According to Canfield:

We say of an idiot that he cannot learn to read, meaning that he lacks the mental ability. We say also, for example, that Jones cannot beat Botvinnik at chess, meaning again that he lacks a certain mental capacity. We say, to take a perhaps doubtful example, that the kleptomaniac lacks the ability to refrain from stealing, or that a certain compulsive cannot refrain from repeating over to himself some particular phrase.[53]

According to soft determinists like Canfield, the individual's power in this context renders him free: "if he can do E and can refrain from doing E, then he is free with respect to doing E."[54] Moreover, if he is free with respect to doing E, then he can be held morally responsible for not doing E (or for doing something else). The virtue of the soft determinists' position here is that both free will and moral responsibility appear to be compatible with a theory of determinism.

Unfortunately, while the capacity of an individual to perform an action which he did not perform may signify that he had at least two potential actions to choose from, it does not signify that he had free choice. In other words, it does not signify that he was free to choose one

52. John Canfield, "The Compatibility of Free Will and Determinism," *The Philosophical Review* 7 (1962), 356.
53. Ibid., 357.
54. Ibid., 368.

action over the other. Furthermore, as long as his choice was determined for him, there is no use in trying to claim that his will was free in the sense relevant to moral responsibility.

One way of getting around this problem might be to view the ability of an individual to do otherwise as the ability to "try" or to "make an effort of the will." One philosopher who views the individual's ability to do otherwise in this way is David Locke. According to Locke, "although our power to try may be limited by many different factors, it is never the principle of causality which annihilates or delimits it."[55] If an individual is "able to try," according to Locke, we can consider him free—and can do so without violating any of our theories of determinism.

While the term "soft determinism" that Canfield, Locke, and other contemporary philosophers use to talk about free will is fairly recent in origin, the position that it represents is not. Both Thomas Hobbes and John Locke dismissed the possibility of contra-causal freedom and argued for its replacement by another sort of freedom in their discussions of responsibility. Hobbes distinguished the traditional "free to will" from his own "free to do if he will." Moreover, he chose to talk about the latter in terms of the "power of an individual to execute his own actions."[56]

In a similar fashion, Locke chose to replace the traditional notion of contra-causal freedom with a softer notion of free will that entailed only the power of an individual to carry out his own intentions. In "The Idea of Power," Locke argues that liberty is not an idea belonging to volition or preference but to the person having the power of doing, or forbearing to do, according to his own choices.

The idea of liberty is the idea of power in any agent to do or forbear any particular action, according to the determination or thought of the mind, whereby either of them is not in the power of the agent to be produced by him according to his volition, there is not liberty. . . . The idea of liberty reaches as far as that power and no farther.[57]

Both of these early positions have their contemporary counterparts not only in the works of soft determinism, but in the arguments put forth by three of the most influential philosophers now writing on free will and determinism: Gerald Dworkin, Gary Watson, and Harry Frankfurt. Dworkin, like Hobbes and Locke, takes a negative approach

55. David Locke, "Ifs and Cans Revisited," *Philosophy* 37 (1962), 246.
56. Thomas Hobbes, *The Question Concerning Liberty, Necessity, and Chance* (London, 1841).
57. John Locke, "The Idea of Power," in *Essay Concerning Human Understanding* (New York, 1959), 316–17.

to free will. "I am free when my conduct is under my control, and I act under constraint when my conduct is controlled by someone else. My conduct is under my control when it is determined by my own desires, motives and attentions, and not under my control when it is determined by the desires, motives and attentions of someone else."[58]

Watson, like the others, argues that human beings are free agents only in a limited number of respects. He himself focuses on the importance of valuation to our sense of free agency. A person is free, Watson claims, when his motivational system allows him to get what he most wants or values. A person is unfree when he is unable to get what he most wants, or values, because of his own motivational system. In this sense, "to circumscribe a person's freedom is to contract the range of things he is able to do."[59]

Frankfurt emphasizes the rational aspect of willing that enables us to govern our own actions, but like the others, he does not reintroduce the notion of an ideal will. Instead, he focuses on what he calls second-order volitions. "A person's will," Frankfurt argues, is the "notion of an *effective* desire—one that moves (or will or would move) a person all the way to action." An individual has an effective desire, or a second-order volition, when he wants "a certain will to be his own." Moreover, it is "only because a person has volitions of the second order that he is capable of both enjoying and of lacking freedom of will."[60]

All three of these philosophers, along with Daniel Dennett,[61] John Fisher,[62] Susan Wolff,[63] and others who are now concerned to carve out a workable theory of free agency provide us with a variety of very important insights into what I would call our social practice of freedom. But they do not rethink the nature of moral responsibility. Nor, for that matter, do those soft determinists who came before them. While soft determinists such as John Canfield and David Locke go to great lengths to develop a notion of free will that is compatible with determinism, they do not follow through on the implications of their softer conception of free will for moral responsibility. Instead, they assume that by developing a notion of free will that is not ruled out by determinism, they have solved the problem of moral responsibility. Canfield writes in

58. Gerald Dworkin, "Acting Freely," *Nous* 4 (1970), 367.

59. Gary Watson, "Free Agency," reprinted in *Moral Responsibility*, ed. Martin Fisher (Ithaca, 1986), 81.

60. Harry Frankfurt, "Freedom of the Will and the Concept of a Person," reprinted in ibid., 74.

61. Daniel Dennett, *Elbow Room: Varieties of Free Will Worth Having* (Cambridge, Mass., 1984).

62. John Fisher, "Responsibility and Freedom," in Fisher, *Moral Responsibility*, 9–61.

63. Susan Wolff, "Asymmetrical Freedom," *Journal of Philosophy* (1980), 151–56.

this context: "Once we realize that free will does not entail the meta-physical powers that we once thought it did, we no longer have to worry about the possibility of moral responsibility itself."[64]

Canfield may have jumped the gun here, though. If he and other soft determinists were to focus on the relationship between their softer conception of free will and moral responsibility itself, they would have to acknowledge two things. One is that while their alternative notion of free will might be compatible with determinism, it is not the sort of thing over which individuals themselves have total control. (Individuals may, for instance, be born lazy or with weakness of will.) The other is that while they might be able to use their alternative notion of free will to shed light on our social practice of blaming, that notion is simply not strong enough to bolster our modern concept of moral responsibility.[65]

Dworkin, Watson, Frankfurt, and their associates are clearly not as attached to our modern concept of moral responsibility as earlier soft determinists.[66] But they do not replace it with an alternative concept of moral responsibility either. If they were to ask themselves, "What is left of the concept of moral responsibility once we stop thinking about free will as contra-causal freedom?" they would presumably have to turn to those "reactive attitudes" that they speak of in conjunction with moral responsibility. Likewise, if they wanted to retain the importance of these attitudes to our judgments of moral responsibility, they would presumably have to develop an understanding of moral responsibility that explained not only how our reactive attitudes shape our various notions of free agency, but how our social practice of blaming takes into consideration our various judgments of causal responsibility.

What if all of the aforementioned difficulties associated with our modern concept of moral responsibility did not exist? Could we then use the concept to talk about the moral responsibility of individuals for external harm? By way of concluding this chapter and introducing the next, let me point out two general stumbling blocks that get in the way of applying the modern concept of moral responsibility to social and

64. John Canfield, "Compatibility of Free Will and Determinism," 357.

65. A. J. Ayer, among others, drew this conclusion early on: "The main objections to soft determinism are that the boundaries of constraint are not all that easy to draw with any precision; and that even if they could be drawn at all precisely, the distinction for which they are needed seems rather arbitrary. Why should a man be praised or blamed if his actions are brought about in one way and acquitted if they are brought about in another? In either case, they are equally the product of his heredity and environment" (A. J. Ayer, *The Concept of a Person and Other Essays* [New York, 1963], 62).

66. Watson suggests that our modern concept of moral responsibility may not be coherent, but he does not pursue this line of argument very far. See his comments on pages 82–83 of "Free Agency."

political affairs. One is what contemporary philosophers talk about as moral luck. The other is the dependence of moral responsibility for external states of affairs on considerations which individuals themselves cannot possibly control.

"Moral luck" as a phenomenon refers to both the element of contingency in an individual's actions and the fact that we nevertheless persist in scrutinizing such actions from a moral point of view. Thomas Nagel captures both aspects in "Moral Luck," where he writes:

> Where a significant aspect of what someone does depends on factors beyond his control, yet we continue to treat him in that respect as an object of moral judgment, it can be called moral luck.[67]

Nagel cites as an example of the precariousness associated with moral luck the case of an individual who launches a violent revolution against an authoritarian regime. If the individual fails, according to Nagel, the individual will surely be held morally responsible for the suffering of its victims. If, on the other hand, the revolution succeeds, which can never be predicted, the individual will probably be excused from all such responsibility. According to Nagel, "from the point of view which makes responsibility dependent on control, this precariousness seems absurd."[68]

Joel Feinberg expresses a similar reaction in *Doing and Deserving*, where he writes of the senselessness of invoking the concept of moral responsibility to talk about the causal relations between individuals and external harm. According to Feinberg, moral responsibility is completely incompatible with the sorts of precariousness that individuals face when they set out to effect change in the world. Hence, while we might want to continue to invoke the concept of moral responsibility to describe the relations between an individual and his own actions, we would be wise to give up talking about the moral responsibility of individuals for external states of affairs. Feinberg makes clear here that

> none of [the above] difficulties need embarrass the champion of moral responsibility. If he is a rational man and a philosopher, he will admit that moral responsibility for external harm makes no sense and argue that moral responsibility is restricted to the inner world of the mind, where the agent rules supreme and luck has no place.[69]

Both Nagel and Feinberg are correct in their assessment of the difficulties associated with the application of moral responsibility as a con-

---

67. Thomas Nagel, "Moral Luck," in his *Mortal Questions* (Cambridge, England, 1979), 32–33.

68. Ibid., 31.

69. Feinberg, *Doing and Deserving*, 32.

cept to relations between individuals and external affairs. But it is important to remember that these difficulties exist only when the concept of moral responsibility that we have in mind specifies the total control by individuals over that which they are being held morally responsible. Indeed, it is only because both Nagel and Feinberg assume the necessity of such control that they find the phenomenon of moral luck troublesome in the first place. (Recall the ease with which Aristotle handled the subject matter.)[70]

The second stumbling block that gets in the way of applying our modern concept of moral responsibility to social and political affairs concerns the multiplicity of causal relations that exist between an individual and external harm and the fact that whichever causal relation we choose as relevant to moral responsibility will inevitably reflect a variety of norms and conventions over which the individual herself can never have control. Here the problem is not so much "luck" as the dependence of our action descriptions on considerations which are, among other things, practical in nature and hence antithetical to the spirit of our modern concept of moral responsibility. I devote a considerable amount of the rest of this study to articulating these considerations, which range from those associated with the prevention of harm to those whose primary source is in the realm of interest. What I have tried to do in this chapter is to explore the modern concept of moral responsibility itself in such a way as to make clear why such considerations are not something which it can tolerate.

70. Interestingly enough, Judith Andre takes the incoherence of our modern concept of moral responsibility vis-à-vis the issue of moral luck as a signal that we should move back to an Aristotelian concept of moral responsibility or in other words, to a morality that focuses not on moral agency but on "What kind of person is X or should X be?" See her arguments in "Nagel, Williams, and Moral Luck," *Analysis* 43 (1983), 202–7.

PART TWO

Moral Responsibility and the Prevention of Harm

Shared Starting Points

Throughout part 2, I focus on the conditions under which individuals are now and might be in the future considered morally responsible for the suffering of others. I do so both by exploring the efforts of several contemporary philosophers to establish these conditions and by adumbrating my own pragmatic perspective. I focus on the efforts of John Harris, John Casey, and Dennis Thompson in particular, not only because they provide us with important insights into our practical judgments of causal responsibility and blameworthiness, but because they demonstrate in very different ways why we need to move beyond the modern concept of moral responsibility as it is now construed if we are to talk about the moral responsibility of individuals for external harm.

While many contemporary philosophers refer to the moral responsibility of individuals for external harm, they do not explore the conditions under which moral responsibility for external harm is possible in general. Instead, like many of the rest of us, they assume that if we want to know whether or not a particular individual is morally responsible for harm, all we have to do is ask whether or not the individual is morally responsible for an action of the form "X brought about harm."

Harris, Casey, and Thompson are not able to make such an assumption themselves because they are confronted with cases in which there is considerable disagreement about whether or not harm can be included in our description of a particular individual's action. Since they cannot, for example, automatically describe a capitalist as causing third world starvation or an abortionist as murdering a child, they find it necessary to establish the conditions under which harm can be deemed the consequence of an individual's actions in general. Likewise, they find it necessary to acknowledge openly what other scholars often ignore: that when we hold an individual morally responsible for actions of the form

"X brought about harm," we make two separate judgments about the individual rather than a single factual discovery. One of these judgments is that the individual's actions were causally responsible for harm. The other is that the individual herself caused—freely willed— her own actions.

Harris, Casey, and Thompson all agree on the importance of both sorts of causal responsibility to our judgments of moral blameworthiness. But they develop what critics talk about as competing or conflicting approaches to moral responsibility itself. Harris develops a consequentialist theory of moral agency as a way of radically extending what we now conceive to be our realm of moral responsibility. Casey tries to reinforce the status quo with respect to moral responsibility by focusing our attention on the importance of social role playing to our description of an individual's action, and Thompson sets out to develop an approach to moral responsibility that builds on the standards of democratic theory.

In the end, neither Harris nor Casey nor Thompson is able to show how the requirements of moral responsibility can be met in cases involving external harm. Nor are they able to develop coherent defenses of their own approaches to moral responsibility. For while they openly recognize the various social and political considerations that ground our judgments of responsibility in practice, they insist on squeezing these considerations into an ostensibly factual discovery of free will. Likewise, while they provide us with a number of important insights into our practical judgments of causal responsibility and blameworthiness, they find it necessary to leave these insights behind as a result of their acceptance of our modern concept of moral responsibility unreconstructed.

I argue that if they were free from the requirements of our modern concept of moral responsibility as now construed, they would be able to develop key aspects of both causal responsibility and blameworthiness. I try to develop these aspects myself in this part of the study within the framework that each theorist provides. I thus concentrate in this chapter on the practical grounds of moral agency, and in chapters 6 and 7 on social role playing and organizational excuses, respectively.

A Radical Extension of Moral Responsibility

John Harris's purpose in "The Marxist Conception of Violence"[1] is to extend radically what we now conceive to be our realm of moral re-

---

1. John Harris, "The Marxist Conception of Violence," *Philosophy and Public Affairs* 3 (1973–74), 192–220.

sponsibility. He does so by showing that we are morally responsible for much of the suffering that we now think of as a "normal" or even "natural" part of our daily lives. Harris contends that such suffering is not caused by natural forces, but is instead the result of human agency. "Much of the suffering that has been thought to be part of the natural hazards of life," writes Harris,

> is not at all natural and if we ask why this harm is occurring when it might have been prevented, we will find that it is in fact attributable to the machinations of men. . . . Far from being the operation of gratuitous and impersonal forces, such harm must be seen as the work of assignable agents.[2]

Who is to be included among the "assignable agents" of third world starvation and the illnesses of industrial workers? Harris chooses to include in this group all persons who let such suffering occur when they could have prevented it. Likewise, he makes clear that these individuals are not only causally responsible for the suffering in question, but morally blameworthy for having brought it about.

Harris does not delve into the nature of moral responsibility as a concept. But he does stipulate at the outset that to discover that an individual is morally responsible for external harm is to discover that the individual is both causally responsible for it and morally to blame. Likewise, he proceeds to establish conditions of moral responsibility that are not only identical to those established in chapter 4 but which would be foreign to any concept other than our modern concept of moral responsibility. While Harris discusses these conditions separately later on in his essay, he expresses them at the outset as part of one overarching principle: that any individual who "himself caused" harm is morally responsible for it.

Under what conditions can an individual be understood to have "himself caused" harm in the sense relevant to moral responsibility? Harris answers this question by providing us with a set of practical considerations that lead us to view actions and omissions together as causally responsible for external harm. Harris first introduces these considerations in his characterization of those cases in which it "makes sense" to question whether or not a particular individual caused the suffering of others. In these cases, we are told, "harm occurs which might have been prevented or in which harm will occur unless it is prevented."[3] Harris then goes on to make the relationship between causation and the prevention of harm explicit. "When we are seeking a causal explanation of the disasters that overtake human beings," writes Harris,

2. Ibid., 194.
3. Ibid., 206.

We are often not seeking to explain why the disaster occurred on this occasion when normally it would not have occurred, but why it occurred on this occasion when it need not have occurred . . . The question that interests us is not "What made the difference?" but "What could have made the difference?" . . . When we are looking for what might have made the difference between harm's occurring and its not occurring, anything that could have been done to prevent the harm in question is a likely candidate for causal status.[4]

Harris does not label his particular approach to causation and responsibility in this context. But he does place the prevention of harm at the center of his attention when talking about causation. Likewise, he does make clear that the causal responsibility of a particular individual for harm depends on what might have prevented the harm from occurring in the first place. Hence, we are justified in talking about Harris as someone who incorporates practical considerations into his judgments of causal responsibility.[5]

While Harris incorporates practical considerations into his judgments of causal responsibility, he is not a pragmatist of the interpretist sort cited in chapter 1. Nor would such a label make sense in the context of his arguments, since he views "preventability", i.e., whether or not a particular individual could have prevented harm, as a purely factual matter unmediated by our own expectaions of the individual. I suggest later on that preventability is not a purely factual matter, but is based on our own social and political norms. Harris denies such a possibility and argues that whether or not an individual is causally responsible for harm has nothing to do with our expectations of him, but depends only on whether the individual himself caused harm.

Harris makes explicit in this context his opposition to that school of thought (represented by John Casey in chapter 6) which contends that failures to act count as causally effective only when the actions in question are ones which we would normally expect individuals to perform.

The idea that a prerequisite of our saying that A's failure to do X caused Y is that X is somehow expected of A, which is employed by D'Arcy, Casey and Hart-Honore, is probably correct for the majority of failures to act.

But, he continues, it is correct for the majority of failures to act only because in general we have come to expect that A do X because A's doing X will prevent Y.

Harris's own concern is with those cases in which our expectations of

4. Ibid., 207.

5. Harris makes his consequentialism more explicit in "Williams on Negative Responsibility," *Philosophical Quarterly* 24 (1974), 265–73.

individuals lag behind the ability of these individuals to prevent harm. In these cases, Harris doubts

whether the techniques of preventing harm must have already become *customary*, the procedures and routines *normal*, the method *standard*, before we can say that their omissions caused some outcome.[6]

Further substantiating this doubt, Harris asks: "at what point does the failure to neutralize the harmful effects of disease come to rank as the cause of the harmful effect?" "On the view outlined above," he writes, "this happens only when the practice of inoculation has become a 'second nature.'" But let us suppose that a vaccine against cancer is discovered, that its discovery is made known, and that no one takes the necessary steps to make it available to those who need it. In this case:

Are we not entitled, indeed required, to conclude that a government, for example, or a drug company, which continues to allow people to die of cancer, when they so easily could be saved, is causally responsible for their deaths? And are we not entitled to say this even though no customary vaccination against cancer has become second nature to the society in question?[7]

Furthermore, what if the normal functioning of society is always a disaster? Every year the poor and the jobless, the aged and the infirm, suffer terribly. What is the cause of this suffering? The myopic view, according to Harris, is that these individuals suffer because they are poor and jobless, aged and infirm. The "World Moral Authority," on the other hand, would

identify the neglect of other members of society or the government as the cause, . . . And surely the "World Moral Authority's" causal explanation is not upset by the discovery that this society normally neglects its weakest members, that there is no difference between what they did this year and what they always do, that caring for the needy is by no means an established procedure with them.[8]

Harris's point once again is that neither personal preferences nor social norms are relevant to the causal responsibility of an individual's actions or omissions for external harm. All that matters is that the individual was able to prevent the harm in question. If he could have prevented it but did not, then his failure to do so can be considered a consequence of his failure to act. In this vein Harris writes: "where Y involves harm to human beings, Y will be a consequence of A's not doing X simply where X could have prevented Y."[9]

6. Harris, "The Marxist Conception of Violence," 203.
7. Ibid., 207.
8. Ibid., 208.
9. Ibid.

Harris provides us in these passages with a very compelling statement of his approach to causal responsibility and makes clear why it might lead us to prevent more harm in society. But he leaves several things out of his arguments which we might have expected him to include. First of all, he does not say why his approach to causal responsibility is better than approaches that take social expectations seriously, other than to point out that when we take social expectations seriously, we do not hold the affluent responsible for a great deal of suffering in the world.[10] Second, he does not fill out or justify his assumption of a "World Moral Authority." Instead, he simply uses it to dismiss the importance of social expectations and to characterize his own judgments of causal responsibility as morally correct.

While Harris does not openly defend his particular approach to causal responsibility, it does seem to constitute a clear improvement over many other approaches to causal responsibility in two important respects. First of all, it recognizes that causal responsibility is not simply a relationship between cause and effect but a relationship between an individual and some occurrence as prescribed by an adjudicator. Second, it enables us to grasp, on a very general level, the sorts of criteria that all such adjudicators necessarily bring to bear on the causal relationships that they construe between an individual and external harm.

These criteria may not always be geared to the prevention of harm, as Harris himself suggests. But they do embody the perspective of practical action, i.e., the perspective that leads us to choose among a variety of contributing factors of a particular state of affairs the one or more causes that we can control in the future so as to ensure that the state of affairs occurs again if it is desirable and does not occur again if it is undesirable. Likewise, while these criteria may not be as objective or as morally correct as those invoked by Harris's own "World Moral Authority," they do embody the sorts of purposes and projects that we as human beings cannot help but bring to bear on our judgments of causal responsibility.

Harris is of course not the only one to view causation from a practical perspective. R. B. Perry, for instance, argues that when we look for the causes of a negative state of affairs, we tend to focus on those forces that

10. While such an argument might be sufficient to bolster a utilitarian argument or Harris's own radicalism, it is not sufficient to justify Harris's claims about the nature of causation, especially since these claims are supposed to be factual. Moreover, such a justification would seem to be especially important in the context of Harris's arguments, since he is concerned with omissions and there are many who contend that omissions are not causally effective. For a discussion of this debate, see Elazer Weinryb, "Omissions and Responsibility," *Philosophical Quarterly* 30 (January 1980), 1–18.

we might be able to control in the future so as to prevent the harm in question from occurring again. According to Perry:

We describe as the cause of an event that practical condition by which we hope to control it. The very meaning to the word "cause" is likely to vary with other purposes. Those who are concerned to produce something beneficial seek the "cause" of what they wish to produce in some new condition. . . . The new condition which is called for to eliminate the bad situation cannot be just any condition. It must be one that can be manipulated and modified.[11]

R. G. Collingwood takes a similar approach to causal responsibility in *An Essay on Metaphysics,* where he argues that the "cause of a thing is the *handle* by means of which we can control a particular state of affairs."[12] Joel Feinberg, who is not himself a pragmatist, argues that we can "describe as the cause of an event that particular condition by which we hope to control it."[13] All three theorists make clear that our own purposes and projects determine in part the cause that we choose to find responsible for harm.

By doing so, they take us beyond the more common assumption that causal responsibility is a mere factual discovery. Likewise, they provide us with a basis upon which to explore the variety of social and political norms that we bring to bear on causal responsibility in our efforts to control a particular situation. I discuss several of these norms throughout the following chapters and focus in particular on those that tell us who is in the best position to prevent harm and how much they should be expected to sacrifice of their own well-being. Harris not only denies the relevance of such norms, but assumes that the question "Who could have prevented harm?" is one that can be answered objectively. Hence, while he sets us off in the right direction, he is held back from exploring in detail the various practical concerns that we bring to bear on our judgments of causal responsibility by his insistence on moral correctness.

How can he assume that his judgments of causal responsibility are not only factually accurate, but morally correct? Harris does not address this question directly. Instead, he simply asserts the judgment of his "World Moral Authority," who is ostensibly able to take an objective and morally correct view of both an individual's practical capabilities and his causal responsibility for external harm. (Harris may of course not believe in either the existence or possibility of such an authority. But he nevertheless uses it to back up his own claim that social and political

11. R. B. Perry, *General Theory of Value* (Cambridge, Mass., 1954), 418.
12. R. G. Collingwood, *An Essay On Metaphysics* (Oxford, 1940).
13. Joel Feinberg, *Doing and Deserving* (Princeton, 1970), 162.

norms are irrelevant to the causal responsibility of individuals for external harm.)

What if Harris's World Moral Authority turned out not to exist? Presumably Harris would be forced either to find another way of characterizing causal responsibility as noncontingent or else acknowledge that the practical considerations that we bring to bear on our judgments of responsibility are themselves mediated by our own social and political norms. How might he attempt to do the former? Since he places the prevention of harm at the center of his attention anyway, he might be tempted to develop a utilitarian approach to moral responsibility. But to do so, I argue in chapter 8, would be highly problematic.

Moreover, the "preventability" of harm might not be as straightforward as Harris suggests. Indeed, it might turn out to depend on the very sorts of expectations from which Harris is trying to distance himself. Recall that Harris views preventability—or what could have prevented harm—as if it were a purely factual matter. "When we are looking for what might have made the difference between harm's occurring and its not occurring, anything that could have been done to prevent the harm in question is a likely candidate for causal status."[14] But surely there are a number of value judgments that we have to make along with our factual analyses, judgments such as how to balance our various needs and projects. Moreover, in doing so, we have to take into consideration not only individual actions, but the concrete institutions and processes through which harm is prevented in the cases about which Harris is concerned.

As things now stand, Harris talks about our causal responsibility for particular cases of harm as if they existed in isolation. Hence, he is able to view certain preventative measures as obviously available. But particular cases of harm—and their prevention—are frequently interconnected and almost always involve institutionalized action. Hence, if we want to talk about the prevention of harm in general, we will have to view particular cases of harm alongside one another so as to figure out how we might channel our resources into the prevention of harm most productively. Likewise, in our efforts to focus on the prevention of harm in general, we will have to rephrase Harris's original statement about causal responsibility to read: Individual X can be considered causally responsible for harm if he could have done something to prevent the harm *without creating more harm elsewhere.*

On the surface, such a statement appears to be relatively straightforward, if not objective. But once we move away from particular cases of

14. Harris, "Marxist Conception of Violence," 209.

harm to harm in general, which we would have to do if we wanted to take the prevention of harm as our central value, we are faced with a great deal more controversy than Harris ever acknowledges. While we may all agree that a particular case of harm needs to be prevented, we will not all necessarily agree that our resources should go to the prevention of that particular case of harm instead of to the prevention of others.

Harris might want to intervene here and claim that if only we put our minds to it, we could prevent all the serious cases of harm in the world. But such a claim would be farfetched, and in any case, questions of priority would still arise. How, for instance, would we know which cases of harm are most urgently in need of prevention? Who would we choose as the moral agents of harm in cases where there are large numbers of equally well qualified candidates and only a few are needed? What would we do in cases where the prevention of harm required us to sacrifice projects that we valued dearly?

It is these sorts of questions that we would have to ask if we were to figure out who could best prevent harm in the cases about which Harris is concerned. While we might be able to answer these questions to our own satisfaction, we could not, as human beings, do so without invoking our own values and personal preferences. Nor could we characterize our judgments of causal responsibility as free from the sorts of personal preferences and social expectations that Harris eschews. Harris's own example of starvation in the third world provides a good case in point. Here we might want, like Harris, to consider all of those who fail to prevent such suffering as moral agents of it. But if we take the prevention of harm seriously in general and acknowledge that no case of harm can be viewed in isolation, we will not make such a move unless we have already convinced ourselves that to do so is in the best interests of preventing harm overall.

As things now stand, there is considerable disagreement among us with regard not only to who is in the best position to prevent starvation in the third world, but to how we can best prevent such suffering in the future. While some of us argue that a large-scale redistribution of wealth to the third world is necessary, others contend that it is more important that we reinvest in our own economic system or even let famine take its own course.[15] Hence, while some of us might be willing to hold ourselves causally responsible for such famine (if we buy Harris's general analysis), others would presumably not be willing to do so.

15. For an example of such an argument, see Garrett Hardin, "Life Boat Ethics: The Case against Helping the Poor," *World Hunger and Moral Obligations,* ed. William Aiken and Hugh La Follette (Englewood Cliffs, N.J., 1977), 11–21.

If we are members of the former group and are willing, say, to transfer a portion of our salary to the third world, we might be tempted to dismiss members of the latter group as selfish or insincere. But to do so would not be fair to at least some of them. For surely there are those who look at the huge amount of suffering in the world and conclude that we can alleviate it better through the sustenance of our own capitalist system than through a wholesale redistribution of wealth. Moreover, even if we could label these individuals "selfish," it is not obvious that selfishness is so bad in this context. Indeed, what we call selfish might be defined by others as a way of placing very high value on their own privacy or personal projects.

The importance of our valuation of personal integrity cannot be underestimated in this context. While the prevention of harm is clearly of value to most people, so too is the ability of individuals to guide their own lives according to the projects that they have established for themselves. The problem is that these projects do not always coincide with the prevention of harm. Hence, we are forced to balance the two in ways that are never totally satisfactory.

Moreover, we do not always agree on the balance to be set. While some of us may argue for complete self-sacrifice, others will stress the importance of developing their own talents. Likewise, while some of us may argue for the expansion of our self-interest to include the whole world, others will respond that a sense of self necessarily requires a much more local focus and perhaps even the exclusion of others' interests.

Presumably those who worry about personal integrity also care about the prevention of harm. But they may view the violation of personal integrity as a harm in and of itself. Who is to say what is harmful and what is not? We may all view starvation as a clear harm, but we will probably not agree on things like the violation of personal integrity or the stifling of creative talents. Moreover, even if we did all agree that the latter were harms, we would probably not be able to agree on how serious they are relative to other harms—which we would have to do if we were to come to agreement on how to prevent harm in general.[16]

I bring these differences up, not to create confusion, but to underscore the dependence of our claims about harm—what it is and how it can be prevented—on a variety of social and political norms which are both personal and culture bound. While we might think of ourselves as

16. For an excellent discussion of the difficulties associated with assessing and comparing various sorts of harm, see Joel Feinberg, *Harm to Others* (Oxford, 1984), 187–217.

merely figuring out who is in the best position to prevent harm, we inevitably fall back on a variety of social and political considerations—considerations ranging in this case from our judgments of relative harm to our valuation of private property. Likewise, while we may think of ourselves as falling back on a neutral conception of an individual's ability to prevent harm in our discovery of causal responsibility, we in fact incorporate into both our conception of an individual's ability to prevent harm and our judgments of causal responsibility a strong sense of when individuals can be expected to sacrifice their own projects for the sake of others' well-being.

What this suggests is that even if we wanted to place the value of preventing harm at the center of our theory of moral agency, we would have to explore the social and political considerations that ground our judgments of causal responsibility in practice. Likewise, we would have to understand the prevention of harm in this context as a socially and politically charged enterprise to the extent that it incorporates into itself the social and political values of its operators.

Since the prevention of harm turns out to be a much less objective enterprise than Harris suggests, we might want to stop and ask whether Harris would still want to place it at the center of his theory of moral agency. Harris, as we have seen, couples his normative judgments with the scientific evidence of his World Moral Authority. Hence, he does not have to confront the manipulation inherent in a purely consequentialist approach to moral responsibility. If he were to do so, he might be a little wary of placing the prevention of harm at the center of his theory of moral agency. For while the prevention of harm is obviously a valid enterprise in general, it does not, like other approaches to moral responsibility, recognize the importance of allowing individuals some awareness of, if not total control over, the way we construct their actions in the world.[17] Nor does it take into consideration the importance of such awareness to our understanding of "fair blaming."

Does this mean that we have to give up on Harris's general practical approach to moral responsibility or take on his World Moral Authority? I do not think so. For we still have the option of combining his practical approach to moral agency with an appeal to the social and political norms that we bring to bear on our practical judgments. I try to develop such an approach throughout the remainder of the study. Suffice it point out here that by turning to the criteria that we invoke in practice

17. I develop this perspective further in chapter 8 within my discussion of the utilitarian approach to moral responsibility.

for deciding whether or not harm was the consequence of a particular individual's actions or omissions, we may gain several advantages over Harris's ostensibly objectivist approach.

First of all, even though we would lose the ability to change the rules of our social practices drastically (by, say, treating actions and omissions as equally causally effective), we would not be obliged to reproduce the status quo. For as Harris's own examples suggest, there is a wide variety of differences among us with regard to our expectations of particular individuals. If we were to discover the relationship between these expectations and causal responsibility in general, and give one set of expectations priority over others, we might be able to extend the responsibility of the affluent for suffering in the third world by relying on existing expectations and the social and political norms on which they are based.

Presumably, to discover such a relationship would also be necessary if we wanted our moral arguments to be taken seriously by those who might apply them in practice. As I have already suggested, we do not have to go as far as to accept the status quo in our efforts to understand our social practices of responsibility. But it would seem helpful to uncover the conditions under which we now hold individuals causally responsible for harm in practice so that if, say, we wanted to extend responsibility as Harris does, we could do so by working within practices that others already accept rather than imposing on them arguments which they can easily reject as utopian.

Third, while we could no longer place the prevention of harm at the center of our pragmatic approach to responsibility, we would not have to give it up either. For when we look at how we construct our judgments of causal responsibility in practice, we see that we often choose as the relevant agent of harm that person whom we consider to have been in the best position to prevent it. But we do not do so on any objective basis. Instead, we construct our judgments of causal responsibility on the basis of a variety of social and political norms concerning who was able to prevent harm without sacrificing too many of her own projects.

I attempt in chapter 8 to show how we incorporate these norms into our practical judgments of responsibility in a variety of controversial cases. While Harris provides us with the basis for such an analysis by underscoring the practical concerns that we bring to bear on our judgments of causal responsibility, he is held back by both his reluctance to take social expectations seriously and his insistence that we discover morally correct judgments of moral responsibility. I suggest below that he is not even able to retain his own practical insights once he confronts the stringency of our modern concept of moral responsibility and the notion of moral blameworthiness inherent in it.

Traditional Constraints and the Deflation of a Radical Theory

In the first part of his essay, Harris describes moral responsibility and the causal responsibility of an individual's action for harm as one and the same thing. In the second part of the essay, he insists that an individual *himself* have caused that for which he is being held morally responsible. "If an individual is to be considered morally responsible for harm, he *himself*, as opposed to his actions, must have caused it."[18] Why the shift? Harris does not address this question himself. But he does make clear that if we are concerned about moral blameworthiness, we will have to focus on an individual himself and not just on his actions.

Harris does not say exactly what he has in mind by moral blameworthiness. But he does make clear that individuals are morally blameworthy solely in virtue of their having themselves caused harm. Moreover, he draws a sharp distinction between what individuals are really blameworthy for and what we blame them for now.[19] Hence, we can assume that he has something like our modern notion of moral blameworthiness in mind, an assumption that is supported further by the conditions that he establishes for showing that an individual *himself* caused harm.

Harris argues that if we want to show that an individual *himself* caused harm, we will have to show not only that the individual's actions or omissions were causally responsible for the harm, but that the prevention of harm was something "eligible" to him. Likewise, he now claims that Y's being a consequence of A's action or failure to act does not yet mean that A is an agent of the harm, or in other words, that A *himself* caused Y. In order for A himself to have caused Y, it is necessary that he have been "able" to perform X. According to Harris, the ability of A to perform X in this context entails that X have been "eligible" to A—which seems to mean for Harris that A was able to perform X without sacrificing too many of his own projects.

By introducing the notion of eligibility here, Harris drastically softens his earlier understanding of an individual's ability to prevent harm. In the first part of the essay, an individual's ability to prevent

18. John Harris, "Marxist Conception of Violence," 209.
19. Ibid.

harm rested solely on his physical and economic capabilities. Now it appears to rest partly on those social and political norms that enable us to claim, for instance, that while personal acts of charity were eligible to a particular individual, full-scale redistribution of his wealth was not.

Why does Harris find it necessary to go back on his earlier claim that social and political norms are irrelevant to questions of moral responsibility? First of all, he has now moved from a discussion of causation to moral blameworthiness. Second, instead of treating causation and moral blameworthiness as part of two separate, albeit related, judgments, he has fused them into one overarching moral discovery. According to Harris:

When we say that someone was the cause of harm (or at least one of the authors), we are saying that he is responsible for it and that he is to blame. . . . If we think that a particular method of preventing harm is for some reason ineligible, then we are unlikely to blame people for not using it.[20]

Once Harris invokes blameworthiness as an aspect of responsibility, his criteria of causation become both stricter and more clearly removed from the prevention of harm. Likewise, he is forced to give up many of the radical claims that he made about causation in the first part of the essay. We see this most clearly in his extended discussion of eligibility, where he argues that whether or not an action was eligible to an individual depends, among other things, on whether or not the individual thinks that it was.

If the individual does not think that the action was eligible to him, then he cannot be understood as having been able to prevent the harm, and he cannot be blamed for it.

Where the doing of X is considered out of the question, we tend to act and talk as though the condition that A could have done X is not satisfied. People will differ as to how "impossible" the doing of X really is, different interests will pull in different directions; what is out of the question for A, B will do without a second thought.[21]

Harris goes on to suggest that whether or not an individual thinks the doing of X is "out of the question" may depend on the individual's station in life.

People are likely to differ crucially about how viable options of saving others are. Suffering people are likely to see the possibility of their suffering as highly eligible, but those who would have to make sacrifices to bring relief are likely to think differently.[22]

20. Ibid., 207.   22. Ibid., 208.
21. Ibid.

Harris does not discuss whose opinion about the eligibility of harm would be accepted in society, but it is safe to assume that it would not be the opinion of those who are suffering (or at least not in the cases with which Harris is concerned). If the opinion accepted in society turned out to be that of the affluent, Harris could no longer consider them to have been able to prevent starvation in the third world. Nor would it seem to make any difference if their actions or omissions were causally responsible for such starvation. For the means of preventing it would be considered "out of the question" and the starvation itself not something for which the affluent could be understood as having "caused themselves" in the sense relevant to moral blameworthiness.

The third condition that Harris thinks must be met in order for individuals themselves to have caused harm undermines even further the radical implications of his practical approach to moral agency. According to this third condition, in order for an individual himself to have caused harm, it is necessary that the individual have "knowingly caused" it.

In saying someone was the cause of harm to human beings, we are singling him out as the author of the harm (or at least one of them), we are saying that he is responsible for it and that he is to blame. Blame is usually appropriate where harm to human beings is knowingly caused.[23]

Two things become clear from this passage. One is that the individual's state of mind—his free will—has taken precedence over the causal responsibility of his actions or omissions for external harm. The other is that this shift is necessary to sustain Harris's secularized Christian conception of moral responsibility, according to which individuals are considered morally blameworthy in virtue of their having themselves caused something bad.

Harris, unlike the theorists whose work we explore in chapters 6 and 7, does not talk about free will openly. But he does specify that in order for an individual to be morally responsible for external harm, he must have "knowingly caused it" or not have been in the position to claim "excusing conditions." Harris appears to have two things in mind here. One is that if an individual cannot justifiably fall back on "excusing conditions," he can be understood to have himself caused his own actions. The other is that if he can be understood to have himself caused his own actions, he can be considered blameworthy.

But Harris is not concerned simply with the moral responsibility of an individual for his own actions. He wants to show that individuals can

23. Ibid., 207.

be considered morally responsible for external harm as well. Hence, he finds it necessary to merge the moral responsibility of an individual for his own actions with the causal responsibility of his actions for external harm into one factual discovery: that the individual himself caused harm in the sense relevant to moral blameworthiness.

Can Harris pull off such a merger? The answer to this question would seem to be a flat-out "no," since the first notion of causal responsibility that Harris needs—free will—is ostensibly (and necessarily) under an individual's own control, and the second notion depends on a variety of considerations that we ourselves make after the individual has acted. (In other words, while the first notion of causal responsibility that Harris needs is an aspect of moral agency, the second notion depends on a variety of social and political considerations over which the individual himself has no control.)

Harris needs to be able to merge these two judgments if he wants to talk about individuals as having themselves caused harm in the sense relevant to moral responsibility. (In other words, he needs to merge them if he wants to talk about moral responsibility as an aspect of causation over which individuals themselves have total control.) I have already suggested that such a merger is not possible, since at least one of these judgments (the causal responsibility of an individual's actions for harm) is relative to a variety of considerations over which the individuals cannot possibly exercise such control.

How, then, does Harris appear to be able to show that an individual himself caused harm in the sense relevant to moral blameworthiness? He does so by running together two very different moral perspectives. One of these perspectives locates moral responsibility in something over which individuals supposedly have total control and which is ostensibly independent of all practical considerations. The other perspective recognizes the extent to which the responsibility of an individual is relative not only to what we have come to expect from individuals in general, but to the distribution of power on which these expectations are partly based.

In part 3 I argue that the impossibility of merging these two perspectives means that we will have to view our judgments of causal responsibility and free will separately as part of our social practice of blaming. Below I focus my attention on Harris's efforts to merge these two judgments in the context of his discussion of moral responsibility. I do so not simply to show why he fails, but to underscore the way we ourselves often merge our judgments of causal responsibility and free will in practice, or in other words, treat as an aspect of moral agency external judgments which are clearly out of an individual's own control.

The Subjectification of Social Blame

Harris does not set out to teach us about how we subjectify social blame, i.e., treat it as an aspect of moral agency. Instead, he tries to establish the conditions under which individuals are in a purely factual sense morally responsible for external harm. But he nevertheless teaches us two very important things about our practical judgments of responsibility. One is the dependence of these judgments on practical considerations which are, I have suggested, themselves mediated by our own social and political norms. The other is the process through which we incorporate our judgments of causal responsibility into our descriptions of an individual as bringing about harm before we blame him.

Harris does not openly acknowledge the difficulties associated with trying to hold individuals morally responsible for external harm on the basis of their having themselves caused the harm. But at the end of his essay he does replace his original claim (that an individual is morally responsible for harm in virtue of his having himself caused it) with a related, but significantly different claim: that an individual is morally responsible for harm in virtue of his having himself caused an action described as the bringing about of harm.

By shifting our attention away from harm itself and toward our own actions, Harris is able to talk about something over which we presumably have control. Moreover, by assuming that our causal responsibility for harm is registered in or ascribed by locutions such as "X brought about harm," he is able to obscure the open-endedness of these judgments. The question becomes what he, or anyone else, can possibly mean by ascription in this context.

While Harris does not make explicit his reliance on an ascriptivist approach to causal responsibility, many other philosophers do, including John Casey, whom I will be discussing in chapter 6. Since I will be discussing ascriptivism in some detail there (and in chapter 8), let me simply point out here what ascriptivism entails in general and what kind of ascriptivism Harris needs to invoke in order to render comprehensible his claim that individuals are morally responsible for harm in virtue of their having themselves been the author of an action of the form "A brought about harm."

By ascriptivism I do not mean the brand of linguistic philosophy that enabled scholars such as H. L. A. Hart to solve a variety of puzzles associated with the philosophy of action.[24] Instead, I use the term more loosely

---

24. For a sense of the controversy surrounding ascriptivism in its original form, see P. T. Geach, "Ascriptiveness," *Philosophical Review* 69 (1960), 221–26; H. L. A. Hart, "The

to refer to the sense in which responsibility can be understood as registered in locutions such as "X brought about harm" or "Y did it." Most philosophers who rely on an ascriptivist approach to actions assume that *causal responsibility* is ascribed to individuals by such locutions.[25] Other philosophers, such as H. L. A. Hart and John Casey, assume that both *causal responsibility* and *moral responsibility* are ascribed to individuals by them.[26] Moreover, there are those, including Hart, who contend further that such locutions always ascribe responsibility to individuals, or in other words, that the function of action sentences in general is to ascribe responsibility rather than to describe individuals.

What Harris needs to assume here is only that *causal responsibility* is ascribed to individuals by locutions such as "A brought about harm." In other words, he does not need to assume that such locutions ascribe moral responsibility or any other sort of liability to the individual. Nor does he need to assume that the exclusive function of action sentences is to ascribe responsibility, although, for reasons which I expand on later, he does need to assume that locutions such as "A brought about harm" *always* ascribe causal responsibility to individuals, even when we think of those locutions as primarily descriptive.

Since Harris does not assume that *moral* responsibility is ascribed to individuals within locutions such as "A brought about harm," he is not faced with Hart's and Casey's problems. (I discuss these problems in chapter 6.) But he is nevertheless faced with two potential difficulties. One is that while we may ascribe causal responsibility to individuals within locutions such as "A brought about harm," we do not generally ascribe causal responsibility to individuals within locutions such as "A failed to prevent it." The other is that even if we could ascribe causal responsibility within such locutions, causal responsibility would still be relative to a variety of social and political considerations over which individuals do not themselves have control, and hence such considerations would not be the sort of things in virtue of which individuals could be held morally blameworthy.

The first difficulty is one that Harris expressly avoids by translating

Ascription of Responsibility and Rights," *Proceedings of the Aristotelian Society* 49 (1948–49), 171–94; George Pitcher, "Hart on Action and Responsibility," *Philosophical Review* 69 (1960), 226–35; S. Stoljar, "Ascriptive and Prescriptive Responsibility," *Mind* 68 (1959), 350–60.

    25. See, for example, Feinberg, *Doing and Deserving*, 119–51.

    26. See Hart, "Ascription of Responsibility and Rights." While Hart views moral responsibility as an aspect of our linguistic practices, he does not, as is often suggested, want to use his ascriptivism to dismiss the problem of free will or to deflate the seriousness of moral blameworthiness. Indeed Hart states outright his wish to "distinguish from [his] own thesis that which is often maintained as a solution or dissolution of the problem of free will" (194).

the individual's omission into what he calls a "negative action." According to Harris:

It is only if the bringing about of Y is a negative action of A's that his causal responsibility for Y will raise the question of whether or not he might also be morally responsible for Y.[27]

By translating an individual's failure to act into a "negative action" and then holding the individual morally responsible for it, Harris appears able to hold the individual morally responsible not only for his omission, but for the harm itself (again presumably because causal responsibility for the harm is ascribed to the individual by locutions such as "A brought about harm"). But Harris appears able to hold the individual morally responsible for such harm only because of his peculiar understanding of a "negative action." Normally, a negative action is understood as an action of the form "A failed to do X" or "A did not do X." For Harris, a negative action is more than this: it is essentially a positive action of the form "A brought about Y."

Harris writes in this context:

A's failure to do X with the result Y will make *the bringing about of Y a negative action of A's*, only where A's doing of X would have prevented Y and A knew or ought reasonably to have known this, and where A could have done X and knew, or ought reasonably to have known, this (Emphasis added.).[28]

What Harris ends up doing here is describing the individual simultaneously as "failing to prevent harm" and as "bringing harm about." Such a dual description of the individual is necessary in the cases with which Harris is concerned. But it appears to be contradictory, given his ascriptivist assumptions about responsibility. On the one hand, Harris must begin by describing the individual in the way we now describe him, as failing to prevent harm. On the other hand, because we do not ascribe causal responsibility to individuals by locutions of the form "A failed to prevent harm," Harris must redescribe the individual as bringing about harm. The problem with such a dual description is that it both ascribes and does not ascribe causal responsibility to the individual.

While omissions create a special problem for Harris in this context, his dilemma is not restricted to them. The same dilemma would have arisen if Harris had chosen to describe the individual as, say, participating in the capitalist system.[29] On the one hand, he would have had to

27. Ibid., 210.

28. Ibid., 209.

29. It is puzzling why Harris did not describe the affluent as participating in the capitalist system initially—given (1) that the causal effectiveness of actions is much less controversial than that of omissions; (2) that he is defending the Marxist conception of

begin by describing the individual as participating in the capitalist system—or in other words, as we now describe him. On the other hand, because we do not ascribe causal responsibility for harm to individuals by locutions of the form "A participated in the capitalist system," Harris would have had to redescribe the individual as bringing about harm.

While the need to describe the individual in both ways is problematic, it is not as contradictory as it might at first appear, if we are willing to view our redescription of individuals as part of a dynamic social process. Harris himself makes clear that in order to describe an individual as having brought about harm, it is necessary to show that three conditions have been met. These conditions are first, that a causal connection existed between the individual's action or omission and harm; second, that the individual was able to prevent the harm; and third, that the prevention of harm was "eligible" to him.

The problem here is not only that these conditions cannot all be satisfied in the cases with which Harris is concerned, but that if we thought at the time that they *could* be satisfied, we would, according to Harris's analysis, have already described the individual as having brought about harm rather than as having failed to prevent it or as having done something else altogether. What this suggests is that if we want to redescribe an individual in this context, we must have changed our minds about the individual's situation after our initial description of him.

With respect to third world starvation, such a change would entail either that we have discovered a new set of causal relations between the affluent and third world starvation or that someone else has persuaded us to change our minds about which actions are eligible to the affluent. Neither such a discovery nor a change of mind on our part is difficult to imagine. The discovery of causal connections is often a matter of publicity, and the alteration of expectations is something that goes on around us all the time.

Interestingly enough, Harris relies on both modes of change in order to redescribe the affluent as bringing about harm. He begins by trying to establish that omissions are causally effective for external harm—even if we do not now realize it. He then goes on to assert (via his World Moral Authority) that the affluent can be expected to be much more active than they now are in preventing third world starvation. By doing both things together, he is able to consider third world starvation a consequence of

violence; and (3) that he says that he is establishing the criteria under which individuals are morally responsible for both their actions and their omissions. By focusing on omissions rather than on actions in this context, Harris manages to avoid having to draw specific connections between capitalist activity and the suffering of the poor. But he renders his argument much less effective than the Marxist argument itself (which relies on "positive actions").

the actions of the affluent, although it is not clear whether he has persuaded anybody else to accept his analysis.

As things now stand, he does not even recognize that he has changed descriptions of the affluent or that the process of description and redescription is a dynamic process based on changing conceptions of responsibility. Since Harris wants to characterize his own judgments of responsibility as morally correct, he might not want to acknowledge such dynamism. But he would have to do so if he were to take seriously the process through which he has redefined the actions of the affluent.

While the dynamic nature of our judgments of responsibility challenges the "moral correctness" of Harris's position, it does not undermine the possibility of talking about moral responsibility in general. Indeed, it does just the opposite by enabling us to grasp not only how we change each others' minds about responsibility, but what happens in the process vis-à-vis our description of a particular individual's actions. Two levels of analysis become important here. The first requires us to look at the way we incorporate harm into our description of an individual's action. The second requires us to recognize the importance of more purely political practices such as those of empowerment to the process of redefinition itself.

Harris does not explore the process of action description in much depth. While he redefines individuals' actions on the basis of their causal responsibility for harm, he does not distinguish between deeming harm a consequence of the individual's action and the redescription of that individual as bringing about harm. In other words, he does not acknowledge what philosophers of action call the accordion effect, i.e., the capacity of action descriptions to elide into other action descriptions of greater or lesser scope.[30] If he were to do so, he would have to acknowledge that there is a major difference between harm's being considered the consequence of an individual's action and the individual's being described as bringing about harm.

I argue in chapter 8 that we generally describe individuals as bringing about harm only if we perceive the causal connections in question as "direct." Nor surprisingly, the nature of "directness" comes to be of utmost importance here. I argue that the directness of a particular causal connection depends not only on physical proximity, but on several purely social and political norms, including whether or not we consider the action in question to be a standard means of bringing about harm.

While we agree on many of these norms, we disagree on others. In

30. For an excellent discussion of the accordion effect, see Eric D'Arcy, *Human Acts* (Oxford, 1963), 2–39.

the case of, say, shooting, we generally agree that firing a gun is a standard means of bringing about harm. Also the causal connection between an individual who shoots a gun and another's death is very close. Hence, we feel free to describe the individual as bringing about harm directly, or in other words, as killing.

In other cases we may disagree either about physical proximity or about whether a particular act can be considered a standard means of bringing about harm. If we are a factory worker, we may consider unhealthy working conditions a standard means of bringing about harm and hence may describe the causal connection between these conditions and our bad health as direct. If, on the other hand, we are a factory owner, we may deny that these conditions are a standard means of bringing about harm and consider the causal connections in question to be indirect.

Not surprisingly, our decision to describe the factory owner as either bringing about harm or as doing something else will not be without its practical consequences. As Judith Shklar makes poignantly clear in *The Faces of Injustice*, how we describe a particular individual with regard to harm will make an extremely important difference not only to our prevention of the harm in question, but to our sense of justice and injustice. If we see harm as caused by human agents, we will view it as an injustice. If, on the other hand, we see the harm as caused by natural forces, we will view it as a misfortune only.[31]

How can we decide between these two ways of describing an individual's action? I argue in chapter 8 that we can never make an objective choice between the two descriptions, since they are inevitably based on both particular interests and subjective perspectives. Nor can we hope to persuade individuals, within a purely intellectual process, that our description is correct and other descriptions incorrect.

Instead we have to take seriously the possibility that our action descriptions in this context are part of a social and political process through which we impose our own descriptions on others by virtue of our own power or respect. In the case of third world starvation, we do not see much change in our description of the affluent. But in cases such as apartheid in South Africa and industrial diseases at home, we see a great deal of change, change which presumably has a great deal to do with the empowerment of those suffering.

31. Judith Shklar, *The Faces of Injustice* (New Haven, 1990). "When," Shklar asks, "is a disaster a misfortune and when is it an injustice?" "Intuitively, the answer seems quite obvious. If the dreadful event is caused by the external forces of nature, it is a misfortune and we must resign ourselves to the suffering. Should, however, some ill-intentioned agent, human or supernatural, have brought it about, then it is an injustice and we may express indignation and outrage" (1).

Harris now appears able to redescribe the affluent as bringing about harm without having imposed his own political perspective on us only because he has made two false assumptions. One is that we can ascribe causal responsibility to individuals within locutions such as "X failed to prevent harm" (or in other words, that we can treat negative and positive actions as equivalent in this context). The other is that we can describe an individual as having brought about harm without having to take into consideration whether or not the connection was direct.

As I have suggested, neither of these assumptions is true. But let us suppose for the sake of argument that Harris is able to describe the affluent as bringing about starvation in the third world.[32] Likewise, let us assume that the particular affluent individuals in question had no "excusing conditions" to fall back on. Could Harris conclude from the fact that they freely willed an action of the form "X brought about harm" that they are morally responsible for the harm itself? Again, the answer would have to be a flat-out "no," if what we mean by moral responsibility is consistent with our modern concept of it. For while causal responsibility might be registered in locutions such as "X brought about harm," it is still relative to a variety of social and political considerations that we ourselves bring to bear on particular individuals.

If Harris were to acknowledge that we bring such considerations to bear on our descriptions of particular individuals, he would have to concede that individuals cannot themselves be considered morally responsible for external harm by virtue of their having themselves caused an action of the form "X brought about harm." But he would not have to give up on holding individuals causally responsible for such harm or on ascribing causal responsibility to individuals within locutions such as "X brought about harm." Nor would he have to stop blaming them for the harm in such a way that they might be persuaded to "work actively and, in the present state of the world, unremittingly for the relief and prevention of such suffering."[33]

Both judgments—those of causal responsibility and free will—are still intact (even though they cannot be viewed together as one factual discovery of moral responsibility). Moreover, even though Harris has not presented these judgments as judgments, he has provided us with a basis upon which to understand our judgments of causal responsibility as part of social and political practice. If he were to go all the way, he

32. I do not mean to suggest here that such a description is out of the question. Indeed, I point out in chapter 8 that we can describe the affluent as bringing about harm in the third world in a number of cases. But, I argue, we can do so, not because of the causal effectiveness of our omissions, but because we can locate several "positive actions" that connect American capitalists to suffering in the third world.

33. Ibid., 211.

would have to not only separate our judgments of free will from those of causal responsibility, but treat both as relative to a variety of practical considerations which are themselves mediated by our own social and political points of view.

Moreover, in doing so, he would have to acknowledge that when we blame individuals for harm, we often do so by incorporating harm into our description of an individual's action on the basis of both physical evidence and our own social and political norms. In cases where we follow the status quo, we usually do so by falling back on conventional expectations of the individuals concerning the sorts of things that they should have done to prevent the harm. In other cases, e.g., in cases where we want to include more or less harm than others do in our description of the individuals, we have to impose unusual expectations on them and perhaps (like Harris) even try to justify such an imposition by debunking existing conventions and norms of behavior.

Harris, in his efforts to redescribe individuals as bringing about harm, chose not simply to criticize existing conventions and norms of behavior, but to show that both were irrelevant to questions of responsibility. Yet he could do so only by invoking the "correct" judgments of his World Moral Authority, an authority that probably does not exist in a secular context, and in any case is not something for which Harris himself argues. Moreover, Harris has not done away with expectations and norms in the way that he suggests, but has simply replaced those associated with the status quo with his own more radical expectations.

Harris does not acknowledge that he has invoked expectations of his own (or of his World Moral Authority). Nor does he acknowledge the problems associated with both his concept of moral blameworthiness and the notion of free will that it requires. Hence, he feels free to claim that he has *discovered* that the affluent are morally responsible for much more suffering around the world than we now realize. While such a claim is, I have suggested, unfounded, it does enable us to see how in practice we are able to subjectify social blame, or in other words, view it as the sort of moral blameworthiness that has its source in an individual's own will.

How are we able to hold individuals morally responsible for harm in practice? As Harris's own analysis inadvertently suggests, we ascribe causal responsibility to individuals for harm within locutions such as "X brought about harm" and then treat what is an ascription as though it registers willfulness. While our judgment of willfulness may not itself be arbitrary—it may in fact be based on acute psychological observations—it is not an aspect of the causal relationship that we have established between the individual and harm. Instead, it is a further judgment that we make about an individual's state of mind and smuggle into our description of the individual's action.

How do we manage to do the latter? If Harris is at all representative of practical actors (which, I argue in chapter 9, he is), we do so by merging two very different sorts of causal judgments into one ostensibly factual judgment about the individual's moral worth. One of these judgments is that the harm in question is a consequence of the individual's action. The other is that the individual acted willfully and is hence worthy of our blame. Neither judgment is purely factual. But by viewing them as such we are able to assume that the individual is morally blameworthy outside the context of our own interests and purposes. While such an assumption is not logically supportable, it is, as we shall see throughout chapter 9, very helpful to those who want to internalize the standards of social blameworthiness.

6

Social Expectations, Role Playing, and the Primacy of Moral Agency

A Deontological View of Moral Agency

John Casey's overall purpose in "Actions and Consequences"[1] is not to explore the social and political considerations that ground our judgments of responsibility, but to defend the deontological moral tradition. Like Harris, he finds it necessary to focus on the moral responsibility of individuals for their own actions as a way of talking about the moral responsibility of individuals for external harm. But unlike Harris, he does not set out to combine the causal responsibility of an individual's actions or omissions for harm with the causal responsibility of an individual himself for his own will. Instead, he sets out to show that moral, and not just causal, responsibility is ascribed to individuals by locutions such as "X brought about harm" and "Y failed to prevent it" (or in other words, that any individual who can be described as such is morally responsible not only for his own actions but for the harm itself).

Three aspects of Casey's analysis make it a more probable candidate for success than Harris's analysis. First of all, Casey begins with the moral responsibility of individuals for their own actions rather than with the causal responsibility of their actions for external harm. Hence, unlike Harris, he appears able to talk about moral responsibility without having to merge the causal responsibility of an individual's actions for harm with the absence of a volitional excuse. Second, he assumes that moral responsibility can be ascribed to individuals not only within locutions such as "X brought about harm," but within locutions such as "Y failed to prevent it." Hence, he does not find it necessary to go back and forth between negative and positive actions in the way that Harris

1. John Casey, "Actions and Consequences," in his *Morality and Moral Reasoning* (London, 1971).

130

does. Third, he embraces our modern concept of moral responsibility at the outset. Hence, unlike Harris, he does not find it necessary to distort his analysis in the last instance by smuggling a foreign moral concept into it.

Casey's approach to the problem of moral responsibility is firmly within the deontological moral tradition. Although he finds it necessary in the end to invoke the causal responsibility of an individual's actions for harm, he begins by focusing solely on an individual's own moral agency. Likewise, although he finds it necessary in the end to merge the causal responsibility of an individual's actions or omissions for harm with the absence of a volitional excuse, he begins with the much simpler-sounding task of showing that bringing about harm and failing to prevent it are "both ways of being responsible for harm" and hence "equally bad."[2]

As a deontologist, Casey both accepts our modern concept of moral responsibility openly and insists on a separation between moral and social blameworthiness. According to Casey, what characterizes moral responsibility, or the "responsibility of persons," is that it is fundamentally connected with praise and blame. Indeed, the "responsibility of persons" is for Casey so fundamentally connected to praise and blame that it can usually be equated with them. Casey writes, for example, that "responsibility . . . in the sense in which a person can be held responsible for something . . . can be replaced by other terms. For instance, when what is done is wrong, to be responsible is to be blamed for it."[3]

Casey argues that what renders an individual morally responsible is not that we choose to blame him, but that he has caused something bad. Casey, like Harris, feels free to talk about the "responsibility of persons" for harm in terms of the individual's having caused the harm. The in-

---

2. Casey is primarily concerned in this context to defend the deontological moral tradition against those who criticize it for resting on the "irrational view" that there is always a moral difference between bringing about harm and failing to prevent it. In his effort to show that the deontological moral tradition does not rest on such an irrational view, he sets out to demonstrate that individuals are always morally responsible for harm which they fail to prevent. Casey believes that if he can show that individuals are always morally responsible for such harm, he will have shown that the failure to prevent harm and the bringing about of harm are "both ways of being responsible for harm" and hence "equally bad" (161).

With respect to the killing–letting die distinction, Casey writes: "Killing and letting die are both ways of being responsible for a death. The same state of affairs—a death—is necessarily the result of both killing and letting die. The concept of killing and the concept of letting die are connected in such a way that they must necessarily fall under the same moral principle" (160).

3. Ibid., 178.

terchangeability of terms here is possible, according to Casey, because the "most general term for 'being responsible for' is 'being the cause of.'"[4] Yet causation per se is not a sufficient condition of moral responsibility. It is also necessary that the "individual himself, as distinct from his actions or omissions, have caused the [harm]."[5]

Not surprisingly, in establishing the conditions under which an individual can be understood to have himself caused harm, Casey ends up setting down conditions very similar to those articulated by Harris. These are: first, that we be able to consider the individual's action or omission causally responsible for harm; second, that the individual's "value as a person be at stake"; and third, that the individual have no valid excuse for his action or omission.[6]

According to Casey, if an individual can meet all three of these conditions, he can be understood to have himself caused harm in the sense relevant to moral blameworthiness. Casey connects an individual's having himself caused harm with moral blameworthiness implicitly throughout his analysis. He makes the connection explicit in his summing up of the three conditions cited above. According to Casey:

To say that *he* is the cause is to imply that the above conditions are in fact satisfied and that he is therefore a proper object of personal assessment with regard to the production of the state of affairs, a proper object of, say, praise and blame.[7]

The question is how Casey can view these three conditions together as those under which an individual himself caused harm in the sense relevant to moral blameworthiness. Harris failed to view these conditions together because he was willing to acknowledge the dependence of our judgments of causal responsibility on a variety of practical considerations over which individuals could not themselves possibly have control. Casey, if he is to succeed where Harris failed, must do two things. First of all, he must discover a way of talking about the causal responsibility of an individual's actions and omissions for harm that does not depend on such considerations, or for that matter, on anything over which the individual does not himself have total control. Sec-

4. Ibid., 184.
5. Ibid., 183.
6. Ibid., 184. Like Harris, Casey never makes explicit the role that excuse giving plays in holding individuals morally responsible. Nor does he make explicit the particular excuses to which he is referring. But we can conclude from his contention that "there should be no features of the situation which excuse the agent—such as involuntariness, unforeseeability of consequences and so on" (184) that he is referring to the volitional excuses traditionally invoked in discussions of moral responsibility.
7. Ibid., 185.

ond, he must show how moral, and not just causal, responsibility can be ascribed to individuals within locutions such as "X brought about harm" or "Y failed to prevent it."

Casey tries to isolate the causal responsibility of an individual's action or omission for external harm from the contingencies of practical life by arguing that the expectations which we bring to bear on our judgments of causal responsibility are themselves both objective and morally correct. He tries to ascribe moral, and not just causal, responsibility to individuals within the above locutions by assuming that our description of an individual will always coincide with the individual's own intentions. Both tasks are, understandably, very difficult. Casey appears able to carry them out, as we shall see, only by merging the individual with his social role to the extent that the individual is no longer able to exercise that autonomy considered necessary for moral responsibility.

Moral Agency and Social Norms

Casey, like Harris, acknowledges that there are an infinite number of causal connections between an individual's action or omission and external harm. But unlike Harris, he insists that an individual's action or omission can be considered causally responsible for harm only if the individual could have been expected to prevent it. According to Casey:

> If a man does not do X, we cannot properly say that his not doing X is the cause of some result Y, unless, in the normal course of events, he could have been expected to do X.[8]

Whether the individual could have been expected to do X depends for Casey on the individual's social role. (And here we see a similarity between Casey's and Harris's approach to moral responsibility, although presumably Harris would want to limit the importance, or at least the bias, of such roles.) According to Casey, if an individual's social role is such that we can expect her to perform action X, and she does not, then we can hold her causally responsible for the harm that results from X.

Casey's first example is that of an obstetrician who is faced with the possibility that if he does not abort a mother's fetus, the mother will die. Casey's primary concern here is with whether or not the obstetrician, who evidently does not believe in abortion, can be described as failing

8. Ibid., 180. Casey's somewhat negative approach to causal responsibility here can be explained by the fact that what he is concerned to show, on the most concrete of levels, is that an obstetrician cannot be held morally responsible for the death of the mother whose child he refuses to abort—because obstetricians cannot be expected to abort fetuses.

to save the mother's life. The question is obviously very important for Casey, since if the obstetrician can be described as failing to prevent the mother's death, he can, according to Casey's general ascriptivist position, be considered morally responsible for her demise.

His second example is that of a mother who does not feed her baby (which subsequently dies). Here again Casey's primary concern is with whether or not an individual can be described as being morally responsible for another's death. Not surprisingly, Casey is going to want to distinguish between these two cases, or in other words, to show that there is something distinctly different about them such that in one case the individual is morally responsible for harm and in the other case the individual is not.

Casey's third and fourth examples are also paired as significantly different with regard to the question of moral responsibility. One of these examples is that of a doctor who does not contribute £1,000 of his own money to save the life of a patient (who subsequently dies). The other is that of the patient's husband who does not contribute £1,000 of his own money to save the life of his wife (who subsequently dies). Presumably the primary difference between these two cases has something to do with the respective social roles of doctor and husband.

Casey writes with regard to the first example that because a doctor cannot be expected to perform an operation which, in saving a mother's life, results in the death of her unborn child, the doctor's nonperformance of such an operation cannot be understood to be causally responsible for the mother's death. Nor can the doctor be described as having failed to prevent the mother's death or as having let the mother die. With reference to the second example, Casey writes that the role of mother requires that a mother feed her child. As such, when a mother does not feed her child (even though she has the means to do so), her omission can be understood as causally responsible for the child's death and she herself can be described as having failed to prevent the child's death or as having let the child die.

What happens when saving a life involves personal sacrifice? Casey writes that because a doctor cannot be expected to contribute his own money for the treatment of his patients, his not contributing £1,000 for the treatment of a patient cannot be understood to have been causally responsible for the patient's death and hence he cannot be described as having failed to save her life. On the other hand, because a husband *can* be expected to contribute his own money for the treatment of his wife, his not contributing such money (assuming that he has it) can be understood as having been causally responsible for his wife's death and he can be described as having failed to save her life or as having let her die.

By invoking an individual's social role in these cases, Casey enables us to understand how our expectations of an individual shape both our judgments of causal responsibility and our descriptions of the individual's actions. If an individual whose actions were causally connected to the suffering of others could have been expected to take that suffering into consideration before acting, we are more likely to hold her causally responsible for the harm than if we had not considered the harm to be any of her business. Likewise, if the connection were one that we considered direct, which is of course a relative matter, we might go as far as to include the harm in our description of the individual's action, or in other words, describe the individual as bringing about harm.

Casey treats actions and omissions together in this context. But for his examples he focuses primarily on omissions. Hence, it is necessary before underscoring the general contributions of his theory to extend his analysis into the realm of actions by reexamining his examples. Take, for instance, Casey's example of the mother who did not feed her child. Casey argues that since mothers in general can be expected to feed their children, the woman in question can be held responsible for the child's death due to starvation.

But what about the more positive actions that she might perform qua mother? Here we might want to focus on the mother's child-rearing practices. Say, for example, she lets her child watch violent music videos on the television, with the result that the child becomes violently aggressive toward members of the female sex. Can we consider the mother's child-rearing practices to be causally responsible for her child's violent behavior? Can we describe her as having turned her child into a misogynist?

While many of us might agree on the causal connections between the child's misogynist behavior and the heavy metal rock videos that the mother allows her child to watch, we would probably disagree on whether or not the mother herself could be held causally responsible for her child's violence. The differences between us presumably would come down to what we felt we could expect from the mother qua mother. If we felt that as a mother she had an obligation to monitor her child's television viewing, we might want to consider her child's violence a consequence of her child-rearing practices. If, on the other hand, we did not feel that she was obliged to monitor her child's television viewing, we might not go so far, although we would probably find someone else to blame.

The most likely candidate for blame in this context would be the heavy metal group itself or the video's director. Here our sense would be not only that their rock video inspired violence against women, but that they themselves could have been expected to think about the effects of their misogyny on young children. Not all of us, of course, would share these expectations of the group or its director (even if we were willing to condemn misogyny in general). Indeed, those who argue for creative freedom often argue that it is not the responsibility of the music industry, but that of the child's parents, to sustain moral education in the home.

Such disagreement is not uncommon in cases where there are many causal factors to be considered and an open-textured set of social roles. Take Casey's own obstetrician, who was last seen in an abortion clinic. This same obstetrician may at one time have prescribed fertility pills to women who gave birth to deformed babies. Could the obstetrician have been held causally responsible for the suffering of both mother and child? Could he have been described as ruining their lives?

Once again the question comes down to what we take to be the social role of the obstetrician. If we feel that obstetricians are in general obliged to test the pills that they prescribe, we may hold him causally responsible for the pills' results. If, on the other hand, we do not include the testing of drugs as one of the obstetrician's duties, we will probably not hold him causally responsible or describe him as doing anything wrong. But we will probably hold someone else responsible, if not the FDA, then the drug company itself.

Both cases demonstrate that while our judgments of causal responsibility, and hence our description of an individual's actions, depend partly on causal evidence, they also depend on the expectations that we bring to bear on an individual and his situation. Likewise, each case demonstrates that while these expectations are in one sense conventional categories through which we perceive an individual's actions or omissions, they are also grounded in, and supported by, a configuration of social roles that we generally respect. Hence, while they may have become second nature to us, they must also be understood as normative expectations, or at least expectations that we feel justified in imposing on others.

While these expectations are most evident in cases where we disagree among ourselves about who is causally responsible for harm, they are also present in our less controversial judgments of causal responsibility. Take, for example, the case of a woman who accidently shoots her neighbor while cleaning her gun. Here we perceive a very direct causal connection between the woman and her neighbor's death. But we do not simply discover causal responsibility as we might discover one among many causes of harm. Instead, we make a very quick, if not automatic, judgment that the individual's actions contributed directly to her neighbor's death and that the individual could have been expected to take her neighbor's well-being into consideration before she picked up her gun to clean it.

This particular case brings out two important aspects of responsibility that Casey and others who want to ascribe moral responsibility to individuals by locutions such as "X brought about harm" or "Y failed to prevent it" are obliged to take into consideration. One is that we do not automatically describe individuals as "bringing about harm" simply because harm is a consequence of their actions. Instead, we describe them as such only if we perceive the causal connection as very direct. The other is that we do not automatically assume that individuals who are causally responsible for harm are morally responsible for it. In the case of the woman who accidently shot her neighbor, we may automatically describe her as causally responsible, but we do not hold her morally responsible until we have discerned the nature of her intentions.

The fact that we do not automatically describe an individual as bringing about harm simply because the harm was a consequence of the individual's actions would seem to be just as troubling for Casey as it was for Harris, in that he too is concerned not only to hold individuals morally responsible for actions that are not now of the form "X brought about harm," but to ascribe moral responsibility to individuals within such locutions themselves. I do not think that we normally ascribe responsibility of any sort to individuals within locutions such as "X failed to prevent harm." Nor can we translate such "negative actions" into positive ones within our ascriptive framework without acknowledging that according to our original description of the individual, she was not responsible for the harm in question.

But what about actions that are already of the form "X brought about harm"? Here we might be able to ascribe causal responsibility to individuals within such locutions. But Casey wants to do more. He wants to ascribe causal responsibility *and* moral responsibility to individuals within locutions such as "X brought about harm" and "Y failed to prevent it." Whether or not he can do so is the question that I place at the center of my discussion of responsibility in the next section.

Social Norms, Role Playing, and the Collapse of a Conservative Perspective

If Casey is to justify his particular approach to moral responsibility, he will have to do two things. First of all, he must show how individuals can be both causally *and* morally responsible for harm in virtue of their having brought it about or having failed to prevent it. Second, he must show how we can incorporate social role playing into moral agency without violating individual free will—or in other words, how judgments of causal responsibility which are based on an individual's social role can be conceived of as independent of social and political practice.

Casey attempts to carry out the first task by arguing that moral responsibility and causal responsibility can be registered together in our description of an individual as either having brought about harm or failed to prevent it. According to Casey, locutions such as "X brought about harm" or "X failed to prevent harm":

Each describe a man's action as the cause of something, and they describe *him* as the cause in all cases where no excusing conditions are present to reject the ascription of responsibility.[9]

Casey makes it clear here that:

A man may let something happen unintentionally, and we cannot therefore claim there is a conceptual identity between "letting something happen" and "being morally responsible for its happening," even though the first will always amount to the second in cases where excusing conditions are absent.[10]

With this last claim, Casey cannot help but undermine his own general theory of moral responsibility, since as is evident from the above passage, one of the most important conditions that must be met in order for an individual to be considered morally responsible for harm can be met only *after* the individual has been described as either bringing about harm or failing to prevent it. I refer here to whether or not the individual was in the position to offer a volitional excuse. If this condition can be met only *after* the individual has been described as bringing about harm or as failing to prevent it, then the individual cannot be considered morally responsible *in virtue of* his having brought about the harm itself.

How, then, can Casey possibly argue that individuals are morally responsible for harm in virtue of their having brought it about or having failed to prevent it? Presumably, he can do so only by assuming that individuals can never be in the position to offer a volitional excuse for bringing about or failing to prevent harm, or, in other words, that in every case in which we consider an individual's actions or omissions to be causally responsible for harm, the individual intended them to be so. Such an assumption is not only very strange in and of itself but is in clear conflict with Casey's own claim that individuals may bring about

9. Ibid., 185.
10. Ibid.

harm unintentionally. Nevertheless, it is the assumption that Casey chooses to make and then justify.

Casey's "justification" amounts to the assertion that the descriptions under which an individual thinks of himself as acting will always coincide with *our* description of the individual. The two descriptions will always coincide, according to Casey, because both are based on the individual's social role. According to Casey:

Not only will our conception of a man's social role govern what we can properly describe him as doing, but *his* conception of his role and its duties will determine the description for him under which he acts.[11]

In his effort to ensure that the two descriptions of the individual's action coincide, Casey resorts to merging the individual with his social role to the extent that the individual is no longer able to step outside of his role in order to assess it and the duties attached to it. Not surprisingly, by merging the individual with his social role, Casey ends up taking away from the individual that "ability to do otherwise" traditionally considered necessary for moral responsibility.

The case in which he first merges the individual with his social role is that of the obstetrician faced with aborting a fetus in order to save its mother's life. Casey writes:

Given the conception of the role of the physician, it is clear that there can be no question of killing the child in order to save the life of the mother. This simply does not present itself as a possible course of action. To say that it *is* a possible course of action is to assume that the medical function is different from what we imagine it to be. For example, it might be said that there is here a straight choice between the woman's life and the child's. But a straight choice for whom? If our understanding of the obstetrician's role rules out the possibility of the child's being killed in order to save the mother, then we would certainly not agree that such a choice is open to the obstetrician, nor would the obstetrician think that such a choice is open to him. Killing the child is not an option.[12]

Or rather it is not a "live" option.

It is clear (and the obstetrician may be presumed to know it) that if the obstetrician were to kill the child the mother would live. In this sense various courses of action are "presented." . . . Killing the child, however, doesn't present itself as possible in any sense stronger than this: it is not a live option. So, the traditionalist might argue, to say that the obstetrician who does not operate "could have done otherwise" is to use "could" in an over-simple, role-neutral fashion,

11. Ibid., 194.
12. Ibid., 167–68.

and to ignore the sense, which, as an obstetrician, he could not have done otherwise than he did. . . . Given this conception of the obstetrician's role, the obstetrician is not "presented" with a straight choice between the mother's life and the child's, he doesn't "let her die," nor does he "refrain from saving her life."[13]

Rendering this rather restrictive understanding of social roles less implausible is the fact that for Casey neither social roles nor the actions which they prescribe are morally neutral. "One's willingness to take a particular role seriously," writes Casey, "may already presuppose a judgment of values."[14]

To accept that there could be a role of "father" or "physician," and at the same time deny that there could be a role of "sadist" or "Jew baiter" presupposes some sort of moral approval of fathers and physicians and disapproval of sadists and Jew baiters. It may be that one cannot speak non-paradoxically of a good doctor without supposing that a doctor is a good sort of thing to be, or that this is a way of being, or at least does not conflict with being, a good man.[15]

The "goodness" of roles, Casey continues, is not necessarily a matter of utilitarian consideration.

It is by no means self-evident that the moral judgment in favor of a particular role can always be expressed in utilitarian terms—that the exercise of a particular role has, for instance, socially desirable consequences. It might rather be based on the view that a particular role or particular pattern of activity embodies certain characteristic human excellences or virtues. The acceptance of a role might, then, involve certain moral pre-suppositions, but might nevertheless not be vulnerable on moral grounds to re-examination in light of particular consequentialist considerations.[16]

It is important, I think, to examine Casey's assumptions here one by one, starting with his assumption that social roles are not morally neutral. In the first place, to say that a social role is not morally neutral is not to say that it is morally good. There do exist social roles which we do not consider to be morally good, e.g., that of bully or tyrant. Casey avoids having to address such roles by assuming that if a social role is not morally good, it is not a social role. By doing so, he distinguishes himself from much of the scholarly work done on social roles, which views social roles not in terms of their moral value but in terms of either their general function in society or their relationship to other social roles.

Casey is of course under no obligation to accept this sociological perspective. But since it is the perspective generally taken among those who talk about social roles, he does need to clarify his own nonsociologi-

---

13. Ibid., 169–70.   15. Ibid.
14. Ibid., 195.   16. Ibid., 195–96.

cal perspective more than he now does. Since he begins with the assumption that social roles are morally good qua social roles, he might want to put forward a perspective on social roles that views them according to a set of role responsibilities which they embody, role responsibilities which are themselves construed as contributing in a positive way to society's well-being.

By focusing on positive role responsibilities as a defining feature of social roles, Casey could reject both Jew baiters and sadists as candidates for social role status. (Presumably neither has positive role responsibilities attached to it.) Likewise, by showing how role responsibilities are sustained by specific occupations, memberships, and social relationships, Casey could easily translate these role responsibilities into expectations that we bring to bear on the situation of particular individuals, expectations that are both conventional and normative and which shape our judgments of causal responsibility in practice.

But he could not assume that social roles are themselves uncontroversial. For even if we were to accept Casey's premise that we only invoke social roles that we consider to be morally good, we would not necessarily agree on the goodness of particular social roles. Take, for example, the social roles of guru, Marxist revolutionary, capitalist, husband, and priest. All of these roles have responsibilities attached to them. They are all considered by at least some people to be socially functional. But not all of them can be considered morally good, or at least not all of them together. Indeed it is likely that at least one of these roles (e.g., that of Marxist revolutionary) would have to be considered morally bad, if the others were going to be considered morally good.

Since there is disagreement among us about whether or not particular social roles are valuable, Casey cannot assume that it is "out of the question" for an individual to question his social role. Nor can he assume that we will always associate an individual with the same social role that the individual himself embraces. Take, for example, the case of an individual X who considers himself to be the family patriarch. Since individual X attaches to the role of family patriarch responsibility for all of his young relatives' finances, he may describe himself as contributing to their financial demise if he does not stop them from making unwise financial decisions. But a person who never accepted the role of family patriarch in the first place will probably not describe individual X as such and may even describe him as minding his own business for once when he fails to give his relatives financial advice.

While our disagreements about a particular social role sometimes concern the very existence of that role, as in the case just cited, they are more often than not about how we are to interpret a social role that we all accept. Here we should expect discrepancies to arise in our descriptions of an individual's actions in two sorts of situations. The first is the sort that occurs when an individual rejects the standard interpretation of his social role which we ourselves accept. The second is the sort that occurs when we reject an individual's own interpretation of his social role.

A case which illustrates the first·sort of discrepancy is that of soldier X, who refuses to use napalm in a situation where several of his friends are killed by the enemy. Soldier X's superior, Captain Y, claims that the responsibility of a soldier in wartime is to defend his countrymen at any cost to the enemy. On the basis of this claim, Captain Y charges soldier X with having been causally responsible for the deaths of soldier X's fellows. Soldier X responds to Captain Y's charge by pointing out that it would have been morally wrong to use napalm. Soldier X may even argue that it is not the duty of a soldier in wartime to defend his countrymen at any cost to the enemy. Either way, soldier X denies having been causally responsible for his fellows' deaths—and refuses to be described as bringing those deaths about.

A case which illustrates the second sort of discrepancy is that of a political radical who rejects the normative value of the social role of capitalist investor. Among the responsibilities of a capitalist investor is that of making as much money as possible without breaking the law. It is not illegal to invest in companies which do business with South Africa. Investor Z invests in such a company. Because he accepts his role as capitalist investor, he does not think of himself as being causally responsible for the oppression of South African blacks. The political radical, however, who rejects the responsibilities of investor Z, argues that investor Z is causally responsible for the oppression of blacks in South Africa, and persists in describing investor Z as bringing about harm.

It is important to note here that the political radical is able to describe investor Z in this way not just because he has rejected the standard interpretation of the capitalist's role, but because he has substituted his own interpretation for that one. Presumably this revised interpretation requires capitalists to examine the social and political consequences of their investments. Hence, the political radical is able to assume that when capitalists do not examine the social and political consequences of their investments in an oppressive regime, they can be held causally responsible for aspects of the oppression itself.

While the discrepancies between our various interpretations of an individual's social role may be more apparent in cases such as these than in other cases, they are much more widespread than we now realize. It is hard to dispute Casey's own examples of the mother and the husband (although to do so is not out of the question). But what if we substituted "wife" for "husband" in Casey's example? Here we would be confronted with a wide variety of differing interpretations, interpretations ranging from those that require total self-sacrifice to those that require equal or superior decision making. Moreover, we could expect these differences in our interpretation of the social role of wife to lead to discrepancies in our judgments of causal responsibility in a wide variety of cases.

Take, for example, the case represented by Daniel Patrick Moynihan's 1965 report on the status of black women and men in America.[17] In this report, Moynihan blamed the low morale of black men on the higher achievement level of black women. Although Moynihan never made his assumptions explicit, we can conclude, along with feminist critics of the report,[18] that Moynihan had to make two assumptions to come to such a conclusion. One is that there exists a causal relationship between the morale of husbands and wives. The other is that wives can be expected to do worse than their husbands financially so as to protect their husbands' egos.

While feminist critics of the report were not upset by the first assumption, they were clearly upset by the second. Likewise, while they were willing to acknowledge the interdependence of husbands' and wives' well-being, they were not willing to accept Moynihan's interpretation of the social role of wife.[19] Nor were they willing to acknowledge that wives should be expected to suffer in order to make their husbands feel superior. Hence, they were, not surprisingly, unanimous in their rejection of Moynihan's judgments of causal responsibility.

The discrepancies in causal judgments are even more strident in the abortion case which Casey cites. Recall that Casey made the case out to be totally uncontroversial by assuming that obstetricians can never be expected to perform abortions. (Such an expectation is "out of the question.") But surely there are many of us who think that obstetricians should perform abortions—or should at least not stop others from doing so. Indeed, we may, if we feel very strongly about the situation,

17. The "Moynihan Report," or the "Negro Family: The Case For National Action," was published officially by the U.S. Labor Department in the fall of 1965.

18. Paula Giddings provides an excellent overview of the feminist perspectives on Moynihan's report in *When and Where I Enter: The Impact of Black Women On Race and Sex in America* (New York, 1984), 325–35.

19. Nor, for that matter, were they willing to accept the relationship between wives and husbands as the relevant one in the context of a discussion of the low morale of black males. Surely, they argued, if any relationship was to be invoked, it should be that between whites and blacks.

hold an obstetrician responsible for the death of a woman whose fetus he refused to abort on the grounds that he should have performed the abortion in order to save the woman's life.

In cases such as these, the grounds by which an individual becomes attached to a particular social role come to be of utmost importance. If Casey were able to show that an individual's attachment to a particular social role is objective, then he would not have to worry about discrepancies between the individual's self-description and the description of that individual by others. He could simply point out that one of these two descriptions of the individual is mistaken—either because it fails to take into consideration the individual's real social role or because it is based on a mistaken interpretation of that role.

Moreover, if Casey were able to show that social roles have an objective or absolute value, he might be able to bring role playing back into the realm of moral agency, although he would never be able to merge moral agency with role playing itself. Casey does attempt to show that the value of a particular role is not always relative to utilitarian considerations. But such a demonstration is not sufficient. If Casey is going to give social roles the importance that he does in ascribing moral responsibility, he must show that the value of a particular role *never* depends on utilitarian considerations. As things now stand, Casey does not succeed in supporting even the weaker of these two claims.

While he comes very close to providing us with a deontological justification for the goodness of roles such as "father" and "doctor," he does so only by blurring the distinction between social roles and those "characteristic human excellences or virtues" embodied in them. While taking on a father's role might lead one to become a generous person, such generosity is a consequence of taking on that role, not part of the role itself. Likewise, while taking on a doctor's role might lead one to prevent sickness, the prevention of sickness occurs as a result of the individual's own moral agency and hence cannot be considered a characteristic of her social role.

Finally, even if Casey *were* able to come up with a deontological justification of social roles, he still could not merge individuals with their social roles in such a way as to ensure the coincidence between *our* description of the individual and the individual's own description of himself. For social roles are not as well-defined as Casey makes them out to be. Rarely do they specify exactly what an individual should do in a specific situation. This is particularly the case when the social role in question is very general, such as that of "parent" or "friend."

While a parent is supposed to take care of his children, it is not clear how far that care ought to extend. Should he watch his child's every move or should he let the child take responsibility for some of her own actions? Should he make all of his child's decisions for her or should he let her make mistakes on the basis of her own untutored judgments? The answers to these questions are far from obvious. Hence, even though we might agree on the value of a particular mode of child care, we could not conclude automatically from our designated role responsibilities what we should do in particular situations. Nor could we expect others to come to the same conclusions as we did.

Furthermore, even in cases where the individual's social role is sufficiently well-defined, there is no reason to expect the individual to occupy it forever. Just as individuals take on social roles, they can, and sometimes do, step back from those roles in order to decide whether or not to continue occupying them. Likewise, individuals can, and sometimes do, step back from their social roles when the dictates of one role clash with the dictates of another, e.g., when being a parent clashes with being a citizen. And finally, it simply may not be possible *not* to step back from one's social role. Gerald Cohen, among others, argues that a sane man can think and believe only "as a man" and not as the occupant of a particular social role.[20]

All of this is to suggest not only that individuals *should* back away from their social roles, but that they already *do*—or at least they do if they are sane. What are the implications here for Casey's approach to moral responsibility? On the one hand, the ability of individuals to step back from their social roles does not imply that Casey cannot invoke such roles in order to decide whether or not an individual is causally responsible for harm. I concentrate throughout chapter 9 on showing how our judgments of causal responsibility are grounded in our conceptions of an individual's social roles. On the other hand, it *does* imply that he will have to allow for the possibility of a discrepancy between our description of an individual and the individual's own description of himself.

Likewise, he will have to allow for the possibility that individuals will

20. See Gerald Cohen, "Beliefs and Roles," *Proceedings of the Aristotelian Society* 67 (1966–67), 17–34. Cohen also has a very persuasive normative argument that to associate individuals totally with their roles is to treat them as things (33–34). For an example of someone who argues that individuals are in fact a mere sum of the roles that they play, see Erving Goffman, *Asylums* (New York, 1959), especially 251–53.

For other views of the relationship between social roles and moral agency, see R. S. Downie, "Roles and Moral Agency," *Philosophy* 39 (October 1968), 29–36, and *Roles and Values* (London, 1971); Dorothy Emmet, *Function, Purpose, and Powers* (London, 1958) and *Rules, Roles, and Relations* (London, 1966); Benjamin Freedman, "A Meta-Ethics for Professional Morality," *Ethics* 89 (October 1978), 1–19; and Charles Fried, "Rights and Roles," in his *Right and Wrong* (Cambridge, Mass., 1978).

not always intend to bring about the harm which we describe them as bringing about or as failing to prevent. Once he is forced to admit the possibility of such a discrepancy, he will no longer be able to ascribe moral responsibility to individuals by describing them either as bringing about harm or as letting it occur. The most that he will be able to conclude is that the individual is morally responsible for an action which we deem causally responsible for harm, and even then, it is not clear that he will be able to construe moral responsibility as a fact about individuals rather than as a judgment that we make on the basis of our own social and political norms.

Casey is committed to the modern concept of moral responsibility and to the assumption that moral responsibility is something to be discovered about individuals, rather than ascribed to them. Likewise, he is committed to the modern notion of moral blameworthiness, according to which individuals are blameworthy, not in virtue of our social practice of blaming, but in virtue of their having themselves caused—freely willed—something bad. Hence, he finds it necessary to write blameworthiness into moral agency itself.

But to do so is not possible, for reasons I discussed in chapter 4. Moreover, to make the effort in the case of external harm is downright absurd, since as Casey himself has shown, the causal responsibility for external harm depends on both an individual's social role and our expectations of him. Casey appears to get around the dilemma created by the dependence of causal responsibility on an individual's social role only because he both misrepresents social roles in general and merges individuals with their social roles to the extent that they lose the very freedom necessary to moral responsibility.

Moreover, he is only able to merge individuals with their social roles by presenting us with a very confused understanding of ascription. On the one hand, since he views moral responsibility as ascribed to individuals by locutions such as "X brought about harm," and "Y failed to prevent it," we cannot help but assume that he has appropriated the understanding of ascription developed by H. L. A. Hart and others, according to which responsibility is relative to the structure of language and hence dependent on its rules. On the other hand, he treats moral responsibility not only as a fact about individuals but as part of their moral agency. Hence, we are left not knowing where to locate the source of moral responsibility itself.

What if he had developed an understanding of ascription similar to that which I sketched in chapter 5? In other words, what if he had viewed responsibility as a judgment that we make about an individual and incorporate into our judgments of her? Presumably he would be faced with the same dilemma that confronted Harris. On the one hand, he would be obliged to acknowledge the practical considerations that ground our ascription of responsibility to individuals for external harm. On the other hand, he would need to view responsibility itself as something independent of these considerations.

The fact that Casey and Harris end up with the same dilemma is surprising, since they begin at opposite ends of the moral and political spectrum. As a deontologist and conservative, Casey is concerned primarily with moral agency and the preservation of our current expectations of individuals. In the interests of bringing these two concerns together, he places social expectations at the center of his theory of agency. Harris, on the other hand, rejects the value of such expectations altogether. As a consequentialist, he is concerned primarily with the prevention of suffering, and as a political radical, he attempts to prevent such suffering by extending drastically what we now conceive to be the realm of moral responsibility of the affluent.

Because both he and Casey try to apply our modern concept of moral responsibility to social and political practice, they are forced to compromise their respective moral and political positions. On the one hand, because Harris incorporates the modern concept of moral responsibility into his consequentialist arguments, he ends up having to require not only that we can expect an individual to prevent harm, but that the individual was the author of his own actions. On the other hand, because Casey chooses to focus on the relationship between individuals and external harm, he ends up having to smuggle into what he calls "agency" the causal responsibility of an individual's actions or omissions for harm. Since, as Casey himself makes clear, causal responsibility is relative to the individual's social role, and social roles are by nature functional, Casey cannot help but let consequentialism in through the back door.

What this suggests is not only that Harris and Casey are forced to develop internally inconsistent approaches to moral responsibility, but that they do so by taking on each other's moral perspectives. In the end, Harris finds it necessary to invoke moral agency. Casey, if he wants to continue his reliance on social roles, will have to acknowledge various consequentialist considerations. How can we explain the congruence of their respective theories? I submit that such congruence is not coincidental, but rather a factor of their shared enterprise—an enterprise which pulls them in opposite directions at once. On the one hand, in order to hold individuals causally responsible for external harm, they must invoke both social expectations and the pragmatic considerations on which these expectations are based. On the other hand, in order to hold the individuals morally blameworthy as traditionally understood, they must couch moral responsibility for external harm in the subjectivist language of moral agency.

In the end, neither Harris nor Casey succeeds in accomplishing what he sets out to accomplish. On the one hand, because Harris finds it necessary to invoke moral agency, he is not able to extend an individual's realm of moral responsibility. On the other hand, because Casey is forced to acknowledge the importance of social roles, he is not able to close himself off from relativism in the realm of consequences. Nor is he able to dismiss offhand the contention that even maintenance of the status quo in this realm serves to protect those interests around which social roles are organized. What these interests might be—or rather, how they are organized—is something which we begin to glimpse in the next chapter.

7

Moral Agency and the Distribution of Organizational Blame

Moral Agency and Democratic Accountability

In a recent series of articles,[1] Dennis Thompson sets out to establish the conditions under which public officials can be held "personally responsible" for harmful policies developed and carried out within government bureaucracies. The first condition that Thompson cites requires that an individual's action or omission have been causally responsible for harm. The second requires that the harm itself have been "a product of the individual's own free will,"[2] a condition that Thompson thinks can be met by showing that the individual was not in the position to provide us with a valid excuse.

Thompson's conditions are unique in two important respects. First of all, unlike most of those now writing on moral responsibility, Thompson stipulates that the absence of a volitional excuse registers not only that an individual's will was free, but that harm was a product of the individual's own free will. Second, he suggests that the criteria of causal responsibility be kept extremely open so as not to get bogged down in the various social expectations and practical considerations that we bring to bear on the causal responsibility of particular individuals for external harm. According to Thompson, in order to show that an individual's action was causally responsible for harm, it is necessary to show only that "the harm would not have occurred without the action's having been performed."[3]

---

1. Dennis F. Thompson, "Moral Responsibility of Public Officials: The Problem of Many Hands," *American Political Science Review* 74 (December 1980), 905–16; "Ascribing Responsibility to Advisers in Government," *Ethics* 93 (1983), 546–60; "Moral Responsibility and the New York City Fiscal Crisis," in Joel Fleishman et al., eds., *Public Duties* (Cambridge, Mass., 1981), 266–85. Thompson repeats many of these arguments in *Political Ethics and Public Office* (Cambridge, Mass., 1987).
2. Thompson, "Ascribing Responsibility to Advisors in Government," 2.
3. Thompson, "Moral Responsibility of Public Officials," 908.

Thompson's decision here to rely on such an open criterion of causation follows from his recognition that what we take to be the cause of an outcome is often relative to the purposes of inquiry.

The event or events we take to be the cause will depend on what the purposes of our inquiry are (e.g., explanation, social reform, or moral criticism). It is therefore better to adopt a weak criterion of causal responsibility, requiring only that a person be *a* cause of an outcome in the sense that the outcome would not have happened but for this act or omission.[4]

Thompson's criterion of causation, as well as his unique approach to volitional excuses, would seem to give him a strong edge over the approaches to moral responsibility developed by both Harris and Casey. Since his criteria of causation is so open—"weak"—Thompson does not find it necessary either to explore the social expectations and practical considerations normally associated with causal responsibility or to explain how they could ever be associated with free will. Moreover, since he views the absence of a volitional excuse as registering not only that an individual's will was free, but that harm itself was a product of the individual's own free will, he appears able to avoid having to merge the absence of a volitional excuse with the causal responsibility of an individual's action or omission for harm. Indeed, he appears able to dispense with the causal responsibility of the individual's action or omission for such harm altogether.

But he appears able to do so, as we shall see, only by joining together two significantly different sorts of excuses—and by smuggling into the second sort a causal connection between the individual and harm. The first sort of excuse refers to an individual's state of mind, or in other words, to whether or not his will was free. The second sort of excuse refers to the individual's organizational role and registers not that the individual's own will was free, but that the organization to which he belongs expects certain sorts of behavior from him.

Thompson's blurring of the distinction between these two sorts of excuses becomes apparent when we examine more closely his understanding of "willing." Unlike most theorists, Thompson does not develop a theory of responsibility on the basis of his understanding of "willing." Instead, he develops his understanding of willing on the basis of the criteria which he thinks a theory of responsibility would have to meet in order to be an adequate theory of bureaucratic responsibility. As such, if we want to grasp what Thompson means by free will, we will have to turn first to his discussion of responsibility in the bureaucracy.

4. Ibid., 909.

Thompson begins this discussion by rejecting the traditional under-standing of willing as intention. He does so on what are essentially prac-tical grounds. According to Thompson, if it were necessary that a public official have intended harm in order for that harm to be con-sidered a product of the official's free will, then officials could not be considered morally responsible for much of the harm produced within the bureaucracy. For as Thompson makes clear, such harm is the prod-uct of "many hands," and is not always intended by those individuals who cause it.

Thompson's primary example here is that of an official whose advice to another produces harm. Thompson obviously thinks that the official should be held morally responsible for the consequences of his advice in particular circumstances. Hence, he rejects the interpretation of will-ing as intention.

Some theories of responsibility would obviate the problem of many hands by making officials responsible only for what they intend, not at all (or at least never as much) for what anyone else does as a result of their decisions. . . . The implausibility of this view in ordinary moral life is magnified in public life. . . . We would surely hold the official morally responsible for failing to take precau-tions to avoid harmful consequences of others' responses to his or her deci-sions.[5]

It is not clear from the above passage whether Thompson is saying that the interpretation of willing as intention is implausible because of-ficials cannot be held morally responsible for what they *are* morally re-sponsible for or because officials cannot be held morally responsible for what Thompson thinks they *should be* held morally responsible for in the interests of, say, democratic accountability. Since the first claim would involve circular reasoning, I take Thompson to be making the second. That he is making the second claim would seem appropriate, moreover, given that he criticizes two other theories of responsibility for "weakening democratic accountability" and defends his own theory of personal responsibility on the grounds that it "supports democratic accountability."[6]

The two theories of responsibility which Thompson criticizes in this context are those of hierarchical and collective responsibility. Before going on to examine Thompson's own theory of responsibility—and in particular the understanding of "willing" on which it is based—let me summarize briefly his criticism of these two other theories of responsi-bility. For it is within his criticism of them that he makes most explicit

5. Ibid., 913.
6. Ibid., 915.

the criteria which he thinks a plausible theory of responsibility should meet.

According to Thompson, the hierarchical model of responsibility will not do for two reasons. First of all, it "does not coincide with current forms of bureaucratic decision-making." In particular, it neglects the "problem of many hands"[7] by assuming that responsibility for policy always falls on the officials holding the top positions in the hierarchy. Second, it is incompatible with moral responsibility as traditionally understood—given that the officials holding the top positions in the hierarchy end up being held responsible for policies over which they have no control.[8]

According to Thompson, while the collective model of responsibility recognizes the problem of many hands, it shares with the hierarchical model a denial of moral responsibility. Its denial of moral responsibility is for Thompson a consequence of its "rejection of the notion that responsibility for an outcome depends in part on the contribution an individual actually made, or could have made, to that outcome."[9] It is because of this rejection, Thompson makes clear, that the collective model of responsibility cannot support a notion of "individual moral blame."[10]

From his criticism of responsibility as intention, hierarchical responsibility, and collective responsibility, we get a sense of the demands that Thompson will be putting on his own theory of "personal responsibility." In the first place, personal responsibility will have to coincide with moral responsibility as traditionally understood, i.e., it will have to embrace both free will and moral blame. Second, personal responsibility will have to be ascribed to individual officials for at least some of the harm which is the product of "many hands." And finally, personal responsibility will have to be ascribed to individuals for such harm in a way that enhances democratic accountability.

Thompson's relation to the tradition of discourse on moral responsibility cannot help but be somewhat puzzling here. On the one hand, he not only associates moral responsibility with both free will and moral blame, but contends that the notion of personal responsibility that he develops is registered in the absence of a volitional excuse. On the other hand, he rejects the traditional understanding of willing as intention on what are essentially practical grounds. According to Thompson, if it were necessary that a public official have intended harm, then officials

7. Ibid., 905.   9. Ibid., 908.
8. Ibid., 906.   10. Ibid.

could not be considered morally responsible for much of the harm produced within a political setting. For such harm is often the product of "many hands" and as such is not always intended by those who cause it.

If Thompson's conception of personal responsibility were essentially different from the conception of moral responsibility that we have been focusing on, it would not be appropriate as an object of analysis in this context. But Thompson demands of his conception not only that it support democratic accountability, but that it coincide with moral responsibility as traditionally understood. Likewise, he insists that all three of the requirements cited above can be met by developing a theory of responsibility around two conditions of moral responsibility that are very similar to those established by Harris and Casey. The first of these conditions is that the individual's action or omission be considered causally responsible for harm. The second is that the harm be considered a product of the individual's own free will.

Organizational Excuses

Since the first condition can be met so easily within Thompson's schema, he concentrates on the second. In doing so, he makes clear that if we want to figure out when harm can be considered the product of an individual's own free will, we will have to concentrate on the volitional excuses that we invoke to excuse ourselves from blame. Thompson joins other political theorists and moral philosophers here in focusing on two excuses in particular: compulsion and ignorance. But he departs from the analyses offered by the others in claiming that the absence of such an excuse registers not only that an individual freely willed his own actions, but that harm was a product of the individual's own free will.

How can Thompson hope to show that external harm has its source in an individual's own free will? He attempts such a demonstration within an extended discussion of the conditions under which volitional excuses are "acceptable." At first glance, these conditions appear to be Aristotelian, although less so when Thompson goes on to view ignorance and compulsion in the context of institutional behavior. According to Thompson:

Following Aristotle, we may consider two kinds of volitional excuses—those of ignorance and compulsion. Ignorance (not knowing that a certain description applies to one's action) does not always count as a valid excuse, or even as grounds for mitigation. Only if the ignorance is not negligent (only if, for instance, the official should not have been expected to know that his action would have certain harmful consequences) would we be prepared to accept the ex-cuse.[11]

Thompson argues that whether the individual should have been ex-pected to know that his action would have certain harmful conse-quences itself depends on the individual's social, or rather institutional, role.

In the case of public officials, standards of negligence largely depend on how we understand the formal requirements of roles or offices. . . . Similarly, we cannot decide whether compulsion should excuse officials without deciding what their roles require of them.[12]

Thompson's first example is that of a public official who pleads igno-rance. According to Thompson, an official who admittedly contributes to an objectionable outcome may in some cases be excused from per-sonal responsibility for that outcome if he could not have been ex-pected to know that other officials before him had acted wrongly. For example, when as U.N. ambassador in 1961, Adlai Stevenson denied that the United States had anything to do with the invasion of Cuba, he could not have been expected to know that the United States *did* have something to do with the invasion. As such, writes Thompson, "Steven-son cannot be held personally responsible for the negative conse-quences of his denial."[13]

At the other end of the chain, writes Thompson:

An official may sometimes be excused for consequences of a decision when he or she could not have been expected to foresee the wrongs that other officials would commit implementing that decision.[14]

More often than not, pleas of ignorance are *not* acceptable. For in order to reject such a plea:

We do not have to show that such an official should have foreseen the specific act of some particular official . . . it is sufficient that the official should have realized that mistakes of the kind that occurred were likely.[15]

A case in which Thompson finds the plea of ignorance unacceptable is that of Sargeant Shriver, who, disappointed by the number of re-quests he had received from foreign governments for Peace Corps projects, urged his subordinates to seek out more requests and, accord-

11. Thompson, "Moral Responsibility and the New York City Crisis," 268.
12. Ibid., 268.
13. Thompson, "Moral Responsibility of Public Officials," 913.
14. Ibid., 913.
15. Ibid., 914.

ing to one account, let those subordinates know that if they did not come back with such requests, they would be fired. Thompson suggests that if this account is true, Shriver should be considered personally responsible for the fictionalized projects which his subordinates subsequently created. For he "should have foreseen that this injunction could have induced such behavior."[16]

Pleas of compulsion more often seem acceptable to Thompson. The compulsion he is concerned with is "not the extreme physical and psychological kind that philosophers and lawyers usually discuss"[17] but rather the kind that results from the organizational setting in which public officials act. An example of this kind of compulsion is

a case in which no explicit order has been given but a subordinate believes that a superior expects him or her to pursue what is seen as a morally dubious course of action.[18]

Other examples of such compulsion are the constraints imposed on officials by bureaucratic practices and procedures, constraints which in effect circumscribe an official's range of choices. Thompson argues that almost all of these constraints result in some way from the hierarchical patterns of authority according to which bureaucracies are structured.[19] Most of the others result from specialization and routinization.

Under what conditions can pleas of compulsion of this sort be considered "acceptable"? Thompson does not offer specific conditions here as he does in the case of ignorance. He does say, however, that if we were to come up with specific conditions,

we would need some criterion based on a hypothetical average performance— what the average official could be expected to do under the circumstance.[20]

From the above examples, we can infer the general conditions under which ignorance and compulsion are "acceptable excuses" in the bureaucratic context. Ignorance is an acceptable excuse if the public official could not have been expected to know that his action or omission would be causally responsible for harm. Compulsion and coercion are acceptable excuses if the official could not have been expected to act otherwise than he did act.

Two things become apparent from Thompson's discussion of volitional excuses in this context. One is that while these excuses may be crucial to our understanding of bureaucratic responsibility, they are

16. Ibid.
17. Ibid., 915.
18. Ibid.

19. Ibid.
20. Ibid.

not the volitional excuses with which Thompson says that he is concerned—i.e., excuses of the form "I didn't know what I was doing," or "I couldn't have done otherwise than I did." Instead they are excuses of the form "I couldn't have been expected to know that my action would cause harm," or "I couldn't have been expected not to cause the harm."

The other is that the absence of such an excuse does not register anything about the individual himself or herself. Nor does it register anything about a causal connection between the individual and external harm. Instead, it registers something about the organization to which the individual belongs. The absence of an excuse of the form "I couldn't have been expected to know that my action would cause harm" underscores the extent to which the individual's organization expects officials to know what their subordinates are doing. The absence of an excuses of the form "I couldn't have been expected not to cause harm" underscores the extent to which the individual's organization expects individuals to act against the wrongdoing of their superiors.

Since excuses of the form "I couldn't have been expected to follow the orders of my superiors" do not register anything about the individual's state of mind or about a causal connection between the individual and external harm, how can Thompson conclude from their absence that harm was the product of an individual's free will? The short answer is that he cannot conclude this. The long answer is that he appears able to do so now only because he joins together two significantly different sorts of excuses and then smuggles into one of them a causal connection between the individual and harm.

The first sort of excuse is that traditionally invoked in discussions of moral responsibility and usually takes the form "I didn't know" or "I was compelled." The second sort of excuse is the one that we just explored; it usually refers to the individual's social role or the responsibilities attached to it. Thompson does not treat the two as different sorts of excuses. Instead, he treats the second as a mere variation on the first. But they are clearly different. While the first sort of excuse refers to an individual's state of mind, the second refers to our own expectations of the individual.

Thompson needs the first sort of excuse to show that the individual's will was free (and even then it is highly unlikely that the absence of such an excuse could ever register the sort of free will required by the modern concept of moral responsibility). Thompson needs the second sort of excuse, along with our recognition of a causal connection between the individual and harm, to show that the individual's action or omission was causally responsible for an external state of affairs. He cannot merge them into one excuse because the second sort of excuse rests on social and political considerations over which the individual has no control, and the first sort of excuse ostensibly registers free will.

If Thompson were to separate the two sorts of excuses on which he is relying, and make explicit that he is incorporating into the second a causal connection between the individual and harm, he might be able to show that an individual is causally responsible for an action which we deem causally responsible for external harm. But he could not show that the harm was a product of the individual's own free will or that the individual himself caused harm in the sense relevant to moral responsibility. Instead, he would have to concede that like Harris and Casey before him, he had provided us with two separate judgments, one that the harm was a consequence of a particular individual's actions, and the other that the individual is worthy of our blame.

Moral Tasks and the Distribution of Power

While Thompson may not be able to use his volitional excuses to show that harm was the product of an individual's own free will, he does not need to leave these excuses behind altogether. Indeed he might use them very productively to reconstruct our judgments of causation and blameworthiness as part of social and political practice. As we have already seen in our discussion of Aristotle, excuses such as "I didn't know," or "I was compelled," are an important part of our social practice of blaming. Likewise, excuses such as "I couldn't have been expected to know," or "I couldn't have been expected to disobey orders," could, if viewed along with a causal connection between an individual and harm, be used to explain our judgments of causal responsibility.

Thompson does not explore the nature of causal responsibility in any detail. Indeed, he provides us with such an open—"weak"— conception of causal responsibility that we are able to assume it is in the background and concentrate on volitional excuses. But once we recognize that Thompson has smuggled causal responsibility into the absence of a volitional excuse in his efforts to conclude that an individual himself caused harm, we are justified in viewing the social expectations inherent in his volitional excuses as among the criteria of causal responsibility. Likewise, we are justified in carving out of his analysis a model of causal responsibility that not only places social expectations in an organizational setting, but stresses the relationship between the goals of the organization and our judgments of causal responsibility themselves.

Since Thompson is concerned about government bureaucracies, he

is led to stress the relationship between our judgments of casual responsibility, on the one hand, and the needs of a democratic polity, on
the other. But his analysis is not strictly tied to his own examples. Indeed, if we could show that society is organized, even loosely, around a
set of social roles which are themselves supported by particular interests, if not purposes and principles, we might be able to apply
Thompson's analysis to judgments of causal responsibility that we
make outside the context of governmental institutions.

Take, for example, the case of a parent whose child is sick. While
famillies are not bureaucracies, they are organized loosely around a set
of roles and expectations which are themselves grounded in a variety of
goods, including physical health. Likewise, when we invoke these roles
and expectations, either by themselves or within our judgments of responsibility, we necessarily reinforce their importance, and if our judgments lead to practical action, ensure that they are met.

Not surprisingly, the situation becomes more complicated when the
stated goals in question differ. In the case of the family, we generally
agree on certain goals, even though we do not necessarily agree on who
should meet them. In the cases about which Harris is concerned, on the
other hand, we disagree about general goals. While American capitalists may not think that famine in sub-Saharan Africa is a top priority,
those dying in the famine presumably do. Likewise, while factory
owners in this country (or in Harris's own England) may not consider it
part of their job to promote the health of their workers, their employ-
ees presumably do. Hence, we should expect considerable differences
to arise between the two groups with regard to causal responsibility.

Whose opinions can be expected to win out in society? If the industrial diseases case is at all telling, we can expect the opinions of those
with more clout, and not a World Moral Authority, to win out over those
with less clout. Likewise, we can expect their judgments of causal responsibility to take precedence over those of others and eventually to
become the conventional wisdom that many, if not all of us, share. But
we cannot treat either our judgments of causal responsibility themselves or the expectations on which they are based as isolated phenomena. For as Thompson's analysis suggests, both our expectations of
individuals and the causal judgments that follow from them are clearly
dependent on, among other things, the larger complex of expectations
and judgments of which they are a part.

Since Thompson's examples are all of government bureaucracies,
which are by nature self-consciously organized, we should not be surprised to discover that the expectations which he talks about are all designed to mesh together in such a way as to be ideally conducive to

democratic accountability. But this does not mean that we cannot talk about such a configuration of expectations in less self-consciously organized settings. Indeed, we may have to do so if we want to understand how our judgments of causal responsibility function together in society.

In the cases that Thompson cites, expectations are distributed with task efficiency in mind. While "efficiency" is too strong a word to use in other cases, we may be able to talk about the distribution of moral tasks. Take, for example, the case of the mother who let her child watch violent music videos on television. In this case, we saw a clear relationship between our expectations of the mother and our expectations of the heavy metal band itself. If we viewed the mother as responsible for the content of her child's television viewing, we were less likely to view the heavy metal band itself as responsible for the consequences of their videos on small children. Likewise, if we viewed the band itself as responsible for the consequences of their videos on small children, we were less likely to place the burden of responsibility on the child's mother.

Such a trade-off in expectations was also evident in the case of the doctor who prescribed harmful pills to his patients. If we lived in the early 1800s, we might have expected our doctor to test his own medicines before prescribing them to us. Likewise, we might have held him responsible for our subsequent illnesses if he did not. But as members of late-twentieth-century society, we expect pharmaceutical companies to test the pills which they distribute and are more likely to blame the pharmaceutical company or the FDA, and not the doctor herself, if the pills which she prescribes turn out to be harmful.

In these two cases, social expectations are organized with a sense of distribution, if not efficiency, in mind. But we cannot assume that such organization is self-conscious, as in the case of a bureaucracy. Nor can we assume that it is neutral with regard to particular interests. Most of us do not explore the source of our expectations or even think about them as expectations. Moreover, even if we did, we would have to acknowledge that they are organized in light not only of tasks to be accomplished, but the distribution of power in society.

Take again the case of a pill manufacturer and a doctor who prescribes his pills. In this case, or cases like it, we see a struggle between the medical establishment and the federal government over who should be responsible for safety, a struggle that is clearly tied up with the power of both groups. Likewise, in the case of violent rock videos, we see a power struggle over responsibility between various watchdog committees and the entertainment industry, a struggle that is taking place in both the media and the courts.

Interestingly enough, Thompson's own bureaucracy may involve more of a power struggle over expectations than he acknowledges. While bureaucracies may have stated goals and rationalized procedures, they are far from neutral with regard to particular interests. Bureaucrats fight over goals, and very rarely, if ever, do rationalized procedures not favor one group over another. Indeed, the concept of rational organization may itself obscure the extent to which particular bureaucracies fight over their turf and have a clear interest in the way stated goals are to be achieved.

Not surprisingly, the struggle for power over expectations is clearest in those cases where there is open conflict over both social roles and the goods around which they are organized. While not all factory owners are purely self-interested, they do tend to construe their social role as factory owner in ways that sustain both their own interests and the endowments of power on which those interests are based. Likewise, while not all factory workers self-consciously mold their conception of the factory owner's social role according to their own interests or desires, they do generally develop expectations of factory owners which, if respected, lead to the benefit of workers in general.

How could expectations, social roles, and judgments of causal responsibility possibly have such practical effects? Two responses come to mind here. One has to do with the organization of social roles. The other has to do with our social practice of blaming. Thompson addresses both of them in his discussion of how the practice of personal responsibility might lead to more genuinely democratic decision making in the future if it were taken seriously by government officials.

While Thompson never spells out the relationship between democracy and the particular expectations about which he is concerned, he does assume that the best distribution of expectations would be one that would make democratic accountability possible in the bureaucracy, or in other words, would give to public officials the sort of responsibility for shared outcomes necessary for democratic review by either the legislative branch or the population as a whole. Likewise, while he does not make explicit the exact effect that responsibility—and the notion of moral blame inherent in it—would have on public officials, he does express faith that they would be led to make wiser decisions in the future if they were blamed for their mistakes.[21]

Thompson's faith rests on his functionalist understanding of roles in an organizational setting. According to Thompson, roles are constructed with efficiency in mind. Likewise, by taking these roles seriously, and basing our judgments of responsibility on them, we can

---

21. Thompson, "Ascribing Responsibility to Advisors in Government," 905.

both ensure conscientious behavior on the part of officials and promote the ends of their bureaus.

The idea of a role delineates a moral division of labor which, within limits, may be justified on the grounds that it promotes a more efficient pursuit of moral ends, just as a political division of labor ideally contributes to political efficiency.[22]

Thompson essentially has two points here. One is that our practice of personal responsibility promotes conscientious behavior on the part of government officials by virtue of the motivational powers associated with blame, public criticism, dismissal from office, and exclusion from public office in the future. The other is that by holding individuals personally responsible for their actions, we not only reinforce the social role on which our actions descriptions are based, but promote the ends around which our social roles are organized.

In the cases which Thompson cites, we promote the ends of an individual's bureau by holding him personally responsible for the consequences of his actions. We do so because what counts as a consequence is determined in large part by the individual's organizational role, a role which was established with the bureau's ends in mind. If applied to society at large, this model of responsibility could be used to explain, among other things, the relationship between our particular ends, social expectations, and consequences. Likewise, it could be used to understand how, in holding each other morally responsible, we both reinforce our social expectations of individuals and help to maintain the distribution of power on which the expectations are based.[23]

But we could not use it for these purposes without also delving into the practical effects that might accrue from associating our judgments of causal responsibility with blame. Thompson himself points to the practical effects that blaming might have in society by showing how our holding individuals personally responsible could "influence the conduct of public officials." According to Thompson:

Those who took the ideas of personal responsibility seriously would perhaps make decisions with greater care, and if they did not, citizens or other officials could reinforce ascriptions of responsibility with sanctions, such as public criticism, dismissal from office, or exclusions from public office in the future.[24]

Thompson adds here that "whether personal accountability could actually support democratic accountability in this way depends partly on

22. Thompson, "Moral Responsibility of Public Officials," 269.
23. I develop this model of responsibility much more fully in chapters 8 and 9.
24. Ibid., 905–6.

the nature of the social and political structures in which citizens and officials act."[25]

While Thompson begins to develop a consequentialist approach to blaming, he stops short of developing such an approach fully and stresses once again that individuals are personally responsible for harm only when harm is itself a product of individuals' free wills. By stressing this Thompson places himself back in the mainstream of those who view blameworthiness as an aspect of an individual's own moral agency. Likewise, he places on himself the burden of showing how individuals can be blameworthy outside the context of our social practice of blaming. Not surprisingly, he is unable in the end to shoulder such a burden, since he develops his whole theory of personal responsibility around the practical needs of a democratic polity.

What if we were to ignore Thompson's comments about free will and take his consequentialist approach to blameworthiness seriously? Two things presumably would follow. One is that we would no longer need to pretend that the absence of a volitional excuse registers free will. The other is that we could view the conditions of blameworthiness— including the individual's ability to do otherwise—as shaped by the sorts of demands that we place on individuals as members of a particular community.

Thompson's second sort of volitional excuse would seem to be perfectly suited to such a view. While excuses of the first sort—"I didn't know" or "I was compelled"—are often placed at the center of discussions about moral responsibility, excuses of the second sort—"I couldn't have been expected to know" or "I couldn't have been expected to do otherwise"—are also extremely important.[26] If Thompson were to treat excuses of the second sort as criteria of blaming rather than as conditions of free will, he might be able to avoid the sorts of contradictions that other philosophers and political theorists create for themselves by invoking volitional excuses to talk about moral responsibility and free will.

But he would have to cease talking about moral responsibility as grounded in free will and begin talking about it as part of two separate judgments that we make about individuals on the basis of our own social and political points of view. (One of these judgments, as we have seen, is that harm is the consequence of a particular individual's action. The other is that the individual is worthy of our blame.) Likewise, he

25. Ibid., 906.
26. The reason why such excuses are now generally ignored may have something to do with the fact that they are so clearly removed from the notion of free will required by our modern concept of moral responsibility.

would have to cease talking about blameworthiness as an aspect of moral agency and begin talking about it as part of a relationship between individuals and actual blamers.

Since Thompson already situates personal responsibility as part of our practice of excuse giving—which involves at least two people—he would seem to be fairly well equipped to perform the latter task. Likewise, since he in effect, if not intentionally, lays out the various social and political considerations that go into our judgments of causal responsibility in practice, he would appear to be able to perform the latter task without contradicting too much of the rest of his theory. But he does not choose to pursue either task. Nor could he do so without leaving the modern concept of moral responsibility behind.

While Thompson provides us with a basic model for understanding moral responsibility as part of social and political practice, he cannot pursue that model himself without violating his own understanding of moral responsibility. As things now stand, he, like Harris and Casey, provides us with two conflicting strands of thought. On the one hand, he develops a theory of causal responsibility around the needs of a democratic community. On the other hand, he tries to couch this theory in the language of moral responsibility as traditionally construed.

By way of summing up this part of the study, let me state briefly what I think Harris, Casey, and Thompson are trying to accomplish, why they fail, and what we can learn from their respective efforts. On the most general level, they are trying to hold individuals morally responsibility for harm that they would like to see prevented in the future. In most cases, this means harm for which we do not now hold individuals causally responsible, either because we conceive of it as having natural (i.e., nonhuman) causes or because we conceive of its human causes as indirect (in the case of omissions) or even distant (in the case of harm which results from many hands).

Since all three theorists begin with controversial cases, they find it necessary in dealing with these cases to set down the conditions under which individuals are morally responsible for harm in general. One of these conditions is that the individual's actions or omissions were causally responsible for the harm in question. The other is that their actions or omissions were a product of their own free will. While Harris, Casey, and Thompson all agree on the nature of the second condition, they differ with regard to their interpretations of the first. Harris focuses on the practical considerations that ground our judgments of causal responsibility for external harm. Casey concentrates on the social expectations that we invoke in deciding whether or not a particular individual is causally responsible for harm. And Thompson sets out to show how our social expectations and judgments of responsibility are organized around the ends of our particular community.

Each theorist provides us with important insights into the nature of causal responsibility by virtue of his particular focus. But all three are forced to leave their insights behind as a result of the modern concept of moral responsibility which they share. While Harris and Casey are led to conclude from the ability of an individual to meet the two conditions cited above that the individual himself caused harm in the sense relevant to moral responsibility, Thompson is led to go as far to talk about harm as the product of an individual's own free will.

Since the causal responsibility of an individual's actions or omissions for harm is relative to a variety of social and political considerations over which the individual himself has no control, it is not something that we can possibly subsume under an individual's own free will, as all three analyses clearly demonstrate. What, then, are we to do? I suggest in part 3 that we cease trying to view the two conditions as part of a purely factual discovery of moral responsibility and begin viewing them as two related judgments that we ourselves make about an individual on the basis of our own social and political perspectives.

PART THREE

8

Actions, Consequences, and the Boundaries of Community

Alternative Approaches

In parts 1 and 2, I explored several difficulties inherent in any attempt to apply our modern concept of moral responsibility to social and political controversies. In part 3, I attempt to overcome these difficulties by taking two sorts of pragmatic perspectives on our judgments of moral responsibility. One requires making explicit the various social and political considerations that we incorporate into our judgments of causal responsibility and blameworthiness in cases where we are concerned to discover who is morally responsible for external harm. The other requires making explicit how our modern concept of moral responsibility enables us to conflate our practical judgments of causation and blameworthiness into one ostensibly factual discovery of moral responsibility.

The pragmatic approach that I take to our judgments of causal responsibility and blameworthiness is of course not the only means of avoiding the difficulties in question. At least three other ways of doing so come to mind. The first entails simply dropping the modern concept of moral responsibility altogether and going back to its Aristotelian counterpart. Such an alternative is particularly attractive, since, as I argued in chapter 2, the Aristotelian concept of moral responsibility is coherent on its own terms. But I choose not to take this approach for two basic reasons. First of all, even though the modern concept of moral responsibility is not coherent on its own terms, it still plays an important role in our own social and political judgments. Hence, unless we are willing to leave these judgments behind altogether, we would be well advised not simply to abandon the concept, but to reconstruct it as part of social and political practice. Second, even though Aristotle successfully articulated the conditions under which we consider individuals blameworthy, he did not explore the nature of those practices that enable us to deem harm the consequence of a particular individual's action or to describe the individual as bringing about harm. Hence, while we can rely extensively on Aristotle's criteria of blameworthiness in our discussions of moral responsibility, we will have to go elsewhere in order to reconstruct our judgments of causal responsibility.

Implicit in my own project is the assumption that in order to develop a coherent understanding of moral responsibility, we need to be able to talk about causal responsibility and blameworthiness together. But not everyone accepts that assumption. H. L. A. Hart and A. M. Honoré, for instance, argue that we would be better off simply pointing out two different ways in which the term "moral responsibility" is used in contemporary society. According to Hart and Honoré, the term is sometimes used to highlight a causal connection between an individual and his actions. In other cases, it refers to blameworthiness. In these cases:

The expression "responsible for" does not refer to a factual connection between the person held responsible and his actions, but simply to his liability under the rules to be blamed.[1]

While such a bifurcation of the concept may enable us to avoid any difficulties now associated with moral responsibility, it has several drawbacks which lead me to reject it as an alternative from the start. Among other things, since Hart and Honoré's first notion of moral responsibility does not involve blameworthiness, it is not clear how it could be conceived of as a concept of *moral*, as opposed to purely *causal*, responsibility. Likewise, since Hart and Honoré's second notion of responsibility explicitly leaves out any causal connection between the individual and that for which she is being blamed, it is not clear why it should be called responsibility at all, rather than simple "liability under the rules to be blamed."

One way of characterizing the notion of responsibility as blameworthiness in moral terms without invoking causation might be to develop a utilitarian approach to moral responsibility. J. J. C. Smart, Richard Brandt, and others attempt to do so by leaving the notions of causation and free will behind altogether and concentrating on the consequences of blame in society.[2] Moral responsibility, not surprisingly, turns out to be a matter of blameworthiness itself.

While the utilitarian concept of moral responsibility is usually associated with contemporary utilitarians such as Brandt, it has its source in earlier works. Hume, for instance, both rejected the possibility of contra-causal freedom and asserted the importance of retaining our

---

1. H. L. A. Hart and A. M. Honoré, *Causation in the Law* (Oxford, 1959), 61.

2. J. J. C. Smart, "Free Will, Praise, and Blame," *Mind* 70 (1961), 291–306; Richard Brandt, "A Utilitarian Theory of Excuses," *Philosophical Review* 78 (1969), 337–61.

modern notion of moral blameworthiness. According to Hume, since we cannot ground blameworthiness in contra-causal freedom, we will have to turn both to the "mind of men" and to utilitarian-bound custom. Hume argues in this context that the "mind of men" is naturally inclined to feel sentiments of praise and blame, and that while such sentiments are themselves part of what it means to be human, the standards of appropriate behavior which we invoke in praising and blaming others are more purely conventional or utilitarian. According to Hume, those characteristics which lead us to praise others are "chiefly those that contribute to the peace and security of human society." Likewise, the characters which lead us to blame others are "chiefly those that tend to public detriment and disturbance."[3]

Hume did not explicitly call such an approach to blameworthiness utilitarian. But his nineteenth-century counterpart J. S. Mill did. Indeed, Mill is often cited as developing the first utilitarian concept of moral responsibility as a result of both his explicit association of moral responsibility with blameworthiness and punishment and his willingness to justify both on utilitarian grounds. "What is meant by moral responsibility?" Mill asks. "Moral responsibility means punishment. When we are said to have the feeling of being morally responsible for our actions, the idea of being punished for them is uppermost in our mind."[4]

Mill makes clear in this context that moral responsibility is based on both utilitarian rules and a "natural sentiment" toward justice. It is thus two-pronged as a concept. On the one hand, there are those rules and laws whose violation goes against the common good. On the other hand, there is a sense of guilt, which Mill characterizes as the product of both our natural instincts and the socialization process. According to Mill, while moral responsibility embraces the "natural sentiment of retaliation," it is enhanced by moral education.

From our earliest childhood, the idea of doing wrong (that is, of doing what is forbidden, or what is injurious to others) and the idea of punishment are presented to our minds together, and the intense character of the impressions causes the association between them to attain the highest degree of closeness and intimacy.[5]

Contemporary utilitarians pick up on Mill's definition of moral responsibility in their efforts to develop a full-blown utilitarian concept of

3. David Hume, "Of Liberty and Necessity," in *An Inquiry Concerning Human Understanding* (New York, 1907), 100.
4. J. S. Mill, *An Examination of Sir William Hamilton's Philosophy* (London, 1867), 454.
5. Ibid., 456.

moral responsibility. But they self-consciously avoid Mill's own reliance on "natural sentiments" and focus instead on both the standards and laws that we are expected to follow as members of a particular community and the practices of blaming and punishment that follow from our acts of defiance. Likewise, they justify both not on the basis of nature and utility combined, but solely with reference to the consequences that each can be expected to have for individuals and society as a whole.

Richard Brandt, one of the most persuasive among contemporary defenders of the utilitarian concept of moral responsibility, argues that our modern notion of moral blameworthiness has a variety of important consequences for both individual behavior and the ability of a community to sustain its conventions and values. According to Brandt, guilt feelings and a sense of blameworthiness "increase motivation in a desired direction—that is, improve the corresponding kind of character."[6] Moreover, once a sense of blameworthiness comes to be associated with the more general idea of a particular action, the unpleasant associations provide a "boost" in the "right direction" for similar situations in the future.[7] And finally, if the agent's blameworthiness comes to be known to others, it takes on the more communal function of impressing on all parties the conventions of acceptable behavior.

As Brandt himself makes clear, the utilitarian concept of moral responsibility is distinct from its Kantian counterpart not only because it invokes utilitarian considerations but because it focuses on moral blameworthiness and not on free will. Likewise, while utilitarians such as Brandt may want to take the causal effectiveness of an individual's action into consideration when talking about moral responsibility, they do not include it in their concept of moral responsibility itself. Instead, they focus on both the utilitarian value of moral blameworthiness and the social conventions that support its place in moral discourse.

By equating moral responsibility with various sorts of social and political approbations and then justifying it on utilitarian grounds, utilitarians such as Brandt are able to develop a moral concept that has several potential advantages over its more traditional counterpart. First of all, when we incorporate it into our discourse on moral responsibility, we no longer have to show how individuals can be considered blameworthy simply in virtue of their having freely willed harm to others. Nor do we have to assume either that contra-causal freedom is possible or that moral blameworthiness is independent of our social practice of

6. Brandt, "Utilitarian Theory," 357.
7. Ibid.

blaming. Instead we can concentrate on the seemingly straightforward utilitarian considerations that go into our judgments of blameworthiness.

While the utilitarian concept of moral responsibility is thus more accessible than its metaphysical counterpart, it is not without its own drawbacks. In the first place, once blameworthiness is construed in terms of utility rather than in terms of a causal connection between individuals and external harm, it loses much of the motivational power that utilitarians themselves rely on to justify moral responsibility. Recall Richard Brandt's arguments here. Brandt argues, among other things, that moral responsibility can be justified on utilitarian grounds because the shame associated with it leads individuals to avoid performing harmful actions in the future. Brandt's arguments might work if shame could be disconnected from the causal connections that we establish between individuals and that for which they are being blamed. But shame in modern society requires that individuals be able to think about harm as the consequence of their own actions. Hence, it cannot help but lose much of its motivational power once a purely utilitarian perspective is introduced.[8]

Moreover, the utilitarian concept of moral responsibility, if put into practice, might well subvert our modern notion of just deserts. For the modern notion of just deserts requires that our reaction to an individual follow from something that the individual actually did, and according to the principle of utility, it makes no difference who produces harm, as long as that harm is prevented. While utilitarians may not want to see individuals blamed for harm they did not bring about,[9] they do not appear to be able to sustain their desire as utilitarians in cases where such blame is utile. Nor do they appear to be able to sustain a notion of "unfair blaming" in cases where our rules of fairness are trumped by utilitarian considerations.

Finally, by placing blame in a purely utilitarian context, Brandt and others may unconsciously undermine the value of personal integrity.[10]

8. Interestingly enough, a utilitarian perspective might work better in a less-individualistic context. For an excellent discussion of shame in a collective context, see H. D. Lewis, "Collective Responsibility," *Philosophy* 23 (1948), 3–18.

9. Certainly this is a concern that utilitarians frequently express in light of criticisms made of their argument. See, for example, Smart's contribution to J. J. C. Smart and Bernard Williams, *Utilitarianism: For and Against* (Cambridge, England, 1973), especially 62–73.

10. I am relying on Bernard Williams's definition of "personal integrity" here. According to Williams, personal integrity is bound up with a class of projects to which the individual is particularly committed. In criticizing utilitarianism from the perspective of such integrity, Williams asks: "How can a utilitarian agent come to regard as one satisfac-

For as I argue more fully in chapter 9, blaming as a practice is necessary to the construction by individuals of a relationship between them and the external world, a relationship which partly defines, and in turn helps to maintain, their personal integrity. If blaming were to become associated with utilitarian calculi, which are themselves necessarily in flux, it could not help but rob individuals of a steady sense of who they are and what they are doing in the world.

The issue of personal integrity becomes even more serious when we begin talking about the "responsibilities" of an individual in utilitarian terms. Take, for instance, what Peter Singer has to say in "Famine, Affluence, and Morality."[11] According to Singer, the affluent have a responsibility to relieve suffering around the world whenever they are in the position to do so and as long as they do not sacrifice a greater moral good. Singer backs up his claim here with an argument about general utility and qualifies it with the principle of impartiality. According to Singer, the affluent have a responsibility to relieve the suffering of others no matter who these others are or what their relationship is to the affluent.

While Singer's arguments are attractive in a variety of respects, there are several problems inherent in them which bring into question the viability of his general utilitarian approach to moral responsibility. In the first place, it is not clear at what point the affluent begin to sacrifice a "greater moral good." Do they do so when they slow down their own economy or when they drain their children's college tuition accounts? Singer does not provide us with any way of answering these questions. But if he wants to develop a convincing utilitarian account of moral responsibility, he will have to do so.

Likewise, he will have to take into consideration the requirements of personal integrity as bound up with a class of projects to which the individual is particularly committed. As things now stand, Singer does not appear to be able to assure individuals that their responsibilities will not change with every new utilitarian calculus.[12] Nor does he appear to be

---

tion among others, and a dispensable one, a project or attitude around which he has built his life, just because someone else's projects have so structured the causal scene that is how the utilitarian sum comes about? The point is that he is identified with his actions as flowing from projects and attitudes which in some cases he takes seriously at the deepest level, as what his life is about" ("A Critique of Utilitarianism," in Smart and Williams, *Utilitarianism,* 116).

11. Peter Singer, "Famine, Affluence, and Morality," *Philosophy and Public Affairs* 2 (Spring 1972), 229–43.

12. This is not to suggest that responsibilities should not change as society changes. (For they should.) Rather it is to suggest that if an individual's integrity is to be preserved, the alteration of her responsibilities will have to be accompanied by a conscious decision on her part to take on a new social role.

able to assure them of any control over the definition of their responsibilities. Since such control is what enables individuals to develop their sense of autonomy, Singer may be understood in this context as threatening both personal integrity and that very freedom which supposedly distinguishes an individual's responsibilities from her obligations.[13]

Furthermore, if we were to replace our affective moral ties with the principle of impartiality, which is what Singer and many other utilitarians suggest, we might lose something very valuable. For such ties not only help us to organize our expectations of individuals, but give to individuals a basis on which to develop their sense of communal responsibility. As such, they—and the responsibilities which they entail—may in the end be what enables our community to function without recourse to an authoritarian state. (This, at least, is what I argue in chapter 9.)

Finally, impartiality itself may simply not be possible. As I suggest later on in the chapter, even universal moral principles such as utility develop out of worldly communities and must be understood as part of them. Likewise, when we apply these principles in practice we necessarily interpret them in ways that reflect our own interests and perspectives. Hence, we cannot present them as objective or as scientific in the way that many utilitarians now do.

But we do not have to reject consequentialist considerations altogether. Nor do we have to conclude that extending an individual's realm of responsibility in the way Singer suggests is not desirable or that it always violates an individual's sense of herself as an individual. For as human beings we necessarily invoke consequentialist considerations whenever we act. Moreover, by extending individuals' realm of responsibility in the cases about which Singer is concerned, we may well enhance, rather than violate, their personal integrity, especially if in extending their realm of responsibility, we extend their affective ties as well.[14]

13. For an excellent discussion of the distinction between an individual's responsibilities and her obligations, see Roland Pennock, "The Problem of Responsibility," in *Nomos III: Responsibility,* ed. Carl Friedrich (New York, 1960).

14. And here I both agree and disagree with Williams's approach to personal integrity. On the one hand, I agree with Williams's contention that utilitarianism requires an individual to abdicate the direction of her own life in the interests of general utility—and that in doing so, utilitarianism violates an individual's personal integrity. On the other hand, I do not want to go as far as to say that we violate an individual's personal integrity when we require her to sacrifice some of her own projects for the sake of satisfying the needs of others. Nor would I want to argue that the individual herself violates her own personal integrity when, over time, she comes to think of helping others as one of her personal projects. Indeed, I would agree in this context with John Harris, who contends in "Williams On Negative Responsibility," *Philosophical Quarterly* 24 (1974), that "Williams does not persuade us that our integrity is of such over-riding importance as to justify our

How might we extend an individual's realm of responsibility in the cases about which Singer is concerned? Singer assumes that he can persuade individuals to take on new responsibilities by demonstrating to them an overall gain in happiness around the world. But most individuals are not motivated by utilitarian calculations alone, especially in cases where they are being asked to give up much of their wealth for the sake of a stranger's well-being. Nor are they inclined to think about the well-being of strangers as part of their moral business.

What, then, are we to do? If, like Singer, we want to extend an individual's realm of responsibility in a practical fashion, we will have to explore the institutions and practices that motivate individuals to accept responsibilities in general. Likewise, if we want the individual to feel responsible for those in need of help, we will have to rethink the status of those suffering or, in other words, figure out how we might include them in the individual's realm of concern.

Robert Goodin offers an extremely interesting solution to the problem at hand, in *Protecting the Vulnerable*, by rethinking the moral relations between us and strangers.[15] While Goodin does not reject consequentialist considerations, he argues that if we want to expand an individual's realm of responsibility, we will have to show that the individual has a special duty to relieve the suffering of those we are capable of helping. How might we manage such a demonstration? Goodin himself zeroes in on the fact that strangers are frequently dependent on us in ways that render us responsible for their well-being. Likewise, he makes clear that such dependence is the basis upon which we develop special responsibilities to others.[16]

Goodin's arguments are attractive in a number of respects. In the first place, unlike most of those who write on responsibility, Goodin does not rest his case on abstract moral principles. Instead, he taps into concrete duties that we impose on each other in practice. Likewise, he remains in touch with those social forces that motivate individuals to accept or reject a particular duty to relieve the suffering of others. Hence, he is able to avoid the utopianism of his Kantian and utilitarian counterparts.

Second, he does not allow strangers to remain strangers. Instead, he incorporates them into our community of concern by showing that they are dependent on us. By doing so, he makes clear that our duties to strangers are not all that different from our duties to those in our more

---

not bothering to decide in any particular case whether our project is sufficiently important for us to pursue at the cost of the harm which we might bring about" (269).

15. Robert Goodin, *Protecting the Vulnerable* (Chicago, 1985).

16. Ibid., 11.

immediate circles. Both sorts of duties rest on relationships of vulnerability.

> What is crucial is that others are dependent on us. . . . The same considerations of vulnerability that make our obligations to our families, friends, clients and compatriots especially strong can also give rise to similar responsibilities toward a much larger group of people who stand in none of the special relationships to us.[17]

Not surprisingly, Goodin's definition of vulnerability becomes key to understanding his theory of responsibility. According to Goodin, individuals are vulnerable if they can be wounded or are susceptible to injury. To be vulnerable is a matter of "being under the threat of harm."[18] In cases where harm can be prevented by others, those who are vulnerable become dependent on those who are capable of saving them.

Where does responsibility enter the picture? According to Goodin, the capacity of individuals to "produce consequences that matter to others"[19] renders them responsible for their own actions and choices. Likewise, responsibility itself "amounts to an individual's being accountable for those consequences of his actions and choices" on those who are vulnerable.[20] "If A's interests are vulnerable to B's actions and choices, B has a special responsibility to protect A's interests; the strength of this responsibility depends strictly upon the degree to which B can affect A's interests."[21]

Goodin makes clear in this context that our particular responsibilities are relative in large part to the causal connections between us and those suffering. "Analytically, the notion of consequences seems central to the notions of both vulnerability and responsibility."[22] But he does not want to focus on either our causal responsibility for past actions or the sort of blame that we associate with causal responsibility. For, to do so, he argues, would be to reintroduce the difficulties associated with discerning causal responsibility for past harms and would not in any case be all that helpful in discerning future responsibilities. "Backward notions of causal responsibility are related only imperfectly to the forward looking problem of task responsibility."[23] Hence, Goodin concludes, it is better to focus on the special duties that we have to prevent harm in the future, duties which require us to think about the consequences that our actions might have on others.

I agree wholeheartedly with Goodin that we need to develop a stronger practice of future-oriented responsibility. But I wonder

17. Ibid.
18. Ibid.
19. Ibid., 110.
20. Ibid., 114.
21. Ibid., 118.
22. Ibid., 114.
23. Ibid., 126.

whether we can develop such a practice without also taking seriously the judgments of causal responsibility and blameworthiness that Goodin chooses to view as secondary. Goodin is concerned that if we focus on such judgments we will not prepare ourselves for practical action. If we "assign responsibility for the task of getting people out of a jam to those who were causally responsible for getting them into that jam in the first place," we may never get around to preventing the harm.[24] Goodin's worry is not only that blame focuses our attention away from those suffering, but that causal responsibility for past harm is extremely complicated. "The notion of 'causal responsibility' is not the unambiguous, technical term it seems. The ascription of causal responsibility for an outcome represents the conclusion of a moral argument, not the premise of one."[25]

Goodin is certainly correct to point out that the ascription of causal responsibility for external harm is not only extremely complicated, but relative to other normative considerations. Likewise, he is certainly justified in worrying that a focus on blame may channel our energies away from those suffering and even reinforce our own narcissistic tendencies.[26] But he is premature, I think, in downgrading the importance of our judgments of causal responsibility and blameworthiness. For while these judgments may not correlate exactly with the special duties that Goodin has in mind, they are, I argue below, necessary to the reinforcement of such duties in practice.

Moreover, thinking about future consequences may not be all that different from ascribing past ones. In other words, our future judgments of responsibility may rest on many of the same norms and expectations that ground our judgments of causal responsibility for past harm. Goodin acknowledges that "whom we are answerable *to* necessarily depends upon social conventions," but he claims that "what we are answerable *for* is less variable. It seems always to be for the *consequences* of our actions and choices: the events or states of affairs thereby produced."[27]

While Goodin is correct to point out that what we are responsible *for* are the consequences of our actions, he underestimates the controversial nature of consequences themselves. As we have seen, what we take to be the consequences of our actions rests on a variety of social and

24. Ibid., 125.
25. Ibid., 26.
26. Goodin argues in *Political Theory and Public Policy* (Chicago, 1982) that if responsibility were a mere "problem of getting one's hands dirty," we would be justified in viewing it as a "narcissistic fixation on moral character" (12).
27. *Protecting the Vulnerable*, 113.

political norms that grow out of interests as well as observations. Like-wise, we rarely agree on what the consequences of our actions are in controversial cases or on who is in the best position to prevent harm. Hence, even a focus on future-oriented responsibility will have to ex-plore the nature of our judgments of causal responsibility, judgments which are just as important to our future location of consequences as they are to our social practice of blaming.

Finally, while Goodin goes way beyond most other theorists in devel-oping our special duties out of social and political practice, he may be too sanguine about our willingness to accept, rather than simply ac-knowledge, such duties. He clearly articulates "what lies hidden within our ordinary moral judgments"[28] and "shows that there is nothing so very special about our special responsibilities. . . . They derive from the same sorts of moral considerations as our general duties."[29] More-over, he shows how we are motivated by our role responsibilities to pre-vent the suffering of others. But he may have too much faith in these responsibilities as a motivating force. We may in practice have to invoke external moral incentives—such as those of blame—if we want to ex-tend an individual's realm of responsibility in the way both he and Singer want to do.

Thus we are led back to the judgments of causal responsibility and blameworthiness with which we began. I argue in the next section that both judgments effectively reinforce the special duties that we rely upon when thinking about the consequences of our actions and enable us to expand or contract our realm of responsibility in practice. But I do not, like those who adhere to the modern concept of moral responsibil-ity unreconstructed, view the two judgments as part of a single factual discovery. Instead, I view them as part of our social practice of blaming.

The Practice of Moral Responsibility

As things now stand, we make both judgments all the time as part of our so-called discoveries of moral responsibility. But we do not always do so self-consciously. Indeed, more often than not, we make one of the judgments implicitly on the basis of conventional criteria and treat the other as purely factual. Take, for instance, the controversy now sur-rounding our moral responsibility for apartheid in South Africa. Here we publicly disagree about whether or not American capitalists are causally responsible for the suffering of South African blacks. But we

28. Ibid., 10.
29. Ibid., 11.

do not argue openly about who is blameworthy for their suffering. Instead, we generally assume that if American capitalists are causally responsible for apartheid, then they are also blameworthy for it.

I say that we "generally assume" as much here because there are situations in which we are willing to excuse individuals from moral responsibility, situations in which, for instance, an individual acted out of compulsion or ignorance. In these situations we assume that the individual was not in control over her own actions and hence not morally responsible for them. In the apartheid case, we do not always know the individuals being held morally responsible on a personal basis. Nevertheless, we assume that they were in control over their actions and hence morally responsible for that which their actions caused.

In cases where we do know the individual personally, or where we can take the causal responsibility of her actions for granted, we focus more directly on her state of mind rather than on the causal connections between her and external harm. Take, for example, the case of a woman who shoots her neighbor. Here we can assume that the neighbor's death was a product of the woman's having shot him. Hence, we do not ask whether or not her actions were causally responsible for harm. But we do find it necessary to ask a series of more purely subjective questions: "Was the woman in her right mind? (Were her actions calculated? Or were they the result of an overriding obsession?)" "Did the individual know what she was doing? (Was she sure that her victim was not a burglar?)" "Was it her choice to pull the trigger? Or was she forced to do so by a third party?"

If, in having these questions answered for us, we are convinced that the individual knew what she was doing and that she was not compelled or coerced into shooting her neighbor, we conclude not only that her actions were a product of her own free will, but that she was morally responsible for the death of her neighbor. Moreover, we do so not only because we have evaluated her state of mind at the time of the shooting but because we have made two further assumptions. One is that the individual's actions were causally responsible for her neighbor's death. The other is that she is morally blameworthy for the harm by virtue of having herself caused it.

The conflation of causation and blameworthiness into one causal discovery is even more apparent in the apartheid case. Here we assume that under normal circumstances, capitalist investors are in control over their own actions. Hence, we feel free to focus our attention on whether or not they are causally responsible for the survival of the white South African regime. Not surprisingly, we do so along clearly social and political lines. But we do not take into consideration the possibility that our ascriptions of responsibility are themselves partly social or political. Nor do we stop to wonder what our own role is in blaming these others. Instead, we assume that we have discovered the real causes of harm and that those who disagree with us have not.

What do we mean by the "real" causes of harm? We rarely ask ourselves this question. But presumably we have in mind those particular causes of harm, among others, that we consider worthy of our blame (or in the case of a purely scientific analysis, our experimental attention). Yet instead of making our criteria of relevance explicit, we tend to assume that some causes are "naturally" more relevant than others or that there exists, in John Harris's words, a "World Moral Authority" who can distinguish the real causes of harm from those that are secondary or not relevant to moral responsibility.

The problem is, as I suggested in chapter 5, that there is no World Moral Authority, or at least not one in a secular context. Nor can we talk about a notion of causal responsibility that is purely objective or independent of our normative expectations of those being blamed. Moreover, even our willingness to view a particular case of harm as having been caused by human agents, rather than by, say, nature, has a great deal to do with our own abilities to control the situation and our sense of how powerful or important those being harmed are. Hence, we have to view our talk about "real" causes as itself grounded in more purely practical and political considerations than those considerations generally acknowledged by individuals who accept the modern concept of moral responsibility unreconstructed.

What are these considerations? As we saw in chapter 5, whenever we choose to view one cause among others as *the* cause of harm, we inevitably focus on those forces that we might be able to control in the future so as to prevent the harm in question from occurring again. But we do not do so as neutral bystanders. Instead, we incorporate our interests, perspectives, and priorities into our sense of when and how a particular case of harm might be prevented. Likewise, we incorporate this sense into our judgments of causal responsibility before we go on to ask whether the individual is worthy of our blame.

Causal Responsibility and Practical Control

What interests, perspectives, and priorities do we incorporate into our judgments of causal responsibility? How exactly does such an incorporation work? Both questions are rendered particularly difficult by the fact that in most cases, convention allows us to assume that harm is, or is not, the consequence of a particular individual's action. In these cases we do not consciously deliberate about whether, say, the election of a president is the consequence of her having been voted into office. Nor do we find it necessary to refer back to a general set of rules according to which harm is considered the consequence of something the individual did or failed to do. Instead, we simply assume that it is natural that certain consequences follow from certain actions.

In more controversial cases, though, such as those surrounding drug addiction and apartheid in South Africa, we not only disagree openly with one another about who is causally responsible for harm, but do so along what appear to be social and political lines. Hence, in these cases we might expect ourselves to have come to an understanding of the social and political norms that ground our judgments of causal responsibility. But such an understanding is nowhere to be found, or at least not in a well-developed form.[30]

Nor is much attention paid to the term "causal responsibility" itself in discussions of moral responsibility. While those who invoke the term clearly want to distinguish between it and causation per se, they rarely make explicit the sense in which causal responsibility, like all other sorts of responsibility, entails that individuals be held accountable by an external authority. Indeed, more often than not, those who write about causal responsibility focus almost exclusively on establishing the conditions under which individuals are causally responsible for external harm without acknowledging the importance of either *relationships* of responsibility or the source of those conditions considered to be relevant to their causal judgments.[31] The result is that contrary to their intentions, they end up presenting causal responsibility as a mere relationship between cause and effect.

But causal responsibility is much more than a mere relationship between cause and effect. It is a relationship between an individual and an external state of affairs as prescribed by an adjudicator. In many cases, we are not aware of the adjudicator as prescriber. Nor does it occur to us to think of the adjudication process itself, since we generally view judgments of causal responsibility as purely factual. But we do nevertheless incorporate the adjudicator's prescriptions into our judgments of causal responsibility and, in doing so, shape our discoveries of moral

30. As I tried to show throughout part 2, contemporary moral philosophers have begun to expose many of the social and political norms that ground our judgments of causal responsibility. But they are clearly held back by their need to view causal responsibility and blameworthiness together as a single moral fact about individuals.

31. There are, of course, exceptions here. See, for example, William Blizek's discussion of responsibility and adjudication in "The Concept of Social Responsibility," *Southern Journal of Philosophy* 9 (1977), 7–9.

responsibility accordingly. As we saw in part 2, Harris, Casey, and Thompson all assumed an adjudicator, but did not make its role explicit. Harris invoked a "World Moral Authority" to justify his judgments of moral responsibility. But because he assumed that his World Moral Authority was objective, he did not find it necessary to ask how this authority (or his own interests) may have shaped his causal judgments. Casey also appeared to have had a World Moral Authority in mind, although he did not need to mention it by name as a result of his assumption that there are absolutely good and bad actions, as well as absolutely good and bad interpretations of an individual's social role. Thompson was clearly more willing than the others to deem a group of individuals—the democratic polity—the appropriate adjudicators of responsibility, but even he was hesitant to construe moral agency as part of the adjudication process itself.

What would have happened if these three theorists had acknowledged the role of adjudicator and the rules of adjudication that ground our judgments of causal responsibility and blameworthiness in practice? Among other things, they would have had to ask not only who the adjudicator is in the particular cases with which they are concerned, but what her criteria of judgment are and how these criteria reflect her own purposes and interests. I address these three questions more fully below in my discussion of causal responsibility. Suffice it to point out here that the identity of the adjudicator is relevant not only to the causal connections that we construe between individuals and external harm, but to the criteria of causation that we invoke in doing so. Likewise, while the interests and purposes of the adjudicator become especially important to the designation of particular consequences, they do not rule out the possibility that we can talk about general criteria that all adjudicators invoke in their judgments of causal responsibility.

Presumably some of these criteria have to do with the closeness of the physical connections that exist between an individual and external harm. Hence, we cannot, like postmodernists, dismiss traditional considerations about proximity or the place of a particular action in a causal chain that links the action and the harm in question. Nor can we accept a "nonfactual" or "purely social" account of causal responsibility or view causal responsibility as a simple creation of the arbitrator. For to do so would, among other things, be to ignore the physical world that we shape with our judgments of causal responsibility.

My assumption here is that if we want to understand our judgments of causal responsibility, we will have to take the chain of events that we are presented with seriously. Likewise, we will have to figure out where in that chain of events we now locate the particular action that renders

an individual causally responsible. While such a project does not require the assumption of an ideal scientific analysis, it does require that
we take causation seriously as part of our moral judgments.

What sort of criteria do we now invoke in deciding how far back to go
in any one chain of causal events to locate the cause responsible for
harm? In most cases, we zero in on a variety of physical considerations
concerning how important a particular action was to the harm in question. Likewise, we take into consideration whether or not the harm
would have occurred without the action's having been performed and
how many links in the causal chain exist between it and the action itself.
Hence, we feel free to view ourselves as making purely factual judgments which are also objective.

But such judgments are either purely factual nor objective. Nor
could they be construed as such. For even if we could locate distinct
links in a causal chain, which is itself questionable, we would not be able
to justify on the basis of, say, the nature of causation itself, stopping at
one link rather than another. Instead, we would have to go further into
the realm of practice and make clear both how we were using the term
"responsibility" and for what purposes we were ascribing it.

How might we do both of these things? A good place to begin would
seem to be with the notion of control. For it is in order to control states
of affairs in one way or another that we often set about locating the
causes of harm in the first place. Hence, in trying to understand where
we stop in a casual chain in our efforts to discern causal responsibility,
we might zero in on the sorts of control that we assert in our causal analyses, or in other words, we might ally ourselves with those who talk
about causal responsibility and control together. R. B. Perry, among
others, argues that when we look for the causes of a negative state of
affairs, we tend to focus on those forces that we might be able to control
in the future so as to prevent the harm in question from occurring
again.

We describe as the cause of an event that practical condition by which we hope
to control it. The very meaning of the word "cause" is likely to vary with our
purposes. Those who are concerned to produce something beneficial seek the
"cause" of what they wish to prevent in some new condition. . . . The new condition which is called for cannot be just any condition. It must be one that can be
manipulated or modified.[32]

Perry himself uses the term "cause," rather than "causal responsibility," in his discussion of manipulatibility and control. Hence, we might
want to ask whether or not there is any difference between saying "X

32. R. B. Perry, *General Theory of Value* (Cambridge, Mass., 1954), 418.

caused harm" and "X is causally responsible for it." Two possibilities come to mind here. One is that "X caused harm" is a more purely factual statement than "X is causally responsible for it," or in other words, that the notion of causal responsibility brings with it (via the word "responsibility" itself) an element of discretion not present in statements like "X caused harm" or "X is the cause of harm." The other is that the two sorts of statements are structured similarly (with the same element of discretion), but invoked in different contexts.

The first possibility ceases to be tenable once we acknowledge that even statements like "X caused her neighbor's death by shooting him" are bound up with both an adjudicator and a set of practical concerns. In this particular case, the practical concerns (e.g., how to prevent death) may be handed down un-self-consciously from inquirer to inquirer or may be obscured by elements of genuine curiosity. But they nevertheless ground, on a very general level, even the most purely scientific endeavors and hence cannot be construed as either objective or completely distinct from judgments of causal responsibility that are based partly on our own projects and points of view.

What, then, is the difference between saying that "X caused harm" and "X is causally responsible for it?" Since both sorts of statements are relative to our own (albeit very general) practical concerns, they cannot be distinguished on the basis of their factual vs. social status. Nor can they be distinguished on the basis of their association with claims about blameworthiness, since both partake in our social practice of blaming, as well as in a variety of other practices, including those associated with scientific inquiry. But we might be able to distinguish between them—and articulate what is distinct about our judgments of causal responsibility—by zeroing in on the different contexts in which they are invoked.

Both judgments are invoked in "scientific," as well as "moral" contexts. (I argue later on that the two contexts are not as distinct as many presume.) But while statements like "X caused harm" or "X is the cause of harm" are generally made in cases where there is no question about the directness of harm (such as in the case of the woman who shoots her neighbor), statements of the form "X is causally responsible for harm" are generally made in cases where there is disagreement about the importance of a particular cause or in cases where the causation in question is thought to be less than fully direct.

Take, for example, the case of the My Lai massacre in Vietnam. Here we do not generally ask "Did Pentagon officials cause the deaths at My Lai?" Instead we ask whether or not Pentagon officials were causally responsible for them. By doing so, we make clear both our concern for blame and the existence of disagreement among us concerning the role that Pentagon officials played in the My Lai massacre. Likewise, we make clear that while we may all agree on which particular causal factors are worthy of our attention, we do not agree on either their importance or their connection to blame.

In cases where we are in agreement about the causes relevant to blame, we may refrain from using the language of causal responsibility and talk instead about mere causation. But we do not refrain from blaming those individuals or forces that we view as having caused the harm in question. Nor do we always use the same language to describe our causal judgments. Indeed, we often vary our causal language according to the relationship between us and our audience.

If we know that others agree with us, we may feel free to talk about, say, American capitalists as oppressing blacks in South Africa. If, on the other hand, we sense disagreement, we may talk about American capitalists as causally responsible for apartheid. By using the language of causal responsibility rather than that of causation in general, we not only signal our concern about who is blameworthy for harm, but make clear both that we are aware of the other possible candidates for causal status and that we consider our candidate to be the most relevant (or one of the most relevant) to blame.

What, then, does it mean to say that "x is causally responsible for harm"? It does not mean that x is simply *a* cause of harm, although our assumption of causal effectiveness is part of our judgment of causal responsibility. Instead, it means that from our perspective x is the relevent cause with respect to whatever practice of accountability we have in mind, and that while there are other causal factors to be considered and competing analyses to be countered, x is where we choose to focus our attention in considerations of praise and blame.

Not surprisingly, the nature of our causal judgments will depend partly on the particular sort of accountability that we have in mind and on whether the cause in question is human or "natural." If the cause of, say, famine, that we have in mind is natural, then our causal judgments will probably be based on a notion of physical control or prevention. If, on the other hand, the cause is a human action, say, involving an exploitative economic policy, then our causal judgments will probably be based not only on a notion of physical control or prevention, but also on a notion of behavioral control.

Moreover, if it is human actions rather than, say, physical events about which we are concerned, we will most likely have a stronger notion of blame in mind, one that because of its moral impact, requires us to be more selective in our ascriptions of responsibility. Likewise, if it is social blame that we have in mind rather than, say, the sort of blame that we attach to natural causes, we will probably be more narrow in the range of causes that we locate as responsible for harm (and probably more coherent, since, as I suggest in chapter 9, the blaming of natural causes may not make all that much sense).

But we will not differ drastically from those who purport to be searching for the "scientific" causes of harm, since even the most scientific analyses of harm frequently have to do with practical action and are associated with blame. Take, for example, the various recent studies that set out to locate the causes of famine in the Third World. While these studies may be more rigorous in their factual analysis than more popular treatments of the subject, they nevertheless look for those causes that we can so something about, i.e., counter. (In other words, they generally focus not on sunspot action or solar winds, but on something that we can control, whether it be farming methods, politics, or the misuse of natural resources.) Likewise, while they may not moralize, they do pinpoint those causes that we can hold accountable for harm.

What exactly is the relationship between causation and blameworthiness in this context? While blameworthiness may constitute the backdrop of our judgments of causal responsibility, it is not inherent in causation itself. Instead, it provides us with a reason for asking "Who is causally responsible for harm?" a question that we can answer, I suggest below, on the basis of a variety of normative expectations that are themselves grounded not only in our configuration of social roles, but in the interests, power relations, and structures of community that support such roles in practice.

Interests, Expectations, and Social Roles

Most of us do not make explicit the importance of social and political norms to our judgments of causal responsibility for external harm, even in cases where we disagree about causal responsibility along what appear to be social and political lines. Instead, we defend our respective judgments by insinuating that the causal connections in question are more (or less) important than others assume. But when we look at what we mean by "importance" in this context, we cannot help but notice the relevance of more purely social and political considerations such as those associated with our configuration of social roles and our conception of communal membership.

Take, for instance, the controversy now surrounding hard drug use in this country. Here we are presented with a wide array of judgments about who is causally responsible for the suffering associated with drug addiction in the inner city. The country's drug czar points his finger at both urban gangs who sell the drugs and weekend cocaine users, who according to him, sustain the power of the drug establishment in general. Social workers cite the unwillingness of the federal government to provide adequate drug centers, and members of the Moral Majority target those cultural institutions in this country that have defied the standards of fundamentalist Christian morality. Diehard Calvinists argue that individual drug addicts are responsible for their own addiction, and Marxists blame all of the suffering associated with drug abuse on the capitalist system.

Each of these groups finds it necessary not only to establish a causal connection between particular individuals and the consequences of drug abuse, but to insinuate that these connections are themselves crucial. Indeed, if there is anything that these groups have in common with regard to their judgments of causal responsibility, it is their willingness to cite "crucialness" as the primary, if not sole, criterion of causal responsibility itself. Hence, we should not be surprised to discover drug officials arguing with social workers over whether or not impoverishment is a crucial factor in the drug addiction of inner-city youths. Nor should we be surprised to discover Marxists arguing with their opponents over whether or not capitalism is a crucial factor in impoverishment.

What do these individuals mean by "crucial" here? In most cases they do not make their criteria of crucialness explicit. But they do tend to assume that only those individuals who made a very large difference to the harm's having come about should be considered causally responsible for it. Drug officials point out that without drug pushers, drug addicts would not be able to sustain their addictive habits. Social workers argue that if drug addicts were treated, they would not find it necessary to buy drugs in the first place. Members of the Moral Majority contend that if it were not for the legitimacy of drugs in American culture—a legitimacy which, they argue, stems not only from suburban drug use but from those cultural institutions that supposedly glorify the lifestyles of drug users—drug addicts would not be tempted to take the sort of drugs that they now take. Nancy Reagan seems to think that if ghetto children would "just say no," the problem would be solved, and Marxists continue to locate the source of drug abuse in the poverty created by large-scale capitalism.

Two things become clear here. One is that the willingness of the groups in question to hold particular individuals causally responsible for harm depends in large part on whether or not the individuals made a great difference to the harm's having come about. The other is that whether or not these groups think that the individuals "made a great difference" to the harm's having come about depends not only on their judgments of causal proximity, but on their sense of who was in the best position to prevent the harm itself. Not surprisingly, the latter consideration turns out to be very closely bound up with both practical observations about various preventative measures and more purely social and political considerations about whose place it is to prevent drug abuse.

The practical observations here tend to be the most obvious. Federal officials are explicit in their opinion that the most practical way of solving the drug problem is by taking both gangs and drugs off the street. Social workers, while presumably agreeing on the need for these two measures, argue that if we want to get rid of drug addiction, we will have to build more drug treatment centers to cure addicts of their addiction. Members of the Moral Majority seem to think that if we could infuse American culture with their own fundamentalist Christian values, we would not need as much treatment or enforcement as we now do, and Marxists claim that the only way of solving the problem is by getting at its root: capitalism.

All of the groups in question incorporate practical considerations into their judgments of causal responsibility, but they do not do so in an objective or politically neutral manner. Indeed, as we saw in chapter 5, practical considerations can never be construed as independent of the particular identity and interests of the investigator. John Harris may have been able to show that Western capitalists are causally responsible for much more suffering in the world than we now realize, but that was only because he made a variety of normative, as well as empirical, assumptions about what we can expect capitalists to do for others and how much we can expect them to give up of their own personal projects.

The same sort of assumptions ground many, if not all, of the judgments of causal responsibility in the drug abuse case. Clearly all of these judgments rest on a causal analysis of the relationship between individual drug users and various other individuals and social institutions (which is not to say that they all rest on equally sound causal analyses).[33] Likewise, they all clearly take into consideration who among the various candidates for causal responsibility was best able to prevent the

33. I do not mean to suggest here that we cannot criticize each other's judgments of causal responsibility by arguing about the facts of the situation. Instead I mean to suggest that even in cases where we agree on the facts of the situation, we often construe them differently on the basis of different social and political norms.

harm in question. But their practical considerations are clearly not value-neutral. Indeed, whether or not they consider a particular individual, group, or institution able to prevent drug abuse depends partly, if not largely, on whether or not they feel that it was her or its place to do so.

Since social workers generally expect the federal government to take part in the prevention of social problems such as drug addiction, they feel comfortable in holding the federal government causally responsible for such addiction when the federal government does not provide the poor with adequate drug treatment centers. But not everyone agrees with them. Milton Friedman and his followers, for instance, do not think that the federal government should have a role in the development of a welfare state. Indeed, Friedman and his followers, as advocates of a free market system, argue vehemently against the institutionalization of such a role.[34] Hence, even though they might agree that drug treatment centers would prevent drug addiction in the inner cities, they would presumably not be willing to hold the federal government causally responsible for such addiction.

Not surprisingly, we do not always systematize our sense of an individual's place in preventing harm. But nevertheless we assume a set of roles which may themselves be more institutionalized than we now realize. In the drug addiction case, we differ among ourselves with regard not only to the roles that particular individuals occupy, but with regard to how these roles should be interpreted. While proponents of the welfare state construe the role of government officials as one of providing all of the basic needs of individuals, free marketeers do not. Hence, while proponents of the welfare state are willing to hold federal government officials (among others) causally responsible for the drug problem, those who oppose the welfare state are not willing to do so and may well concentrate on blaming someone else.

The same sort of discrepancy in role interpretation becomes apparent in the case of the violent rock video director cited in chapter 6. Even though the director himself might be willing to acknowledge a causal connection between his violent rock videos and the incipient misogyny of, say, a six-year-old child who watches them, he might not be willing to hold himself causally responsible for such incipient misogyny, especially if he denies that his role is to morally educate or to determine the viewing choices of a six-year-old child who watches television unsupervised. The child's parent, on the other hand, might well hold the rock

34. See, for example, Friedman's arguments in his *Capitalism and Freedom* (Chicago, 1962).

video director causally responsible for her child's incipient misogyny, especially if she considers moral education to be part of the director's social role.

In the two cases cited here, we differ openly about the respective roles of a government official and a video director. Moreover, we do so not only on practical grounds concerning who, say, could have best prevented harm, but on the basis of a variety of other purely social and political phenomena, including both our conception of communal boundaries and our perceptions of political power. In other cases, we are not as aware of the importance of our interpretation of an individual's social role to our judgments of causal responsibility, especially if the role in question is one that we all generally agree on or construe as natural. Take, for example, the case of the drug pusher herself. Here we may all generally agree that no member of our community should be able to get away with selling crack cocaine to small children, but we do not explicitly invoke the role of either community member or American citizen to do so. Instead, we un-self-consciously incorporate both the roles and the duties that we associate with them into our judgments of causal responsibility.

The un-self-conscious way in which we incorporate our interpretation of an individual's social role into our judgments of causal responsibility is even more striking in cases where the social role in question is one that we construe as natural. Take, for example, those cases in which the relevant social role is that of wife. While wifeliness may in fact be a social construct, many members of our community assume that both it and the role responsibilities associated with it are natural. Hence, while they may have no facts to back up their particular interpretations, they feel confident in assuming that the role of wife entails a variety of specific duties ranging from child rearing to complete self-sacrifice.

Since they assume that these duties are themselves natural, they are able not only to incorporate them into their judgments of causal responsibility, but to do so without acknowledging the highly controversial nature of these judgments themselves. Take, for example, the arguments of Midge Decter. Since Decter clearly assumes that women's "natural place" is in the home, she is willing not only to chastise women for leaving the home, but to hold them causally responsible for the malaise experienced by men who have been "abandoned" in American society.[35]

While such judgments are becoming steadily less common in Ameri-

35. See Decter's arguments in her *New Chastity and Other Arguments against Women's Liberation* (New York, 1972).

can society, they nevertheless demonstrate both the importance of our interpretation of an individual's social role to our judgments of causal responsibility and the ways in which we can incorporate such an interpretation into our causal judgments without being aware that we are doing so. As we have just seen, the supposed self-evidence of the interpretation of a particular social role is crucial to our lack of self-consciousness, but it is not sufficient. It is also necessary that our social roles have expectations attached to them that are so deeply ingrained that we are able to invoke them automatically along with our physical perceptions.

In cases where we all generally agree on the interpretation of a social role or construe it as natural, we have developed expectations that are so automatic that we might want to consider them purely conventional criteria of causation. But we would still have to recognize them as having a normative component as well, to the extent that they are expectations that we feel justified in having. Likewise, we would have to recognize the extent to which this component is transported into our judgments of causal responsibility by virtue of expectations which are themselves automatic.

In this sense our expectations of the individual are both predictive and normative. They are predictive in that we fully expect the individual to act in a certain way—and are surprised or taken aback when she does not. They are normative in that *what* we expect the individual to do is based on judgments about what we think the individual *should* do in such circumstances, or in other words, on the sorts of actions that we feel she is required to perform.

Clearly such expectations differ widely from person to person. In the drug abuse case, most of our differences rest on both our cultural attitudes concerning how much individuals can be expected to transcend in their own environment (the extreme formulation here being Calvinist) and our sense of how social welfare assistance is to be distributed among particular individuals, groups and political institutions in society. In other cases, such as those that rest on the social role of wife, our differences have more to do with our sense of how to identify a particular individual and what rights we are willing to ascribe to her.

Where do such expectations come from, and how, if at all, is their source registered in our judgments of causal responsibility? The first question is more difficult to answer than the second in that we cannot understand all of our social expectations as having the same source. But we might be able to talk about them in general as having evolved within a complex web of practical considerations, traditional beliefs, and configurations of social roles. Moreover, while we could never provide a detailed picture of such a web, we could at least underscore the extent to which our expectations of individuals, as well as our traditional beliefs, practical considerations, and configuration of social roles, have their source in and are shaped by relationships of power among members of a community.

I bring up these relationships of power not because they are the only source of our expectations of individuals, but because they are the best hidden and hence the most likely to alter our conception of causal responsibility once they are made explicit. As things now stand, we may be willing to acknowledge that our expectations have something to do with the moral culture in which we are reared. But we are not likely to admit that what we expect from a particular individual, and hence whether or not we are willing to hold her causally responsible for harm, has anything to do with where we stand in our community or with the relationships of power that exist between her and those suffering.

Yet once we examine our actual judgments of causal responsibility, we see that our expectations of individuals are not only supported by a particular distribution of power in society, but have social or political power as a constituent part. Take, for instance, the social expectations associated with the role of wife. Traditionalists are inclined to construe wifehood as the primary role of women and to associate that role with various self-denying characteristics. Feminists, on the other hand, do not construe wifehood as the primary role of women. Nor do they accept the traditionalist's interpretation of that role as purely supportive or other regarding. Instead, they expect women to take control of their own lives and develop themselves intellectually and emotionally.

As members of a pluralistic society, we might want to analyze these differing expectations of women in terms of culture or religious beliefs. But we cannot justifiably ignore the fact that what we expect from women has a great deal to do with how much power they wield in our community. Indeed, as social historians from Lawrence Stone to Gerda Lerner have made clear, the willingness of any one community to expect women either to become mothers or to sacrifice their identities as women can be traced back in part to the social and economic power that particular women wield in the private and public spheres.[36]

Not surprisingly, the amount of power wielded by particular individuals also plays a very important part in the cases about which Harris was concerned. While our expectations of the wealthy are clearly related to the good which they can do in the world, they are also grounded in a set

36. See Lawrence Stone, *The Family, Sex, and Marriage in England, 1500–1800* (New York, 1977); and Gerda Lerner, *The Creation of Patriarchy* (Oxford, 1986).

of power relations between the wealthy and those suffering. In cases where those suffering (and their supporters) are able to wield economic or political power over the wealthy (as, say, in certain unions or the antiapartheid movement), we should not be surprised to see those expectations and the distribution of power on which they are based reinforced when they are incorporated into our judgments of causal responsibility.

In none of these cases is our factual analysis or practical viewpoint pushed aside or rejected. Instead, both are shaped according to social and political beliefs about how much particular individuals can be expected to give up of their own interests to prevent harm, beliefs which are themselves clearly related to how much power particular individuals wield in society. While many of us would agree that if the wealthiest sector of the community were willing to devote a large sum of money to the establishment of drug rehabilitation centers, they could go a long way in curbing drug abuse, very few among us would *expect* the wealthy to give up their luxuries to pay for such centers. Likewise, while many of us might concede that American women could, by leaving the work force, make room for men and, given the sexist structure of society, preserve the traditional family, very few of us would *expect* women to do so.

Such expectations could of course change over time. If, for instance, the impoverished of the world were to muster sufficient power over the wealthy to alter our expectations of the wealthy, we might begin to expect the wealthy to transfer their goods to other sectors of society. Likewise, if men and women with sexist views were to muster a great deal more power over men and women of a more egalitarian bent than they now have, we might begin to expect women to stay in the home (and to blame them when they do not).

Two things become clear from all of these examples. One is that neither our expectations of individuals nor our practical analyses are stable over time. The other is that our desire to prevent harm can be deflated by what we expect (or do not expect) from particular individuals or, in other words, by how much we can (or cannot) expect individuals to give up of their own projects for the sake of the happiness of others. Hence, in viewing our judgments of causal responsibility as grounded partly in our need to control or get a handle on a particular state of affairs, we need to become more fully aware of how such a need for control is itself shaped by our social and political contexts.

Likewise, we need to become more fully aware of the tension between the practical grounds of our causal judgments and those social expectations of individuals that we bring to bear on our judgments (and which may have as much to do with political power as with the desire to prevent harm). In many cases we are not aware of a tension between the two. But our expectations of an individual (vis-à-vis the priority that we give to her projects) may nevertheless take precedence over pragmatic considerations, and we may end up arguing that while harm should be prevented, it need not be prevented by the particular individuals in question, even though they have the physical capacities to prevent the harm.

Take, for example, the cases with which John Harris was concerned. On the one hand, Western capitalists clearly have the physical capacities to prevent starvation in, say, Ethiopia. On the other hand, many of us do not expect them to do so, either because we assume that their money could be better used in other ways or because we assume that they have a right to spend their money at home. Hence, even if we agree that starvation should be prevented and that we could prevent it, we do not place such expectations on ourselves or hold ourselves causally responsible for the starvation.

In other cases, our desire to prevent harm is compatible with what we expect from individuals. Take, for instance, the case of a tire manufacturer who places gutted tires on the market. Here our desire to prevent harm is generally compatible with what we expect from the individual. Indeed, the two are so compatible that we simply assume that the manufacturer is causally responsible for the deaths which result from his having marketed bad tires. Yet once we examine this assumption, we see that it is based not only on a causal connection between the manufacturer and the deaths in question, but on the expectation that manufacturers produce only safe tires.

While such an expectation clearly rests on a set of practical considerations, it also depends on a variety of social and political assumptions that we make about the relationship between the manufacturer and his customers, assumptions that we do not generally make about the relationship between American investors and those starving in the third world. One of these assumptions is that the manufacturer has an obligation to take the safety of his customers into consideration before manufacturing his tires. The other is that his own business interests should not be conceived of as trumping the health interests of his customers.

Since these two assumptions are ones that most of us generally accept, we are not always aware of their social and political nature. Take, though, the related case of a factory owner whose workers become seriously ill because of the high concentration of cotton fibers in the air. The factory owner in this case could have cleaned the air by installing a filter system, but he decided against the installation of such a system on the grounds that his profits would drop. As a result, several of his workers contract brown lung disease. But he is nevertheless not considered causally responsible by all members of our community for his workers' suffering.

While more and more of us are inclined to consider industrial diseases a consequence of manufacturing practices, there are still those who refuse to do so on the grounds that factory owners in general should not be expected to sacrifice profits for the sake of their workers' health. Likewise, while we may want to pretend that these differences are purely subjective, they are clearly political in two important respects. First of all, our expectations of factory workers depend not only on political ideology but on whose interests we are concerned to protect. If we are workers, we will most likely assume that factory owners are obliged to take our interests into consideration. If we are factory owners, we will probably assume that our business interests come before all else in particular circumstances.

Second, what expectations come to be accepted by the rest of the community will probably have a great deal to do with the power of one group or another to make their expectations stick. The fact that our expectations of factory owners have begun to change in recent years as a result of the empowerment of labor unions is significant for two reasons. First of all, it suggests that our expectations of individuals depend partly on how we prioritize their interests vis-à-vis the interests of others. Second, it suggests that our expectations presuppose, or are at least sustained by, a particular distribution of power in society.[37]

In the industrial disease case, many of us did not until recently consider the health of industrial workers to be as important as the manufacturer's own business interests. Hence, those among us who felt this way did not expect the manufacturer to ensure the safety of his workers. Nor did we consider the illnesses of these workers to be a consequence of his manufacturing practices in any but the most extreme cases. The situation changes, though, when the object of our scrutiny becomes the tire manufacturer. Here we as a community have generally considered the safety interests of the manufacturer's customers to be more important than his own business interests when it comes to gutted tires. Hence, we have generally expected him to ensure the

37. For a sense of the changes that have occurred in attitudes toward industrial liability and the conditions under which these changes have taken place, see N. J. Wihely, "Industrial Disease and the Onset of Damage," *Law Quarterly Review* 105 (1989), 19–24; "Hazards in the Workplace: What is the Employer's Duty?" *Trial* 24 (1988), 24–27; and "OSHA's Turnabout," *National Journal* 21 (1989), 298–92.

safety of his customers, and when he has not, we consider him to be causally responsible for the harm which results.[38]

In both cases, the amount of power that those being harmed have over the industrialist matters a great deal to how we frame our expectations. Since consumers generally have more power than factory workers do, their ability to shape the industrialist's role is considerably greater than those who remain within the productive sphere, although this situation may be changing with the success of labor unions in imposing their own expectations of industrialists on the population at large. Likewise, since members of the first world have more power than members of the third world, their ability to make their expectations known is much greater than that of those starving in sub-saharan Africa.

The importance of both interests and power to our expectations of individuals is, not surprisingly, clearest in cases where the imbalance of power is greatest. But even in these cases, we cannot go as far as to view interests and power as the only determining forces behind our expectations of individuals. Nor can we view them as the only determining forces behind our configuration of social roles or our judgments of causal responsibility. For clearly our social roles are determined in part by both cultural traditions and a variety of purely practical considerations having to do with task efficiency. Moreover, there are other considerations—such as the value of community itself—which also play an important role in our configuration of social roles and our judgments of causal responsibility, considerations which at least appear to be distinct from the sorts of interests and power that we have been talking about so far.

Causal Responsibility and the Boundaries of Community

Take, for example, the case of third world starvation. Most Americans would prefer not to see individuals starving in sub-saharan Africa. But not all of them expect capitalists to take the suffering of these individuals into consideration when establishing businesses there. Nor do they think that Americans are obliged to give up their personal projects to help those starving in places outside their own borders. Indeed, they may even argue that they as Americans have a special duty to other

38. For a sense of the conditions under which the public places high expectations on the producers of consumer goods, see Robert N. Mayer, *The Consumer Movement: Guardians of the Marketplace* (New York, 1989); Thomas Stewart, "The Resurrection of Ralph Nader: After Ten Years in the Shadows," *Fortune* 119 (1989), 106–8; J. A. Henderson and T. Eisenberg, "The Quiet Revolution in Products Liability: An Empirical Study of Legal Change," *UCLA Law Review* 37 (1990), 479–553.

Americans, meaning in this context either that they should not take the interests of other people into consideration when making their investments or that they should not let these interests interfere with the well-being of their own community.

While such a sense of community may in this case grow out of pure self-interest, in other cases it appears to have its source in a more genuine valuation of community membership, a valuation which may be necessary to the shared life that individuals lead. Although it might be possible to imagine a universally inclusive group of human beings, such a group does not now exist. Nor is it clear how such a group could pursue its activities outside the communal life made possible by smaller groups. For as Michael Walzer points out:

Even the idea of distributive justice presupposes a bounded world, a community within which distributions take place, a group of people committed to dividing, exchanging and sharing, first of all among themselves. It is possible to imagine such a group extended to include the entire human race, but no such extension has yet been achieved. For the present, we live in smaller distributive communities. Were the extension ever attempted, it would depend upon decisions made within these smaller communities and by their members—who distribute decision-making power to one another and avoid, if they possibly can, sharing it with anyone else.[39]

In any case, two things are clear. One is that even if the boundaries of a particular community are tied up with both individual interests and the assertion of power, the valuation of community per se is independent of them and must be taken into consideration as such. The other is that although we ourselves may not be willing to accept as legitimate the value of retaining communal boundaries, we nevertheless have to face the fact that we often incorporate our sense of these boundaries into both our configuration of social roles and our expectations of particular individuals.

In many cases we agree not only on the boundaries of the particular community in question, but on the importance of taking these boundaries into consideration. Take, for example, the case of a father who spends his paycheck on lottery tickets rather than on food for his children. Here most of us would agree that the family unit is not only important, but requires of the man that he pay special attention to those who belong to it, especially his children. Likewise, most of us would agree that if the man lets his children, as opposed to, say, his neighbors, go hungry, he can be held causally responsible for their ill health and perhaps even be described as abusing them.

39. M. Walzer *Just and Unjust Wars* (New York, 1977).

In other cases we clearly disagree about the boundaries of our community and incorporate such disagreements into our judgments of causal responsibility. While some among us consider South African blacks to be part of our community to the extent that we feel that we should take their interests into consideration before making our investment decisions, others do not. Hence, while some of us are willing to hold those who do business with South Africa causally responsible for the suffering of South African blacks, others are not.

While the unwillingness of these individuals to take South African blacks into consideration before investing may in many instances have its source in a general sense that capitalists should remain free from social and political obligations, we cannot automatically conclude that communal boundaries have no place in their judgments of causal responsibility. For in other cases these same individuals might well expect capitalists to take the situation of "native peoples" into consideration before investing. Take, for instance, the recent debates surrounding free trade between the United States and Canada. While very few American businesspersons were willing to give Canadians' interests as high a priority as their own, most were under the impression not only that they were supposed to be concerned about the consequences of their investments on Canadians, but that their concern was in large part the result of the "special relationship" between the United States and Canada, a relationship which is partly economic, but also partly cultural, historical, and (presumably) racial.

While communal boundaries may play a more obvious role in judgments of causal responsibility that involve those suffering outside of our own country, they are also important to judgments of causal responsibility that involve the suffering of our fellow citizens. The case of industrial diseases provides us with a very good example here. While factory workers may be American citizens, factory owners do not in this country always consider their workers part of that group whose interests they are expected to further beyond the requirements of law. Hence, many of them not only balk at providing heath care benefits to their workers, but resist being held causally responsible for industrial diseases when those diseases occur.

Most factory workers, on the other hand, appear to be of a very different opinion about the causal responsibility of factory owners for industrial diseases. Likewise, while the notion of community that they have in mind might not be one based on affective ties, they do insist through their union representatives that the workplace be considered a place of shared power and that factory owners take the workers' interests into consideration before acting on their own. Hence, while the workers may not demand that they be considered part of the factory owner's family, they do expect him to provide for their well-being in the workplace, and when he does not, they hold him causally responsible for their illnesses.

The above case, as I have noted, pertains primarily to American factory owners and workers. The situation of their Japanese counterparts is significantly different. In Japan, factory owners do consider workers to be part of their family, albeit as subordinate family members. Hence, they expect to provide for the well-being of their workers, and when they cannot, they not only feel shame, but hold themselves causally responsible for the harm that has resulted from their failure.[40]

Since both the apartheid and the industrial disease cases are overtly political, we might want to conclude here that they are exceptional, and that other cases may involve social expectations, but not political ones. Such a response would be correct in one respect—that the social expectations that ground our judgments of causal responsibility are in those cases overtly political. But we could not conclude from the overtly political nature of these considerations that other judgments of causal responsibility are divorced from considerations of interest, power, and communal boundaries.

Take, for instance, the less-controversial case of murder. Here we generally consider individuals to be causally responsible for the deaths of those whom they shoot. But we do so only because we have come to expect individuals not to shoot others. While such an expectation might strike us as simply deriving from morality per se, the situation cannot be so simple, since we allow shooting in wartime and in some places as a form of capital punishment. Likewise, while we may want to assert that enemies and the guilty are simply exceptions to our general rules, we cannot do so without making clear why they as guilty persons should be excluded from our community of respect.[41]

All of these examples taken on their own might lead us to conclude that there is one self-evidently relevant community whose boundaries we incorporate into our judgments of causal responsibility. But this of course cannot be true. For we belong to all sorts of communities at once, and the expectations that we attach to them not only overlap, but clash in significant ways. Likewise, even those of us who belong to roughly the same communities often differ with regard to the impor-

40. See Chalmers Johnson's arguments in *Politics and Productivity: The Real Story of Why Japan Works* (New York, 1989).

41. Anthony Quinton provides us with such a discussion in "On Punishment," *The Philosophy of Punishment*, ed. H. Acton (New York, 1969), 55–64.

tance that we attach to each community. While some may feel stronger loyalties to their ethnic communities, others may feel more attached to their professional or work communities. Hence, we cannot always be expected to come up with exactly the same causal judgments.

Take, for example, two individuals whose company dumps toxic chemicals into a town's water supply. Both individuals belong to at least two of the same communities, the company and the town. But they differ with respect to what they think they should do when they discover that the chemicals are toxic. Individual X is totally loyal to the company, and hence refuses to be a whistle-blower, even though her own children may suffer. Individual Y takes her town membership more seriously than her company duties. Hence, she not only becomes a whistle-blower, but holds the company causally responsible for the harm it has caused.

Not surprisingly, the disparity among our various causal judgments increases when people outside of our community judge us on the basis of their own conception of our social role or community membership. In these cases we may be taken completely by surprise at the amount of harm for which others hold us causally responsible. Take, for example, the case of Pentagon officials during the Vietnam War. While they clearly thought of themselves as distanced from the My Lai massacre, their critics did not and argued that they could be held causally responsible for the suffering of Vietnamese children on the grounds that it was part of their role as military leaders to stop the war in general.

The Vietnamese example is an interesting one in that many of the causal arguments made by critics of the war rested not only on different interpretations of the role of a military leader, but on different interpretations of the roles that military leaders should be occupying. While Pentagon officials clearly conceived of their role in large part as one of winning the war, critics often imposed on them the all-encompassing role of American citizen. Likewise, while Pentagon officials often confined their relevant community to their own ranks, critics often expanded the officials' community to include the whole world (or at least Vietnamese peasants).

The effect that such conflicting interpretations had on both groups' causal judgments was of course stark. Since many Pentagon officials expected themselves only to win the war within legal limits, they could not understand why they were being held causally (and indeed morally) responsible not only for the deaths of the enemy, but for the deaths of their own soldiers. Likewise, since critics of the war expected Pentagon officials to take the suffering of Vietnamese peasants into consideration before formulating their military policy, they held these officials causally responsible for the deaths of peasants in both "normal" and "extraordinary" situations.

The Vietnam example is of course not the only one in which individuals' particular social roles are pitted against the more encompassing roles of United States citizen or citizen of the world. While the latter role is often invoked to change the membership of our local communities, the former is often invoked to jar us out of our more particular social roles. The situation of the entertainment industry vis-à-vis drug use provides us with an example of how our membership in a larger community is used to break down our attachment to these roles, or at least to get us outside of them. Here the argument is that while the role of, say, director, is primarily an artistic one, directors are also citizens and have a responsibility to reconstruct their social role in light of its duties (which in this case apparently means deglorifying drug use).

The tension between our role as citizen and our more particular role becomes especially troublesome when our particular role is closely tied to citizenship itself. Here the case of a foot soldier confronted with the problem of stopping his sergeant at the My Lai massacre is illustrative. On the one hand, the foot soldier may have construed his role as United States citizen in terms of obedience to his military superiors in time of war. On the other hand, the role of United States citizen clearly does not include standing by while others rape and pillage. Hence, he is forced to choose between the two roles, fully realizing that if he tries to stop his commanders through physical force, he may be accused not only of disloyalty to the military but of treason against his country.[42]

During the post–Vietnam War period, the press, as well as Congressional oversight committees and makers of Hollywood movies, have been more than willing to remind such soldiers that they were also American citizens and hence had a responsibility either to step outside of their role as soldier or to reformulate that role in a way perhaps not recognizable by their commander. Moreover, they often hold soldiers causally responsible for the suffering of Vietnamese peasants, which effectively reinforces their own conception of a soldier's social role (and clearly illustrates the dialectical nature of the relationship between our expectations of individuals, on the one hand, and our judgments of causal responsibility, on the other).[43]

While reminding individuals that they are citizens as well as doctors, lawyers, soldiers, mothers, and fathers may be enough to get them to

42. The tensions revealed in such a situation are discussed openly in William Peers, *The My Lai Inquiry* (New York, 1979); and Peter French, ed., *Individual and Collective Responsibility: The Massacre at My Lai* (Cambridge, Mass., 1972).

43. I discuss the dialectical nature of this relationship more fully below.

evaluate their particular roles in most cases, in other cases it may be necessary to remind individuals that they are also members of a larger community of human beings. Take, for example, the dilemma facing the civil rights movement in the 1960s. Here it was clearly not enough to remind Southern racists that they were also United States citizens, since the laws that they were expected to obey as United States citizens were also racist. Hence the tendency of civil rights activists to use the conception of a "universal community of mankind" to argue for the inclusion of African Americans into all facets of a society dominated by the Caucasian race.

In a similar fashion, famine relief supporters now remind us that while we may not know where Ethiopia is on the map, we are nevertheless part of a larger community that includes Ethiopians. Likewise, antinuclear activists point out that while we may want to continue the cold war for military reasons, we cannot do so without annihilating a community that is much larger than that designated by mere national boundaries. Both groups incorporate what we might talk about as a universal community of human beings into their analyses in such a way that they are able to conclude not only that a particular individual can be expected not to harm those in that community, but that when she does, we can hold her causally responsible for the harm itself.

The universal community of human beings invoked in these contexts might strike us as significantly different from the more particular communities that we have been discussing so far in that it is purely moral, as distinct from social or political. But once we take a closer look at this community—and at how it gets incorporated into our judgments of causal responsibility, we see that it too is dependent on the social and political norms of our particular communities. Likewise, we see that the universal community is often used to endow our particular communities with the sort of moral authority that our particular communities themselves lack by virtue of their social and political identities.

Although we may be generally conscious of the moral authority that our notion of a universal community wields in society, we are not always aware of its source in our more worldly practices. Indeed we often assume that we are able to talk about a universal community either because to do so is religiously sanctioned or because human beings all have moral worth qua human beings. But we are clearly shortsighted in making such an assumption. For we could not endow all individuals with the same value unless we had already decided to view all of them together as a group whose members all have something very important in common.

The decision to view all human beings together may even underlie the *principle* of universal community that modern philosophers generally assume. Kantians, including Rawls and his followers, assume a Kingdom of Ends in which all human beings are to be treated with the dignity due to them as rational creatures. Likewise, utilitarians insist that when making moral decisions we must take into consideration the happiness of all human beings (and according to some utilitarians, that we must treat all forms of happiness as equally valuable).

While both groups insist that they derive their universal community from purely moral values, neither actually does. Kant, as we have seen, contended that the universal nature of his moral community could be derived from the value of rationality (or law-abidingness) per se. But Kant was never able to convince us that it is rationality per se—as opposed to our own valuation of rationality—that renders individuals worthy of respect.[44] Hence, it would seem necessary for those who want to invoke the universal community of human beings as a moral value to explain it in other terms.

Here we might want to look to the realm of practice and ask why it is that we value rationality in the first place. If we were to do so, presumably we would discover, among other things, that we value rationality as highly as we now do not only because it enables us to cope with the modern world, but because it enables us to claim superiority over other beings who do not exercise rationality. If we were more politically inclined, we might want to take the route chosen by Rawls and argue that the value that we give all human beings qua human beings is relative to the liberal democratic communities of which we are a part.[45]

If we are utilitarians, we may discover that happiness is one of our central values, not because it is intrinsically worthy, but because those who experience happiness value it very highly. Likewise, we may discover that the way we count up happiness modules is not dictated by the nature of happiness per se, but by the particular modes of exchange characteristic of our worldly communities. Where, though, would the notion of universal community enter the picture? If we were to focus on our evaluation of both rationality and happiness in practice, we might discover that it is because we (or some of us) value all human beings to begin with that we are able to ensure a moral value which, not surprisingly, all humans are (we think) capable of achieving.

---

44. Even if Kant's claim that rationality is not contingent on worldly practice were true, it would not be sufficient in this context. See my discussion of Kant in chapter 4.

45. I refer here to Rawls's contextualization of his own *Theory of Justice*. See, for example, his arguments in "Justice As Fairness, Political Not Metaphysical," *Philosophy and Public Affairs* 15 (1985), 223–51; "Kantian Constructionism in Moral Theory," *Journal of Philosophy* 77 (1980), 215–72; and "Priority of the Right and the Idea of the Good," *Philosophy and Public Affairs* 17 (1988), 251–71.

Such a focus would suggest not only that our moral values are generated within our concrete worldly communities, but that the universal nature of our moral community is the result of our own quasi-egalitarian approach to the value of human beings, an approach that is of course given support by the Judeo-Christian tradition of which it is a part. Pre-Christians in Europe did not take such an approach to the value of human beings.[46] Nor did the Nazis, among other modern groups of individuals. If they had, moreover, they would not have been able to sustain their nonegalitarian principles.

By locating the source of the universal community that we incorporate into our judgments of causal responsibility in social and political practice, we are able to avoid the difficulties associated with both Kantianism and utilitarianism. In other words, we are able to focus on the values of both rationality and happiness without having to show why either is intrinsically worthy or superior to the other. Moreover, in doing so, we are able both to grasp the relationship between our particular and worldly communities and to show how they function together in our judgments of causal responsibility.

The latter demonstration would seem to be especially important in the context of this study. For the community of all human beings that we sometimes invoke in our judgments of causal responsibility is obviously very general (if not purely formal) and does not embrace any obligation more specific than that of being concerned about the well-being of others. Hence, if we want to see how it is incorporated into our practical judgments, we have to focus on the relationship between it and the more particular communities that give it practical meaning.

Not surprisingly, once we focus on the concrete contexts in which we invoke the universal community of human beings, we are confronted once again with the primacy of both our worldly communities and the various practical considerations with which we began, considerations which often deflate our universalistic impulses. Take here the case of those concerned to relieve starvation in the third world. By invoking the universal community of human beings, antihunger activists are able to draw attention to the plight of those suffering and argue that they have a right not to starve.[47] But since others invoke a variety of practical considerations that get in the way of redistributing wealth,

46. While the Stoics may have conceived of their moral community as universal, they did not consider all human beings capable of achieving human dignity. Such dignity was for them to be achieved through higher forms of wisdom.

47. See, for example, the arguments made in Peter Brown and Henry Shue, eds, *Food Policy: U.S. Response to Life and Death Choices* (New York, 1978); and Arthur Simm, *Bread For the World* (New York, 1975).

antihunger activists are not able to guarantee, or even substantiate, the claim that these others must be considered equal members of our particular communities. Hence, even though we may be led to include them in our realm of concern, we do not necessarily reformulate our social roles so as to ensure that their interests are realized concretely.

There are of course cases in which we are led to reformulate both our social roles and our conception of communal boundaries as a result of others' invocation of universal community, but even in these cases the concept of universal community is effective only because it is coupled with practical considerations. The experience of the civil rights movement is a good case in point here. By invoking the "universal community of mankind," civil rights activists were able to shift the way in which many of us structured our particular communities. But they were not able to shift the membership of those communities drastically. Nor were their successes in this context a matter of pure moral suasion. Indeed, if members of the civil rights movement had not been able to muster a certain level of power, they would not have been able to impose their notion of universal community on others or to persuade us to include this community in our judgments of causal responsibility.

Two general points emerge here. One is that while the notion of universal community may endow our particular judgments with moral authority, it is by itself too general to be translated into practice as such. Instead, it must be invoked alongside various other worldly considerations, considerations which range from who is in the best position to prevent harm to how much we can expect individuals to sacrifice of their own projects in order to prevent the suffering of others. Since the expectations associated with such practical norms are socially and politically charged, we should not be surprised to discover that two groups can invoke the same universal community of human beings with very different concrete results.

Take, for example, the controversy now surrounding apartheid in South Africa. While there are obviously exceptions, most people outside of South Africa consider South African blacks to be part of the universal community of human beings. But they do not agree on who should ensure that South African blacks are treated as part of that community. Nor do they agree on what it would mean for individuals to be *treated* as part of such a community (as distinct from existing in it on a formal level of concern). Hence, we cannot help but conclude in this context that while the notion of universal community that antiapartheid activists invoke is important to the energizing of the movement and its supporters, it is necessarily mediated by social and political considerations ranging from the valuation of private property to the role of American businesses in the communal life of foreign countries.

The other point that emerges here is that while the universal community that we posit is part of social and political practice, it is not purely ideological in the way that Marxists often suggest it is. Instead, it exists in a dialectical relationship with the particular communities through which it is necessarily mediated. On the one hand, the only way in which we are able to apply our universal notions of community in practice—or simply care for other human beings in general—is by taking into consideration the structures of our more worldly communities. On the other hand, we cannot conceive of our particular obligations and responsibilities as moral unless we make at least one of the following two assumptions. The first is that these obligations and responsibilities either embody or help us to realize our universal moral values. The second is that the individuals who belong to our worldly communities are also members of our universal moral community and hence are worthy of our concern.

Once we recognize that the morality of those worldly expectations that ground our judgments of causal responsibility depend on our acceptance of a set of universal moral values, we are faced with a discrepancy between our particular and universal communities. But such a discrepancy is not as illogical or as immoral as some have made it out to be. For as I have tried to show, while we may legitimate the normative expectations that we have of particular individuals on the basis of universal values, we structure those expectations on the basis of both practical considerations and our own social and political points of view. Likewise, while we may incorporate a concept of universal community into our judgments of causal responsibility, we necessarily do so along with a host of more particular social and political norms.

Shifting Boundaries

In the previous two sections, I articulated a variety of social and political norms that ground our judgments of causal responsibility for external harm. I also pointed out the extent to which our judgments of causal responsibility rest on both our conceptions of communal membership and the interests and power relations that sustain them. I did not deny the importance of causal chains of events, but suggested how we choose within them a particular act or event to hold causally responsible for the harm in question on the basis of both physical and social considerations.

In this section I want to underscore the extent to which our judgments of causal responsibility can themselves alter at least the latter of these considerations under particular circumstances. The particular circumstances that I have in mind are those in which we not only differ about who is causally responsible for harm, but impose our own judgments of causal responsibility on each other. I try to show below in a number of cases how our own judgments of causal responsibility can alter both our configuration of social roles and our conception of communal boundaries—or in other words, alter the very social and political phenomena on which our judgments of causal responsibility are partly based.

The key here is both difference and conflict among competing judgments of causal responsibility. I argue below that it is because we differ so widely among ourselves about causal responsibility in the cases mentioned above that we are presented with the possibility of change vis-à-vis both our judgments of causal responsibility and the boundaries of our community. Likewise, I suggest that what enables such change to occur is the dynamic nature of our practice of causal responsibility itself, a practice within which we are able to change each other's minds about the boundaries of our community and the sorts of harm which we ourselves can be expected prevent.

Take, for example, the case of apartheid in South Africa. Here, as we have seen, individuals differ not only with regard to the causal connections that exist between those who invest in companies that do business in South Africa and South African apartheid itself, but with regard to both the proper role of American businesspersons in general and the boundaries of our moral community. Those who view the role of American businesspersons as requiring them to think about the consequences of their investments on "foreigners" are generally more willing than those who view the role of American businesspersons as strictly economic to hold particular investors causally responsible for the resiliency of South African apartheid itself. Likewise, those who view South Africa as part of our community of concern are generally more willing than those who do not to view the causal connection in question as fairly close.

What happens when the two groups impose their judgments of causal responsibility on each other in public? Presumably, if one group is able to convince the other that the economic connections in question are more (or less) close than has hitherto been assumed, it can change others' minds about causal responsibility on a more-or-less scientific basis. While such changes are not all that common, they have clearly occurred within the debates about South African apartheid, especially in cases where capitalists have been able to show on specific occasions that their investments have created more jobs for South African blacks or in cases where antiapartheid activists have been able to show that the white South African regime would have less legitimacy in the absence of American businesspersons.

But factual claims have not been the only source of change in our attitudes toward the causal responsibility of American investors for the resiliency of apartheid. Equally important have been our judgments of causal responsibility themselves, judgments which, as part of our social practice of blaming, have enabled us to change each other's minds about causal responsibility by connecting particular individuals with apartheid in such a way that we are then led to blame them. Take, for example, the debates that have surrounded divestiture in many university communities. While particular members of such communities may well have been influenced by purely economic analyses, others have clearly changed their minds as a result of the judgments of causal responsibility—and blameworthiness—that have been made about them and those with whom they identify.

Not surprisingly, whether or not we are willing to accept others' judgments of causal responsibility depends partly on how much we care about their blaming us and how much power they have in our community. If we take their judgments of blameworthiness seriously, we will in many cases be led to reevaluate our own causal responsibility for the suffering of others. Likewise, if we reject their judgments of blameworthiness, we will not change our minds about our causal responsibility for the harm in question. Indeed, we may, if we are powerful or influential enough, be able through our rejection of blame to convince others that we are less responsible than they themselves thought.

In the apartheid case, we see a growing consensus that at least some investors are at least partly responsible for the resilience of the white South African regime. Moreover, we see such a consensus developing not only because of the presentation of scientific evidence, but because the divestiture movement has been fairly successful, at least within universities and state governments, in persuading others to accept its judgments of causal responsibility, judgments which, I have suggested, are particularly powerful to the extent that they are coupled with both blame and at least a minimal amount of political clout.

The same process of change is evident in the industrial disease case. During the years in which unions were particularly strong, e.g., throughout the 1960s, industrialists came to be considered by many, in and out of the courts, to be causally responsible for their workers' ill health. In many cases, the increased willingness of both private citizens and courts of law to hold industrialists causally responsible for diseases such as brown-lung disease resulted in part from the scientific health research sponsored by the federal government (often at the request of unions themselves). It also resulted from the growing power of the unions to impose their own causal judgments on others, a power that is now clearly waning and which may lead in turn to less stringent judgments of causal responsibility in the future.

Two things become clear in this context. One is that in cases where our judgments of causal responsibility conflict, we can change each other's minds about causal responsibility within the practice of causal responsibility itself—both because we assert our judgments within power relations and because we frequently couple them with blame. (I discuss the motivational aspects of blame in chapter 9.) The other is that in changing others' minds about causal responsibility for harm, we may also challenge many of those social and political norms that ground their own judgments of causal responsibility, norms that include, among other things, how closely they feel themselves to be related—morally *and* physically—to those suffering and what their role should be in preventing harm.

In the case of South African apartheid, we may have come not only to change our conception of social responsibilities, but to shift the boundaries of what we consider to be our community of concern. In other words, by accepting new judgments of causal responsibility in these cases (as the result of either social pressure or new scientific evidence), we may have changed the very conception of communal boundaries that grounded our judgments of causal responsibility in the first place. Likewise, we may have ensured that in the future we will take the interests of these others into consideration when we think about the consequences of our actions, especially if in locating a causal connection between ourselves and those suffering, we come to include these others in our community concern.

What this suggests is that the relationship between our judgments of causal responsibility and our conception of communal boundaries is a dialectical one. On the one hand, our judgments of causal responsibility are grounded in, among other things, our conception of communal boundaries. On the other hand, by holding each other causally responsible for more (or less) suffering in the world, we change each other's minds in particular contexts about how close we are to those suffering. Or rather we do so if there already exists a difference of opinion about communal boundaries and one group is able to impose its judgment of causal responsibility on others.

The same sort of dialectical relationship exists between our judgments of causal responsibility and our configuration of social roles. On the one hand, our judgments of causal responsibility are grounded in, among other things, our configuration of social roles and the responsibilities that we associate with them. On the other hand, by holding each other causally responsible for more (or less) suffering in the world, we impose our own sense of an individual's role responsibilities on others and, if they accept our judgments, lead them to expect different sorts of behavior from the individual in the future.

The differences between us with regard to social role responsibilities were evident in the apartheid case, where the role of businesspersons was taken to be contestable. Such differences with regard to our understanding of an individual's social role are also evident in the case of the Hollywood entertainment industry. Here there is a great deal of disagreement about whether or not moral education should be included among the role responsibilities of a Hollywood director. Hence, we see very different judgments of causal responsibility made in cases involving, say, violence. On the one hand, those who include moral education among the role responsibilities of a Hollywood director are willing to hold a particular director responsible for the maladjustment of a six-year old who watches the director's violent films. On the other hand, those who insists that moral education is not part of a Hollywood director's social role are not willing to hold a particular director causally responsible for such maladjustment (although they may be willing to hold responsible the child's parent or the local television station which aired the film).

The interesting thing here is the extent to which many directors have changed their own self-conceptions by virtue of the judgments of causal responsibility that others have imposed on them. While such changes have not occurred all that often with respect to the willingness of directors to temper the display of violence on screen, it has occurred with respect to their willingness to show the horrors of hard drug use (or at the very least, they may think they should not glorify hard drug use). Likewise, with changing conceptions of the role of directors, we see in some instances the development of higher expectations of directors, expectations which will inevitably shape future judgments of causal responsibility.

Of course not all efforts to change expectations are successful. Take, for example, the efforts of drug officials to hold suburban drug users causally responsible for drug problems in the inner city. While drug officials may see a direct-enough connection between the two groups, suburban drug users themselves have generally not. Nor have they felt compelled by the blame lodged against them to change their self-conceptions. The same appears to be the case with regard to third world starvation. While individuals such as John Harris have judged the affluent to be casually responsible for starvation in the third world on the basis of their own conceptions of the role responsibilities of the affluent, as a whole the affluent do not themselves appear to have accepted these judgments or to have changed their social role or their conceptions of communal boundaries.

In both of these cases, unlike the first two mentioned, individuals were not able to expand the role responsibilities of others by holding them causally responsible for external harm, either because the causal connections in question were just too weak or because they themselves were not able to muster enough power or influence over those who disagreed with them. The status quo was thus maintained. In other cases, the status quo changed, but not necessarily in the direction of expanded responsibilities or the extension of communal boundaries. Indeed, in a variety of cases we can see both role responsibilities and communal boundaries shrinking as a result of our unwillingness to hold others causally responsible.

Take, for example, recent developments in labor law. While courts in the 1960s were willing to hold industrialists causally responsible for a considerable number of health problems that occurred in the workplace, they are now less willing to do so. Hence, we may expect the public's conception of industrialists' role responsibilities to change and also their expectations of industrialists in general. Likewise, with such changes, we may expect industrialists to be held causally responsible for much less harm in the future and hence not to feel compelled to take their workers' interests into consideration when thinking about the consequences of their actions.

The case of the industrialist here is particularly interesting in that it points to both the way in which silence on questions of causal responsibility can diminish our sense of a particular individual's role responsibilities and the relationship between our judgments of causal responsibility and power. As we have seen, whether or not we expect an individual to prevent harm (and hence whether or not we come to hold the individual causally responsible for it) depends partly on the distribution of power that exists between her and either those suffering or their representatives. Likewise, when we hold the individual causally responsible for the suffering (or refuse to do so) we reinforce the distribution of power that grounds our judgments.

In the case of industrial disease, we may increase the power of industrialists if we cease to hold them causally responsible for the ill health of their workers. Likewise, we may decrease the power of the workers themselves if we ignore their claims about the industrialists' causal responsibility. The same would seem to hold true in the case of newly employed women and minorities. If we choose not to hold these individuals causally responsible for the underemployment of American males, we may empower them as members of our community. Likewise, we may disempower those who have a stake in keeping women in the home—or, at the very least, challenge their conception of a woman's social role.

Each of these examples suggests not only that our judgments of causal responsibility are partly shaped by the distribution of power in our community, but that these same judgments—especially when coupled with blame—can themselves either challenge or maintain the status quo with regard to the distribution of power in society. In chapter 9, I explore this relationship further in the context of a discussion of blame. Here I have tried simply to sketch the dialectical nature of the practice of causal responsibility, a practice which, I have suggested, not only grows out of, but can in turn help shape, social and political practice.

Likewise, I have tried to underscore the sense in which the application of existing norms and expectations does not need to reproduce the status quo, but can change it in important ways, especially if there is considerable disagreement about the norms and expectations to be applied. In the cases cited above, changes occurred not only in the norms and expectations accepted by the majority of the community, but in both the judgments of causal responsibility that followed from them and our own sense of relatedness to others. While this sense of relatedness is in several respects both social and moral, it is also physical, in that it is grounded in, among other things, the configuration of consequences that we ascribe to each other for harm that we ourselves and others experience.

The relationship between our configuration of consequences and our conception of communal boundaries is, I have suggested, mutually determinant. Moreover, it is a dynamic relationship that enables us not only to bring about an expanded sense of community, but on the basis of such an expanded sense of community to discover "new" consequences. John Dewey had something like this relationship in mind in *The Public and Its Problems* when he talked about establishing a Great Community on the basis of scientific inquiry. But Dewey assumed the sort of scientific progress that would ensure the continual growth of community or, in other words, the unlikelihood of communal shrinkage. Likewise, he viewed the discovery of consequences as an objective enterprise based on the neutral principles of scientific method rather than on the imposition of social and political expectations. Hence, he was able to talk about his search for a Great Community and his discovery—rather than ascription—of new consequences.[48]

Like Dewey, I have focused on the relationship between our configuration of consequences and our conception of communal boundaries in such a way as to be able to talk about social and political change. But unlike Dewey, I have not posited a monolithic community or one bound by scientific principles of inquiry. Instead, I have located a number of overlapping and often conflicting communities whose members do not discover new consequences, but ascribe them according to their own social and political expectations. Likewise, I have characterized such ascriptions not as objective or stagnant, but as part of a dynamic process through which we change each other's minds about both communal membership and the consequences of our actions.

Since the process of inquiry that I have located is bound up not only with social and political expectations, but with the dynamics of power, I have not been able to talk about the progressive extension of community. Indeed, I have suggested that on many occasions our communal boundaries shrink as a result of our reluctance to hold particular individuals causally responsible for harm. Likewise, since power politics is by nature oppositional, I have not been able to treat such inquiry as a collective project, but have instead viewed it in part as a contest over the meanings that we associate with our actions.

But I have not viewed it exclusively as such a contest or suggested that we do not act collectively in locating consequences. Indeed, I have gone so far as to suggest that in ascribing consequences to each other for external harm, we not only alter our configuration of social roles and our conception of communal boundaries, but recreate new "we's" from which to read "our" norms and expectations, "we's" which turn out to be much more dynamic than those invoked by Richard Rorty and his followers and which in any case are capable of both shaping and being shaped by our moral judgments.

The Problem of Omissions

In the preceding sections I tried to pinpoint the various social and political considerations that we incorporate into our judgments of causal responsibility in practice. Below I focus very briefly on two other as-

48. I critically analyze the relationship that Dewey posits between his Great Community and scientific inquiry in "Pragmatic Inquiry and Social Conflict: A Critical Reconstruction of Dewey's Model of Democracy," *Praxis* 9 (1990), 365–80.

pects of our judgments of causal responsibility. The first concerns the causal effectiveness of omissions. The second concerns the conditions under which we feel comfortable in describing individuals as bringing about harm (as distinct from being causally responsible for it).

Contemporary philosophers and political theorists, as we saw in chapters 5, 6, and 7, often make two assumptions about omissions in their discussions of moral responsibility. One is that omissions are special kinds of actions and hence are causally effective. The other is that the conditions under which individuals' omissions are causally responsible for external harm are the same as the conditions under which their actions are causally responsible for such harm. Both assumptions are, I think, incorrect—although I suggest below that there are other ways of describing omissions as rendering individuals morally blameworthy for the suffering of others.

Since neither Harris nor Casey nor Thompson tried to justify the causal effectiveness of omissions, we might want to start with the arguments of someone who did: Jeremy Bentham. According to Bentham, omissions (or "negative actions") count as actions because when an individual omits doing something, she performs an inner act of the will.[49] Likewise, since actions are clearly causally effective, so too are omissions.

Several problems confront the contemporary philosopher or political theorist who wants to rely on Bentham's analysis. One is that inner acts of the will may simply not exist. Gilbert Ryle, among others, argues that it is highly unlikely that processes or operations occur that correspond to Bentham's notion of a volition.[50] But even if Ryle is wrong and processes or operations which correspond to Bentham's notion of a volition do indeed occur, Bentham's approach to omissions would not be very useful in the particular cases about which we are concerned. For in these cases the individual is not necessarily conscious of herself as not doing something to help others. Indeed, in cases such as those surrounding apartheid or starvation in sub-Saharan Africa, she may simply think of herself as minding her own business.

Since individuals do not always think of themselves as not doing a particular action that we expect from them, it is important that we distinguish between different ways in which we now use the term "omission." First of all, we sometimes use the term to refer to an individual consciously not performing a particular action. Second, we sometimes

49. Jeremy Bentham, *An Introduction to the Principles of Morals and Legislation* (Oxford, 1967), 72.
50. Gilbert Ryle, *The Concept of Mind* (New York, 1949), 62–82.

use it to refer to an individual's consciously not performing a morally good action or an action that we think she should be performing.[51] Third, we sometimes use it simply to note that an individual is not performing an action which for some reason we expect her to perform.

It is omissions of the first and second sort that Bentham argues are causally effective, but it is omissions of the third sort that we have been concerned about in the study. While we might be able to consider these omissions causally effective in some other way, we cannot consider them causally effective by virtue of an individual's inner act of the will. For in these cases, the individual is not necessarily aware that she is not doing what we expect from her. Indeed, if she can be said to be willing anything, it is an action that we might not ourselves recognize as the one pertinent to our own judgments of causal responsibility.

Moreover, even if we could assume that omissions of the third sort are causally effective, it would be difficult to consider them causally responsible for harm. For such omissions do not necessarily represent the nonperformance of an action which we normally require an individual to perform. Those who appear able to consider such omissions causally responsible for harm often assume not only that the individual consciously refrained from performing a particular action, but that the nonperformance of the action is morally unacceptable in the sense relevant to causal responsibility.

The problem is that such assumptions are rarely justified with respect to omissions of the third sort. Take, for instance, Harris's attempt to extend an individual's realm of causal responsibility. Harris assumes that not contributing money to Oxfam is morally wrong. But he cannot assume that the affluent—or even the poor—consider such an omission morally wrong. Nor can he assume that the affluent, in pursuing their own interests, even think about themselves as failing to help others. Likewise, even if Thompson thinks that not reporting the harmful activities of one's superior is morally wrong, he cannot assume that either the official or the public at large consider such an official morally wrong, although he might in this case be able to assume that the official was conscious of himself as not reporting to his superior.

If the absence of willing in these cases is so problematic, not simply get rid of Bentham's definition of omissions as volitional? Why not, like Harris, assume that there is no moral difference between actions and omissions, and treat omissions as part of a social practice in which we impose expectations on individuals which they do not themselves nec-

51. Such omissions are often phrased in terms of an individual's failing to do x (where x is a morally good act) rather than merely in terms of an individual's not doing x.

essarily share? Two responses come to mind here. One is that to do so would be perfectly acceptable if actions and omissions were really parallel with respect to causal responsibility. The other is that actions and omissions might not really be parallel with respect to causal responsibility—especially if, as Elazer Weinryb and others argue, omissions are not themselves causally effective (because, according to Weinryb, they are not bodily movements, or at least not movements that occur in specifiable timezones).[52]

If Weinryb's analysis is correct, it is not clear how we can construe a direct causal connection between an individual's failure to act and the harm, even though we might be able to show that the harm would not have occurred if the individual had acted. One way of getting around this dilemma might be simply to construe our practice of causal responsibility as not requiring the existence of such a connection. Here we might want to argue that it is sufficient to show that if an individual had acted, the harm would not have occurred. But to do so would presumably have serious practical drawbacks.

Among other things, if we were to incorporate the reformulation sketched above into social and political practice by, say, underscoring the irrelevance of a visualizable chain of events, we might very well threaten the ability of individuals to act in the world. For individuals act in light of the consequences which they hope to bring about around them. If they were no longer able to visualize a causal connection between their actions and external states of affairs, or if they were no longer able to predict the particular states of affairs that others would construe as the consequences of their actions, they would no longer be able to frame their actions clearly. Nor would they be able to figure out ahead of time what they would later be described as doing.

Such a scenerio is not likely to reproduce itself in practice. But it does suggest in extreme form the importance of visualizing consequences both to the framing of our actions and to the development of a strong sense of self. As we saw above, when we extend or restrict the realm of actions for which we can be held causally responsible, we alter both our sense of relatedness to the world and our conception of communal boundaries. If we were not able to visualize such a realm, we would not only lose sight of the world, but lose control of ourselves.

In suggesting here that we not hold, say, the affluent, causally responsible for the suffering of those in the third world on the basis of their omissions, I do not mean to suggest that we stop trying to hold

52. Elazer Weinryb, "Omissions and Responsibility," *Philosophical Quarterly* 30 (1980), 1–18.

them causally responsible for such harm in general. (For clearly we still might want to do so by zeroing in on various harmful actions, such as those associated with exploitative policies.) Nor do I mean to suggest that we construe omissions as morally neutral. Indeed, there would seem to be a variety of circumstances in which we might want to consider omissions morally bad, either because they constituted failures of duty or because they amounted to not causing happiness. (Clearly the latter of these two considerations would be relevant only to utilitarians or to those willing to make consequentialist arguments.)

While moral philosophers such as John Harris have been willing to make such consequentialist arguments, they have generally resisted the positing of a duty of beneficence. According to Harris:

We do not need to postulate a duty of beneficence to explain how the neglect of the passerby might well have resulted in the man's death, rather we need to understand the causal connection between the neglect and death to see why anyone might be required to tend him.[53]

Harris's reasoning here clearly follows from both his concern to move beyond the status quo (there being no such duty of beneficence now generally accepted in society) and his formulation of moral responsibility itself, which focuses exclusively on moral causation rather than on communal accountability.

Not surprisingly, legal scholars, who generally focus on communal accountability rather than moral causation, have been more willing than moral philosophers to construe omissions as the violation of duty in their discussions of external harm. Likewise, since they tend to construe the duties in question—those surrounding Good Samaritanism—as socially construed, they have felt more comfortable than moral philosophers in arguing about whether or not individuals *should* be held accountable for failing to aid strangers in cases of grave danger. (Recall that Harris and Casey tried to move away from such normative discussions so as not to jeopardize the causal objectivity of their moral judgments.)

Although the arguments of legal scholars in this context are clearly motivated by a need to come to terms with the general absence of Good Samaritanism in the legal, as distinct from moral, context, they provide us with two very important insights into our moral categories. One is that the moral status of omissions depends not just on their causal

53. John Harris, "The Marxist Conception of Violence," *Philosophy and Public Affairs* 3 (1973–74), 200.

effectiveness, but on a variety of cultural values that we bring to bear on them. The other is that these cultural values are not incidental, but are deeply embedded in our social and political worldviews.

Take, for instance, the controversy surrounding the well-known judgment of Judge John P. Flaherty that in American law there is no duty to rescue a stranger or to save a stranger's life, a judgment that Flaherty supplanted with the further claim that to institutionalize such a duty would be to "violate the right and the sanctity of the individual." In their rebuttal of Flaherty's claims, Flaherty's critics did not question his knowledge of legal precedent. Instead, they challenged his atomistic conception of individualism and insisted that there does in fact exist a duty to help strangers in grave situations and that such a duty should be embodied in criminal, if not civil, law.

Interestingly enough, legal scholars, in asserting such a duty, have chosen not to couch it in the language of causation or to argue for it on purely philosophical grounds. Instead, they have presented it as part of existing "moral consensus" or have argued that it is necessary to the development of a "humane society." A. M. Honoré claims, in "Laws, Morals and Rescue," that the "law should reflect, reinforce and specify, at least that segment of the shared morality which consists in moral duties to others."[54] J. H. Scheid bolsters this claim by pointing out that individuals do not live in a vacuum, but are interdependent in ways that make Good Samaritan laws crucial. Scheid argues in his "Affirmative Duty to Act in Emergency Situations" that the "law should formally acknowledge the contemporary moral consensus that we are all necessarily inter-dependent and that each member of society has a duty to aid his brother in danger."[55]

Both commentators argue for holding individuals accountable in the case of omissions, not by demonstrating causal effectiveness or by fleshing out abstract moral principles, but by pointing out that contemporary society is not as highly individualistic as people like Judge Flaherty believe it to be. Interestingly enough, it was a much-earlier legal scholar, F. H. Bohlen, who pointed out the specifically political context in which arguments about omissions often take place. Bohlen argued in 1908 that there had been a "complete *volte face* of social thought from individualism to a collectivism verging on socialism"

---

54. H. M. Honoré, "Laws, Morals, and Rescue," in J. M. Radcliffe, ed., *The Good Samaritan and the Law* (Garden City, N.J., 1966), 238.

55. J. H. Scheid, "Affirmative Duty to Aid in Emergency Situations," *John Marshall Journal of Practice and Procedure* 3 (1969), 49.

which had "enormously extended the scope of those duties which a citizen owes his fellows."[56]

Although Bohlen's historical claims may be exaggerated, his analysis is relevant to our discussion of omissions in two important respects. First of all, it suggests that whether or not we are willing to hold individuals accountable for their failures to act depends partly on our normative beliefs about the way in which individuals are related in our community. The second is that if we wanted to argue openly about whether or not we *should* hold each other accountable for our failures to act, we would have to address, among other things, what kind of community we wanted to live in and how much we think people's interests should be meshed with those of others.

As things now stand, we do not view people's lives as so caught up with other people's lives that we hold them responsible for harm which they fail to prevent unless they are somehow connected to those suffering by virtue of a special relationship. But in a more purely communistic or altruistic society, we might easily impose such a duty on all individuals and blame them when they fail to exercise it fully.[57] How, if at all, might we figure out whether or not such a society is worth pursuing? Presumably we would want to ask whether by holding individuals responsible for harm which they failed to prevent we would enhance— or violate—the personal integrity of individuals, as well as the integrity of the collectivity as a whole.

I have not attempted such an analysis myself in this section. Instead, I have made three more general points. First of all, actions and omissions are not parallel with respect to causal responsibility, and even if we wanted to view them as such, we might well threaten an individual's ability to think about herself as acting in the world. Second, we do not need to rely on the causal effectiveness of omissions in many of the cases about which we have been concerned. Instead, we can shift our attention to more positive actions or else view the omissions as a violation of duty. Third, in our efforts to do the latter, we cannot hope to locate natural duties of Good Samaritanism, but we can hope to shape such duties on the basis of our communal norms.

56. F. H. Bohlen, "The Moral Duty to Aid Others on the Basis of Tort Liability," *University of Pennsylvania Law Review* 56 (1908), 219.

57. Gilbert Harman makes a similar argument in "Relativistic Ethics: Morality as Politics," *Midwest Studies in Philosophy* 3 (1978), where he writes: "In a more egalitarian and altruistic society, which did not recognize a moral distinction between harming and not helping, you would be considered responsible if you failed to give the person help when it was needed" (115).

When Do We Become Killers?

In the bulk of this chapter I have concentrated on our judgments of causal responsibility rather than on our incorporation of these judgments into our description of an individual as bringing about harm. But clearly such an incorporation is important to our practice of moral responsibility, since we generally hold individuals morally responsible for harm by holding them morally responsible for actions of the form "x brought about harm." Moreover, as I suggest more fully in chapter 9, whether we choose to blame an individual harshly or mildly depends in large part on whether we describe the individual as, say, contributing to the person's death.

Harris, Casey, and Thompson all assumed that they could move back and forth between descriptions of an individual as causally responsible for harm and descriptions of her as freely willing harm or as doing violence or as killing others. Thompson was concerned to show that top officials can frequently be described as freely willing harm which was the product of many hands. Harris was concerned to view the affluent as doing violence to those whom they do not save. Casey was concerned to show that abortionists are indeed killers.

All three theorists found it necessary to include harm in their descriptions of an individual's action in order to hold the individual herself morally responsible for the harm. Moreover, they did so as a result of their particular understanding of moral responsibility, an understanding which required, among other things, that individuals be in control over that for which they were being held morally responsible. (While external states of affairs are dependent on a variety of occurrences, actions, according to the Kantian view, are something over which individuals themselves have total control.)

Neither Harris nor Casey nor Thompson were, as it turns out, able to hold individuals morally responsible for harm in the cases about which they were concerned. Moreover, each of them ran into the same two problems in trying to do so. First of all, in their efforts to show why particular individuals could be described as bringing about harm or as doing violence or as killing others, they found it necessary to show that the individuals' actions were causally responsible for the harm on the basis of social and political norms over which the individuals could not themselves possibly have control. Second, in their efforts to move from their descriptions of individuals as causally responsible for harm to descriptions of them as bringing about harm more directly, they found it necessary to collapse two significantly different descriptions of the in-

dividuals. While both descriptions might be adhered to by different individuals or by the same individual over time, they could not be held at
the same time by the same individual without internal contradiction.

Why not? As we saw in our examination of Harris's arguments, there
are different levels of responsibility ascribed in the two descriptions.
Moreover, in order to move from one to the other, we must have discovered new causal connections or changed our minds about how important one particular causal factor was to the occurrence of the harm, a
change that itself might result from either new information or an altered sense of what might be expected from a particular individual.
Hence, if we want to view the two descriptions together, we will have to
do so within the context of a discussion of such changes themselves or
of the discovery of new facts.

Both sorts of discussion require that we come to terms with what philosophers of action refer to as the "accordion effect," i.e., the tendency
of action descriptions to elide into other action descriptions of greater
or lesser scope. Moreover, they require that we come to terms with the
accordion effect not only as philosophers, but as social and political theorists, since what is at stake here is not just the nature of actions per se
but the processes through which our action descriptions change over
time. (Presumably these processes have something to do with our social
and political expectations.)

Why bother with the accordion effect? While to analyze it might not
teach us anything new about moral responsibility, it might teach us how
we come to describe individuals as bringing about harm or as killing
others (rather than as being causally responsible for their deaths). Likewise, analyzing the accordion effect might help us to understand our
social practice of blaming, since how we choose to blame an individual
frequently comes down to whether or not we include harm in our description of his actions or treat it as a consequence of his actions.

Absolutists such as Casey—along with a host of others, including,
most notably, Elizabeth Anscombe—deny the truth of the accordion
effect and assert instead that there is only one morally correct description of an individual's action in controversial cases (although they never
make clear why the controversial nature of the case could be at all relevant).

The position represented by such a claim is both conservative and
absolutist.[58] Eric D'Arcy, for example, argues on absolute (and im-

58. Carolyn Morillo underscores the conservative nature of the position in "Doing,
Refraining, and the Strenuousness of Morality," *American Philosophical Quarterly* 14
(1977), 29–37.

plicitly Catholic) terms that "certain kinds of acts are of such significance that the terms which denote them may not, special contexts apart, be elided into terms which a.) denote their consequences and b.) conceal, or fail to reveal, the nature of the act itself."[59] Anscombe emphasizes the absolute nature of action descriptions by showing the same sort of moral absolutism that Casey displayed in rejecting certain action descriptions as "out of the question." According to Anscombe:

> If someone really thinks, in advance, that it is open to question whether an action such as the procuring of the judicial execution of the innocent should be quite excluded from consideration [and here she is alluding to, among other things, abortion]—I do not want to argue with him; he shows a corrupt mind.[60]

The problem with such a claim is that it is difficult to argue with, since, like the religious beliefs with which it is often associated, it is based on faith rather than on a set of propositions or deductive statements. Moreover, even if the position were not based on rocky metaphysical assumptions, it is clearly not the way in which most people now construct action descriptions. Indeed it may only be because Anscombe and other absolutists incorporate their conservative beliefs into their description of an individual's action that they are able to talk about actions as good and bad in the way they do.[61]

I begin, then, with the assumption that there is never only one description of an individual's action and that terms which denote the action may often be elided into terms which denote a consequence of that action. In this sense, "doing x (with the consequence y)" may in some cases be redescribed as "bringing about y." Likewise, "bringing about y" may in some cases be described as "doing x (with the consequence y)."

Take, for instance, the case of an industrialist who dumps chemicals into a town's water supply. While some of us may describe the industrialist as dumping chemicals (with the consequence that several people

59. Eric D'Arcy, *Human Acts* (Oxford, 1963).

60. Anscombe, "Modern Moral Philosophy," 12.

61. J. L. Mackie's argument for why we cannot treat action descriptions as absolute remains one of the strongest of its kind. Mackie argues, in "Responsibility and Language," *Australasian Journal of Philosophy* 33 (1955), that "determining whether a person is responsible for something, whether it is a part of his 'action' in a moral sense, is not a thing that can be done in advance of a moral judgment. We cannot first decide what each person did and then proceed to pose a series of moral judgments; for to decide what each person 'did' in the sense of 'was responsible for' presupposes a system of moral judgments" (145).

die), others may describe the industrialist as killing his neighbors. Under what conditions could we describe the industrialist as killing his neighbors?[62] In the first place, if we already consider the deaths in question to be a consequence of the individual's actions, we presumably recognize a casual connection between the dumping of chemicals and the townspeople's deaths. But we cannot describe the industrialist as killing townspeople until we have come to think of the connection as direct or immediate.

How do we measure immediacy in this context? On the one hand, it is partly a factor of the distance in a causal chain between an individual and external harm. According to Jonathan Bennet, for example, "immediacy consists in the brevity or absence of a time-lag, spatial nearness, simplicity of causal connection, and paucity of intervening physical objects."[63] But physical proximity of this sort is not itself enough to make us consider a causal connection direct. Also necessary is a judgment on our part about *how* proximate a cause must be in order for us to label it as direct or immediate.

If we were taking a purely internalist approach to actions, such a judgment would rest in part on the intentions of the individual. But we are taking an external approach to actions, that is, we are concerned with how individuals describe one another in situations where they do not always know what others intend. Hence, we have to rely on whether or not we consider an individual's action a standard means of bringing about harm.

Consider the case of a man who shoots his neighbor. Most of us consider shooting a gun to be a standard means of killing others. (Indeed, most of us would probably consider killing to be the primary function of shooting a gun.) Moreover, the distance in a causal chain between shooting a gun and another's death is relatively short. Hence, in most cases we consider the causal connection between a man who shoots a gun and his neighbor's death as immediate, even if the man did not intend to shoot his gun.

Consider, on the other hand, the case of the industrialist who dumps chemical waste into public water supplies. Here we can locate a fairly

62. In setting down the conditions under which individuals come to be described as bringing about harm, I am not taking a stand on the nature of actions per se. In other words, I am not trying to *explain* human actions in the way that philosophers of action are concerned to do. Nor am I suggesting that actions are themselves social events, controlled solely by the form of life exemplified in an individual's community. (Indeed it seems to me that even the most strictly social theories of action must take some form of mentalism into consideration.) All that I am suggesting here are the conditions under which we come to *describe* an individual as bringing about harm.

63. Jonathan Bennett, "Whatever the Consequences," *Analysis* 26 (October 1965), 92.

tight causal connection between the dumping of the chemicals and the deaths of local residents. But we do not consider dumping chemicals to be a standard means of killing people. If we did, we would probably consider the causal connection between an industrialist and those poisoned to be much more direct than we now do. Indeed, we might even describe the industrialist as killing others—in which case we would probably cease to consider the deaths in question a mere consequence of the individual's actions.

At this point it becomes necessary to point out that while most members of our community would not describe the industrialist in the above case as killing others, there are those who would. Indeed, many Marxists already describe industrialists in general as killing the poor. Presumably they are able to do so because of their assumption that capitalism is a standard means of destruction. How, if at all, could they convince others to accept their assumption? Among other things, they would have to show not only that the distance in a causal chain between a capitalist and suffering in the world is relatively short, but that capitalism as a system does not have any overriding positive function in society.

Since most Americans assume that capitalism as a system does have an overriding positive function in society, they have been reluctant to accept the Marxist characterization of capitalism as a standard means of bringing about harm. But they have not been unwilling to change their minds about particular capitalist practices. Indeed, we see such changes occurring now not only in the growing tendency of courts to describe a negligent factory owner as killing his workers, but in the growing willingness of the population at large to accept these descriptions.[64]

While such changes do not mean that capitalism has come to be considered a standard means of killing individuals, it does mean that activities such as the conscious exposure of workers to dangerous chemicals is no longer considered an acceptable part of capitalism. Likewise, while it does not mean that we as a community are willing to describe all factory owners as murderers, it does mean that we—or at least the courts and those journalists who cover them—are more will-

64. See, for example, the range of opinions presented in "Getting Away With Murder: Federal OSHA Preemption of State Criminal Prosecution For Accidents," *Harvard Law Review* 101 (1987), 535–54; G. L. Mangum, "Murder in the Workplace: Criminal Prosecution vs. Regulatory Enforcement, *Labor Law Journal* 39 (1988), 230–31; and "Pursuit of the Corporate Criminal: Employer Criminal Liability For Work-Related Deaths as a Method of Improving Workplace Safety and Health," *Boston College Law Review* 29 (1988), 451–80.

ing than we used to be to describe industrialists who endanger the
health of their workers as killing their workers when their employment
practices lead to their workers' deaths.

While describing individuals as bringing about the suffering of
others—or killing them—is clearly intended to signify moral disapproval, it is not in itself sufficient to ascribe blameworthiness to them.
(I discussed the reasons for this extensively in part 2.) It is also necessary that we be able to assume that it was the individual herself, and not
simply her circumstances, that led her to act badly. In chapter 9 I focus
on what such an assumption actually entails by exploring our social
practice of blaming. In this chapter, I have taken the first step in helping us to understand our judgments of blameworthiness by exploring
the extent to which our so-called discoveries of causal responsibility rest
on social and political norms which are themselves frequently obscured
by our modern concept of moral responsibility.

9

Private Blame and Public Accountability

Moral Responsibility, Causation, and Blameworthiness

In this chapter, I want both to articulate the criteria that we invoke for blaming individuals in practice and to suggest what role our modern concept of moral responsibility plays in our social practice of blaming. To do the latter might appear contradictory, since, as we have seen, the modern concept of moral responsibility views moral blameworthiness as independent of all worldly considerations. But, I suggest below, the modern concept of moral responsibility does nevertheless play an important—if paradoxical—role in our social practice of blaming to the extent that it enables us to merge our judgments of causal responsibility and blameworthiness together into one ostensibly factual discovery.

I discussed our judgments of causal responsibility extensively in chapter 8. In this chapter, I want to focus on our social practice of blaming and show how we attach blame to our causal judgments. But first let me reiterate why it is that we need to begin with these two judgments rather than with the modern concept of moral responsibility itself.

In the cases about which we are concerned, we often view individuals as blameworthy for harm in virtue of their having themselves caused it. In other words, we do not take into consideration the possibility that the blameworthiness of these individuals might have something to do with our own role as blamers. Instead, we assume that causation and blameworthiness are both purely factual and can be realized together.

But such an assumption is deeply flawed. First of all, the causal responsibility of an individual for external harm requires both a mediator and a set of social and political norms, neither of which an individual herself can possibly control. Second, it is not clear how individuals can be conceived of as blameworthy or praiseworthy in virtue of the causal effectiveness of their wills. Nor is it clear how their wills can be conceived of as inherently good or bad.

If individuals cannot be conceived of as blameworthy in virtue of their having themselves caused harm, what are we to do? I have suggested that we should not abandon our judgments of causal responsibility and blameworthiness but should instead reconstruct them as part of social and political practice. I tried to do the latter with regard to our judgments of causal responsibility in chapter 8. I now want to concentrate on our judgments of blameworthiness and the social practice of blaming of which they are a part.

There are generally two conditions under which we now blame individuals in practice. The first is that an individual have acted badly—a condition that can be met either by describing the individual as bringing about harm or by showing that the harm is a consequence of her actions. The second condition is that the individual was able to do otherwise than she actually did, an ability that we often try to discern by asking whether or not the individual was in the position to provide us with an acceptable volitional excuse.

The two volitional excuses that we invoke most often in discussions of moral responsibility are ignorance and compulsion. Both excuses were discussed extensively by Aristotle. Each is now construed by philosophers and political theorists in significantly different ways. While utilitarians construe volitional excuses as part of our social practice of blaming,[1] more traditional scholars view such excuses (or rather their absence) as registering both free will and moral responsibility. According to John Hospers:

> If an action arises through compulsion, the agent is not *responsible* for it. We say that a person is *responsible* for performing a wrong act unless he has an acceptable *excuse* for performing it. . . . The underlying idea in the concept of moral responsibility is simply this: a person is morally responsible for an action if he *couldn't help it.*[2]

I suggest below that volitional excuses must be understood as part of our social practice of blaming. But before I do so, I want to show why the absence of such an excuse cannot possibly register moral responsibility as traditionally understood. Hospers and others who invoke volitional excuses as a way of discovering moral responsibility rarely discuss the structure of those excuses in any depth. Nor do they explore the nature of moral responsibility itself. Instead, they simply assume that the absence of a volitional excuse registers not only that an individ-

---

1. See, for example, Richard Brandt, "A Utilitarian Theory of Excuses," *Philosophical Review* 78 (1969), 337–61; and David Lyons, "On Sanctioning Excuses," *Journal of Philosophy* 66 (1969), 649–60.

2. John Hospers, "Blame and Excuses," *Human Conduct* (New York, 1961), 469–70.

ual could have done otherwise than she actually did, but that the individual herself is morally responsible.

If we wanted to render such an assumption comprehensible, we would have to show not only that the ability of an individual to do otherwise registered in the absence of a volitional excuse is equivalent to contra-causal freedom, but that contra-causal freedom is itself something in virtue of which individuals can be considered morally blameworthy. Neither demonstration is possible. But even if both were, we could not possibly conclude from the absence of a volitional excuse that an individual "could have done otherwise" in the sense relevant to moral responsibility as traditionally understood. For excuses are not factual accounts of an individual's state of mind, but rather pleas that we make to one another as part of social and political practice.

Hospers might want to respond here that while excuses are not themselves facts, they represent facts such as "X could have done otherwise" or "X acted out of ignorance." Likewise, he might want to characterize excuses as symbols or shorthand references to more purely physical capacities—a characterization that is not uncommon in the philosophical literature. But he could do not so, presumably, without ignoring two absolutely crucial things about both volitional excuses themselves and the relationship between them and blameworthiness. One is that what enables us to conclude from the absence of a volitional excuse that a particular individual is blameworthy is not just the existence of such an excuse, but a judgment on our part concerning whether or not to view the excuse as valid. The other is that the criteria of validity that we invoke in this context are not designed to show, say, that a particular instance of compulsion is a *real* instance of compulsion, but that it is the sort of compulsion that we think excuses individuals from blame.

Here we cannot help but acknowledge that everyone is compelled to some extent and that no one is completely free from ignorance. The question becomes where to draw the line between pleas of compulsion and ignorance that lead us to excuse individuals from blame and those which do not. Since we cannot rely on any absolute definitions of compulsion and ignorance in this context, we might want to ask how we draw the line in practice. But two facts would seem to get in the way. One is that we do not always agree about when individuals are able to do otherwise in the sense relevant to blameworthiness. The other is that we rarely make our criteria of validity explicit.

While both facts challenge our ability to understand moral blameworthiness as part of social and political practice, neither makes that task impossible. Indeed, by exploring the differences that exist among us with regard to the conditions under which excuses such as ignorance and coercion are valid, we might be able not only to understand the differences that exist among us with regard to blame, but to reconstruct blameworthiness itself as part of our social practice of blaming. This, at least, is the assumption that grounds my analysis in the following section.

Volitional Excuses and the Question of Fairness

On what grounds do we distinguish between pleas of ignorance and coercion which excuse individuals from blame and those which do not? The most obvious criterion in the case of compulsion is simply one of degree. Here we ask not whether the individual is compelled, but how compelled she is by external forces or her own mental demons. If the individual is forced to act by virtue of the fact that another is in control of her bodily movements, then we are likely to assume that she is not blameworthy on the grounds that she was unable to do otherwise. Likewise, if she is so compelled by her own mental demons that she does not know who she is or what she is doing, we are likely to excuse her from blame on the grounds that her will was not free.

In both cases it is the degree of control that we consider an individual to have over her self that leads us to consider her excuses to be valid or invalid. If the individual is not able to control her own bodily movements, we do not consider her actions to be her own. Indeed, we may even consider her bodily movements to be an extension of her tormentor's actions (as in the case of an individual who is physically forced to harm another). Likewise, if the individual is not in control over her own mind to the extent that she does not know who she is or what she is doing, we assume that she does not have sufficient control over herself, or that it was not really she who was acting.

But we do not judge the validity of pleas of compulsion *solely* on the basis of the degree of control an individual was able to exert over herself. Clearly there are cases in which we refuse to accept an individual's plea of compulsion even though we recognize that she had very little control over herself at the time she acted. Take, for example, the much publicized case of the Detroit woman who sold her young daughter for sex and then claimed that she could not have done otherwise than she did because she was addicted to crack cocaine.[3] While the woman was clearly debilitated by her addiction, she was not excused by the area residents who made clear that for them addiction is never a valid excuse for child abuse.

3. *Detroit Free Press*, 15 March–3 April 1989.

Why not? What is it about drug addiction that renders many of us less willing to accept pleas of compulsion than we would, say, if the woman had been insane? In both cases the candidate for blame does not appear to be in control of herself. But in the case of drug addiction, we assume that the individual was once in the position to control herself, and that she was able at that time not to take addictive drugs. Hence, while we may be willing to lessen our blame of her if we feel that she chose to take such drugs as an escape from great poverty or despair, we nevertheless persist in our belief that the individual's plea of compulsion is not strong enough to excuse her from blame.[4]

Two things enable us to maintain such a belief. The first is our tendency to identify individuals not according to their present behavior alone, but according to their behavior over time. While we do not always agree on how far back in an individual's history we can go before we have to conclude that she was a "different person," we do generally agree that we can talk about, say, an individual who is now drunk as the same individual who ten minutes ago chose to drink a pint of scotch. Likewise, we feel comfortable in assuming that, while the individual is now out of control, she (the same person) was able not to get drunk at one time, even if she is now an alcoholic.

The second thing that enables us to reject the individual's plea of compulsion in this context is our own more purely normative sense that the individual could have been expected to take control of her life or, in other words, not to indulge herself in the way that she did. While such a sense rests partly on scientific beliefs about the mental capacities of individuals to control their own psychological processes (we are clearly not now willing to blame the insane), it also rests on a variety of cultural beliefs about where to draw the line on self-indulgence.

While we ourselves do not generally blame the insane for their actions, seventeenth-century Puritans did so on the grounds that if such individuals "really tried," they could overcome their compulsive behav-

4. For a very interesting discussion of how far we can go in taking an individual's background into consideration in judging her blameworthy, see Michael Philips "Rationality, Responsibility, and Blame," *Canadian Journal of Philosophy* 17 (1987), 141–54. In his efforts to develop criteria of acceptable excuse giving, Philips underscores the dangers of dwelling on poverty as an excuse: "Do persons from disadvantaged backgrounds deserve as much blame for their immoral or criminal acts as persons who have had all the advantages? . . . Taken in its most obvious direction, this line of argument has dangerous deterministic implications. The price of diminished blame is diminished responsibility. We absolve the disadvantaged by portraying them as persons with a diminished capacity for free action. In the extreme case, we view them as victims of circumstances, utterly unable to act other than they do. Thus is born the demeaning parentalism of the worst sort" (141).

ior.[5] Likewise, while many of us are not now willing to accept excuses such as those associated with extreme stress, others are willing not only to accept them, but to incorporate them into our legal system. How can we explain the differences between us? While psychological theories may keep some of us apart, two other differences appear to be more relevant. One concerns how much of an individual's environment we can expect her to resist. The other concerns the levels of self-control that we expect the individual to attain.

Not surprisingly, the more we expect individuals to transcend their environment, the less likely we are to accept their excuses of mental impairment in cases where the mental impairment is something that they could have disciplined themselves to resist. Likewise, the more willing we are to indulge individuals in behaviors that may lead them to lose self-control, the less likely we are to resist them when they tell us that they were out of control or unable to act otherwise than they did. In the case of stress, for example, we may all agree that an individual was out of control because of the pressures of professional life. But only those among us who are willing to say that she could not have been expected to arrange her life so that stress did not occur are willing to accept her pleas of compulsion as valid.

How much control can individuals be expected to exert over their external circumstances? If individuals are greatly impoverished, we may not expect them to turn around their own situations in the way that we might expect, say, a professional to get out of the rat race. But we cannot treat such an expectation as if it were something grounded solely in the facts of the situation either. For clearly there are cases in which individuals agree with one another about the factual constraints of poverty, but disagree about the acceptability of poverty as an excuse for, say, lack of initiative.

Take, for example, the debates now surrounding the responsibility of African Americans for the lack of economic initiative in the black community. Both black activists such as Benjamin Hooks and black conservatives such as Thomas Sowell agree (or contend that they agree) on the pressures that confront those living in the ghetto. But they disagree on how far African Americans can go in using such pressures to evade responsibility for their own impoverishment. While Hooks clearly wants to place the blame on the system that takes initiative away from blacks,[6] Sowell refuses to accept the sorts of excuses that Hooks offers

5. For an excellent discussion of this phenomenon, see H. W. Schneider, *The Puritan Mind* (Ann Arbor, 1958).
6. See Hooks's arguments in *Go Tell It!* (New York, 1979).

for the black community and places the blame squarely on the shoulders of African Americans themselves.[7]

What distinguishes the two analyses? On the one hand, it is hard to believe that Hooks and Sowell really agree on the facts of the situation (i.e., on the pressures that confront African Americans who now live in poverty). On the other hand, even if such agreement really does exist, the two men clearly disagree about how much individuals can be expected to transcend their own environments. While Sowell takes a more individualistic or puritanical view, Hooks rejects that view as cruel and replaces it with a view which he describes as based on compassion (and which Sowell rejects as self-indulgent). The two men incorporate distinct norms of acceptable behavior into their analyses of the constraints that face African Americans in the ghetto and come up with very different opinions about blameworthiness.

Excuses based on ignorance appear to be even more steeped in social and political norms than those based on coercion. Take, for example, the case of sexual ignorance. Here most of us agree that ignorance about the effects of unsafe sex can be potentially disastrous. But we disagree about when individuals can use such ignorance as an excuse from blame when they have inadvertently spread the AIDS virus. While some judges have been willing to accept ignorance as a valid excuse in this context, others have not only rejected it, but have made clear that sexually active adults can be expected to educate themselves about the dangers of AIDS and other communicable diseases.[8]

The same sort of expectations come to the fore in cases involving drug use during pregnancy. Here the issue is whether or not pregnant women who have given birth to deformed or addicted babies can be blamed for the state in which these babies find themselves. While some judges have been willing to excuse women in this position from blame on the grounds of ignorance, others have rejected such excuses on the

7. Sowell develops this position in *Compassion versus Guilt and Other Essays* (New York, 1987), and *A Conflict of Vision* (New York, 1987).

8. For a range of opinions on the blameworthiness of individuals who pass on the AIDS virus, see C. A. McLaughlin, "AIDS: Current State of the Law—An Overview," *Journal of Law and Health* 3 (1988–89), 77–115; "The Real Fatal Attraction: Civil and Criminal Liability for the Sexual Transmission of AIDS," *Drake Law Review* 37 (1987–88), 657–97; "Tort Liability for Sexual Transmission of Disease: A Legal Attempt to Cure 'Bad' Behavior," *Willamette Law Review* (Fall 1989), 807–27; "Liability For the Transmission of AIDS and Herpes," *1987 Annual Survey of American Law*, 523–47; "To Have and to Hold: Tort Liability for the Interpersonal Transmission of AIDS," *New England Law Review* 23 (1988–89), 887–917.

grounds that pregnant women can be expected to know that drug use during pregnancy is potentially harmful to the fetus.[9]

Many of the cases referred to as examples of valid or invalid pleas of ignorance involve those who are underprivileged or poor. But there are certainly plenty of cases in which those pleading ignorance are well educated or wealthy. Take, for example, the case of industrial polluters. It is not at all uncommon for industrialists who dump chemicals into public waterways to claim that they were unaware of the consequences of their actions. Nor is it at all uncommon for their critics to claim that they should have looked into these consequences before formulating their policies.

While both groups agree on the industrialists' ignorance, they disagree on how much work the industrialists could have been expected to do to educate themselves about the environment. Those who are sympathetic to the industrialists may argue that industrialists cannot be expected to hire environmentalists to guide them in their policies (because to do so would undermine their ability to make profits and contribute to the capitalist system). Environmentally concerned citizens, on the other hand, may argue that industrialists have an obligation to hire environmentalists no matter what their financial losses may turn out to be.

How are we to decide which party is correct? There does not seem to be any absolute answer to this question. Nevertheless, we persist both in asserting our own expectations of particular individuals, and in couching these expectations in the language of fairness. While we do so in a variety of situations, we do so most vehemently in cases where we do not think that the individuals in question are blameworthy. "It would not be fair to expect poor women to know about the birth defects associated with drug use." "It would not be fair to expect capitalists to trace every connection associated with their investments."

What do pleas of ignorance, or for that matter, coercion, have to do with fairness? Two things come to mind here. First of all, there may be a sense of distributive justice inherent in our claims about how much individuals can be expected to put out for others or the community in

9. The range of opinions on a woman's responsibility for prenatal harm is vast. See, for example, "Setting the Standard: A Mother's Duty during the Prenatal Period," *University of Illinois Law Review* 189 (1989), 493–516; "Maternal Tort Liability for Prenatal Injuries," *Suffolk University Law Review* 22 (1988), 747–77; and "Developing Maternal Liability Standards For Prenatal Injury," *Saint John's Law Review* 61 (1987), 592–614. For a very interesting view of where else responsibility for fetal harm might lie, see "Fetal Alcohol Syndrome: Liability for Failure to Warn—Should Liquor Manufacturers Pick Up the Tab?" *Journal of Family Law* 28 (1989–90), 71–85.

general.[10] If, for instance, we think that an individual's obligation not to pollute the environment is very extensive, then we will probably consider it fair to blame the individual for polluting the public waterways even if she was ignorant of the consequences of her actions. Likewise, if we think that individuals have an obligation to the community not to abuse drugs, we will probably consider it fair to blame a drug addict for abusing others even if she is poor and addicted to crack cocaine.

Although the sense of fairness at work here may not be ideal or even principled, it does embrace those standards of reciprocity that structure our community as a community. Take, for example, the excuses that we make to each other in our capacity as friends, excuses such as, "I was too tired to take your feelings into consideration," or "I was in love; I couldn't help myself." While we may have strong feelings about when such excuses are acceptable, we do not argue about when they register free will. Instead, we pass judgments on them by asking ourselves whether or not the individual who has made them has in doing so undermined the reciprocal relationship that characterizes our friendship.

The same sort of reciprocal relationships may be at the back of our minds when we reject strangers' pleas of ignorance or compulsion in cases where they have harmed the community. Although we may not in these cases feel that intimate bonds of friendship have been violated, we will probably feel that those who have harmed the community have not lived up to their side of the civic bargain—a civic bargain which specifies at the very least that individuals should not abuse themselves to the extent of rendering themselves useless to the rest of the community or in need of communal assistance. (Not surprisingly, pleas of ignorance and compulsion are least welcomed in cases where the individual who has indulged herself then expects others to pick up the tab.)

A sense of reciprocity may also be in the back of our minds in cases where we accept others' pleas of ignorance or compulsion on the grounds that no reciprocal relationship can yet possibly exist. Take, for example, the case of a ghetto mother who pleads extreme stress to excuse herself from blame in a situation where she has done violence to the property of another. Here we may realize that the woman has not lived up to one of the basic responsibilities of all citizens. But we nevertheless feel that it is fair to excuse her from blame on the grounds that she has not been afforded the basic material conditions necessary to the exercise of her civic personality.

10. Elizabeth Beardsley chooses to talk about blameworthiness as a matter of "just deserts," in "A Plea For Deserts," *American Philosophical Quarterly* 6 (1969), 33–42.

Second, the fact that we use the term "fairness" at all suggests that we construe the expectations that ground our judgments of blameworthiness as rules of behavior rather than as purely subjective reactions to particular individuals. While these expectations or rules of behavior may not, as we sometimes assume, be endowed with a higher moral authority, they are clearly part of a system of conventions that govern the relationships between us as members of a blaming community. Hence, we often refer to their infraction as a matter of unfairness.

While contemporary philosophers and political theorists often talk about volitional excuses as registering moral responsibility or even free will, they do not fail to notice the role that fairness plays in our practice of excuse giving. Hospers discusses moral responsibility in a chapter entitled "Fairness and Excuse-Giving," and Hospers is not alone. Indeed, quite a few of those philosophers and political theorists who talk about volitional excuses and moral responsibility/blameworthiness together refer at some point to the unfairness or injustice of excusing (or not excusing) individuals under certain circumstances.

While most of these writers incorporate notions of *fairness* and *unfairness* into their discussions of volitional excuses, some go as far as to talk about *justice* and *injustice*. In *Just and Unjust Wars,* Michael Walzer makes explicit the relationship between volitional excuses and justice which most of these writers seem to be assuming. According to Walzer, a

theory of justice should be able to point us to the men and women from whom we can rightly demand an accounting, and should shape and control the judgments we make of the excuses they offer.[11]

Any theory of justice that could determine for us what sorts of behavior to expect from individuals would seem necessarily to depend on social and political norms, if not actual policy, and indeed Walzer himself contends that the best way of distributing moral responsibility would be through the democratic process.[12] Walzer would seem to be in agreement with Dennis Thompson here. Recall that Thompson argued that his volitional excuses depended on a democratic theory as well as on "a variety of political considerations, such as an assessment of the outcome in question and the nature of the individual's role."[13]

Since Walzer and Thompson are discussing moral responsibility in the context of wars and government bureaucracy, respectively, they stress the political aspects of excuse giving much more than other philosophers do and indeed much more than they themselves would if

11. Michael Walzer, *Just and Unjust Wars* (New York, 1977), 287.
12. Ibid., 299.
13. Thompson, "Moral Responsibility of Public Officials," 906.

they were discussing, say, the moral responsibility of an individual for her own character. Likewise, since they both assume that moral responsibility is registered in the absence of a volitional excuse, they cannot help but confuse the conditions of justice that ground our ascriptions of causal responsibility with those that ground our judgments of free will. But they are nevertheless correct to point out that justice—or a sense of "fair deserts"—often guides us in deciding how much bad behavior individuals can justifiably get away with before being blamed.

What implications follow from an analysis of blameworthiness that takes fairness and justice into account? First of all, blameworthiness turns out to be part of a relationship between individuals who blame and are blamed rather than a moral fact about individuals themselves. Second, it turns out to be relative to the rules and conventions that govern the relations in question rather than to be absolute or inherent in an individual's own will.

Do We Really Need to Talk about Free Will?

Since blameworthiness turns out to be conventional rather than metaphysical, we might be tempted simply to leave the notion of free will behind altogether when discussing moral blameworthiness. But to do so would be premature, since there may be a notion of free will other than contra-causal freedom that remains crucial to our social practice of blaming. What might such a notion of free will look like, given that it would have to be registered in the absence of a volitional excuse?

A prime candidate here would seem to be the freedom of an individual from external constraint. Richard Hunter points out in his discussion of the relationship between freedom, volitional excuses, and blame that the very purpose of excuses such as ignorance and compulsion is often to show that an individual was constrained by forces external to himself.[14] Hence, we might want to talk about the notion of free will registered in the absence of a volitional excuse as the freedom from particular sorts of constraint.

But to do so would not capture our more positive sense that actions performed by individuals are up to them in some important sense that reflects their moral agency. Since volitional excuses are themselves part of our social practice of blaming, we might want to view the notion of free will that their absence signifies as shaped by our criteria of blameworthiness. Likewise, we might want to construe an individual's "ability

14. Richard Hunter, "Acting Freely and Being Held Morally Responsible," *Dialogue* 12 (1973), 233–45.

to do otherwise" as drawing its meaning from considerations we appeal to in deciding whether or not to blame a particular individual. Certainly to do so would seem to be in line with the volitional excuses that we invoke.

Take, for example, the plea of insanity. Most of us view insanity as a valid excuse because we consider it inappropriate to blame an individual whose will is not free. But we did not always accept insanity as a valid excuse. Nor did we always think of insane individuals as unfree. (Seventeenth-century Puritans were convinced that insane individuals freely willed their own actions.) What made us change our minds? Discoveries in psychology and biology certainly played an important part. But such discoveries were not sufficient, and for some were not even necessary. What was necessary was the loosening up of our own sense of how much self-control and restraint individuals could be expected to exert, or conversely, how much self-indulgence they might be allowed to get away with before being held accountable by their peers.

Since such a sense is clearly relative to our own cultural standards, we cannot use it to talk about the ability of an individual to do otherwise in any absolute sense. But we might be able to use it to understand how we circumscribe such an ability according to our own expectations of individuals, expectations which are often coupled with claims about fairness and justice. Take, for instance, the case of an individual whose plea of compulsion and drunkenness is not accepted as valid. By rejecting the individual's plea, we make known not only that she could have performed the required action but that what kept her from doing so was a force (in this sense drunkenness) that she could have been expected not to bring upon herself.

Since we would not have developed expectations such as these unless we had found it necessary to distinguish between blameworthy and nonblameworthy actions in general, we might want to view these expectations as part of our social practice of blaming itself. Likewise, since we rely on these expectations to shape our understanding of an individual's ability to do otherwise in this context, we might want to view that ability as relative to our criteria of social accountability. But if we did so, we might not be able to retain the concept of free will itself. For free will as traditionally construed entails the absence of determinism—or self-determination.

If we wanted to retain the concept of free will in this context, we might take a cue from soft determinists and talk about free will as the absence of those sorts of determinism that keep an individual from performing a particular action that she wants to perform. But to do so would probably not take us very far, since such freedom from determinism (soft as it is) does not tell us anything about the individual's will itself. Instead, it tells us something about the individual's abilities: that she could have performed a particular action if she had wanted to.

While such abilities are clearly important to our social practice of blaming, they do not refer to what we generally talk about as moral agency. Nor do they enable us to understand how we can conceive of an individual's actions as her own. Hence, we cannot rely upon them to explain the sense of moral agency that grounds our judgments of blameworthiness in practice. But we do not have to give up on that sense of moral agency either. For as I have suggested throughout this section, we might be able to reconstruct such a sense of moral agency by focusing on the way in which we circumscribe an individual's ability to do otherwise in the context of our social practice of blaming.

Take, for example, the professional who pleads extreme stress when caught embezzling bank funds. If we accept her excuse and do not blame her, we reinforce our sense that her decision-making processes were not her own when she embezzled the funds, but rather those of her mental demons. If, on the other hand, we do *not* accept her excuse and blame her, we reinforce our sense that her decision-making process is her own and that she, rather than her mental demons, has willed her actions.

In this case the decision-making process is localized. In other cases, the decision-making process, along with the notion of moral agency itself, are spread across several decisions. Take, for example, the case of the drug addict who sold her daughter for sex in order to buy drugs. If we are willing to accept her plea of addiction and excuse her from blame, we reinforce our sense that the woman is not the moral agent of her actions in general. If, on the other hand, we are not willing to accept her plea of addiction and blame her, we reinforce our sense that her decisions over time, i.e., her decision-making process itself, is a reflection of her own moral agency.

Not surprisingly, the notion of moral agency that emerges here is not as strong as that of contra-causal freedom. But it does refer to the individual's own decision-making processes over time rather than, say, simply to her physical abilities. Likewise, while it concedes a great deal more determinism than more traditional concepts of moral agency do, it does not go as far as to dissolve the self in the way that postmodernist accounts of the individual do.[15] Instead, it tries to capture the sense in which we shape, if we do not create, a self for individuals out of their own choices, abilities, and decisions to act in the context of our social practice of blaming.

15. See, for example, Jean-François Lyotard, *The Postmodern Condition* (Minneapolis, 1984); and *Just Gaming* (Minneapolis, 1985).

How important is it that we be able to couch such a notion of moral agency in the language of free will? On the one hand, it is crucial that we be able to retain a sense of individuals as having control over their own actions, since otherwise it would make no sense to blame them. On the other hand, such control does not have to be absolute—especially if we are willing to concede that individuals are not blameworthy *in virtue of* the causal connection between them and that for which they are being held morally responsible. Indeed if we were willing to view individuals as blameworthy in virtue of a decision on our part that they are worthy of our blame, we might be able to capture the extent to which an individual's choices, abilities, and decisions to act are shaped by our social practice of blaming into a notion of free will.[16]

Social Blame and the Regulation of Communal Standards

What exactly is our social practice of blaming? And how does it help shape our notions of blameworthiness and free will? Both questions require that we shift our attention away from the notion of blameworthiness and free will per se to the reactive attitudes that comprise our social practice of blaming itself. Since most philosophers and political theorists view blameworthiness and free will as ideal constructs to which our judgments of moral responsibility should aspire, they do not take our social practice of blaming seriously. Nor do they take into consideration the possibility that our criteria of blameworthiness have anything to do with the nature of blaming as a social practice.[17]

My assumption here is that if we were to start with our social practice of blaming, we might be able to articulate a notion of free will that both refers to an individual's own initiative (or "willing") and takes into consideration that the freedom of such an initiative is circumscribed by our own sense of when individuals' wills reflect their own choices and when their wills reflect external forces which they cannot be expected to control. Likewise, we might be able to grasp the extent to which our own concerns in holding individuals accountable for their actions help to shape both the form and the content of what we talk about as free will. Just what these concerns are is the focus of my attention in this section.

What do we do when we blame each other for acting badly? While

16. This is not to say that the notion of free will per se makes sense only as part of our social practice of blaming. Rather the notion of free will that we invoke in our discussions of blameworthiness makes sense only as part of this practice. "Free will" may mean something very different in other contexts, say, in the context of explanation or deliberation.

17. The major exception here is Peter Strawson. In *Free Will and Resentment* (London, 1974) Strawson views free will as shaped in part by reactive attitudes such as resentment.

the social practice of blaming is not uniform across contexts, it does generally comprise a set of negative attitudes that we take toward others for bringing about harm. Such negative attitudes are not merely a matter of our being dissatisfied with others' actions or omissions. Indeed, when we blame individuals, we express dissatisfaction with them as persons. By doing so we make clear that these individuals have not lived up to either our expectations of them as particular individuals or to our standards of acceptable behavior.

Since we ourselves play an important role in blaming others, blame cannot be understood solely in terms of those being blamed, which is how most philosophers and political theorists now appear to understand it. Instead, it must be understood in terms of a relationship between those being blamed and those doing the blaming, as well as in terms of its function in social and political practice. While the relationship between blamer and blamed is not difficult to discern, the function of blame is elusive—and unless we are willing to commit the functionalist fallacy of jumping from a practice's consequences to its purposes, it is best to remain tentative.

The relationship between those being blamed and those doing the blaming is both grounded in convention and generally reciprocal. On the one hand, both parties must belong to the same community and must share roughly the same criteria of acceptable behavior if blame is to be effective. On the other hand, neither party has to occupy the role of blamer or blamed through time, as in the case of legal punishment. Indeed, one of the interesting aspects of the social practice of blaming is that individuals constantly blame and are blamed by others as part of what looks like a reciprocal relationship. Not surprisingly, the practice begins to look less reciprocal when we take into consideration who has the power to make his or her own judgments of blameworthiness known in the community. But at the level of blame itself there does appear to be room throughout the community for everyone to blame everyone else, although many can do this only in silence.

But what about the roles of blamer and blamed themselves? While to be blamed is to make oneself vulnerable to moral scrutiny, to blame is to place oneself at the moment in question in the role of moral authority. It is to suggest not only that one has access to what the standards of appropriate behavior should be in society, but that one has the right to impose those standards on other individuals when they have violated our trust in them. It is as such a relationship of judge to judged, a relationship that brings with it the right to express disdain for others through shame, condemnation, or exclusion from the community.

How does such a relationship function in society? Most psychologists and philosophers are quick to point out that in blaming individuals, we condition them to act more conscientiously in the future—unless of course they enjoy being blamed. In some cases our conditioning of an individual is intentional, say, if we are a parent or a teacher. In other cases, it is unintentional, say, if we do not care about the well-being of the individual we are blaming. But even when our conditioning of an individual is unintentional, we probably would not have blamed the individual unless we thought that she was capable of acting better in the future. In this sense, as J. J. C. Smart points out, the ability of an individual to do otherwise that is associated with blame clearly involves malleability.[18]

While the conditioning of those being blamed is an important function of blaming in society, it is not the only function. Blaming must be understood not only in terms of those being blamed, but also in terms of the relationship between those being blamed and those doing the blaming. What this suggests is that when we blame individuals for acting badly, we do something for ourselves too. In particular, we let others know that they have violated our trust in them, as well as the conventional standards of decency that govern our actions as members of a particular community. In this sense, blaming has an expressive, as well as a manipulative, function. It lets others know that they have stepped outside the boundaries of what is acceptable to us in our relations with them.

By letting others know that they have stepped outside the boundaries of what is acceptable to us, our social practice of blaming also enables us to impose two sorts of expectations on those being blamed. One has to do with the content of actions that we deem acceptable in our community. The other has to do with the level of self-control that we expect individuals to exert over their own actions. Both sorts of expectations are reinforced by blame in cases where our blame is taken seriously. But they are reinforced in significantly different ways.

Our standards of acceptable behavior are reinforced by virtue of the action description with which we begin. If, for example, a factory owner is willing to accept our description of her as destroying the environment rather than, say, as getting rid of her factory's waste material as efficiently as possible, we will have gone a long way in incorporating our expectations of her into her own worldview, although the negative reactions associated with blame are necessary to reinforce that incorporation. Likewise, if we are able to convince a professional woman to

18. Smart, "Free Will, Praise, and Blame," 208–13.

accept our definition of her as depriving men of their livelihoods rather than, say, as lawyering or doctoring, we will have gone a long way in convincing her to accept our standards of acceptable behavior, especially if she is also willing to accept our blame.

While we impose our standards of acceptable behavior on individuals via our description of their actions, we impose our standards of free will on them as part of our practice of excuse giving. In most cases we simply assume that individuals were in control over their actions. But in other cases we do not know or are challenged in our assumption by those being blamed. While such challenges may in some cases take the form of assertions—such as "I am not in control over my actions," they more frequently take the form of pleas designed to excuse oneself from blame, pleas of the form "I didn't know" or "I was coerced."

While these pleas may themselves appear to register free will, they do not. Nor could they, since they require criteria of validity that we ourselves bring to bear on them. If we decide that a particular plea is acceptable, we are generally willing to excuse the individual from blame on the grounds that her will was unfree. Likewise, if we decide that her plea is unacceptable, we are generally unwilling to excuse her from blame on the grounds that her will was free and she was in control over her own actions.

While the notion of free will that emerges here conditions particular judgments of blameworthiness, it is shaped more generally by our social practice of blaming and the criteria of validity that we associate with volitional excuses. Hence, in trying to discern why we draw the line between free and unfree wills in a particular place along the spectrum of self-control, we need to take seriously not only the particular sorts of relationships in which blame is lodged, but the more general practice of blaming we accept. Likewise, we need to understand our discoveries of free will not only as moral judgments, but as reflections of those standards of self-control that we impose on each other as part of either a particular relationship or a larger community.

Interestingly enough, neither the behavioral standards associated with our description of an individual as bringing about harm or the standards of self-control associated with our discoveries of free will make any sense outside the context of a relationship between individuals and those who may potentially blame them. While the behavioral standards that we incorporate into our description of an individual's action do not necessarily have anything to do with blame, they do presuppose communication among individuals about what others are doing. Likewise, while the standards of self-control associated with our discoveries of free will may be very general, they do require an openly recognized relationship between blamer and blamed when incorporated into our practice of volitional excuse giving.

Since both sorts of standards and our expression of them presuppose a relationship between us and members of a particular community, and since relationships of all sorts are based on, among other things, acceptance of shared standards, we should not be surprised to discover that our social practice of blaming is not only expressive, but regulative of the very relationships of which it is a part. In most cases blame regulates relationships among persons in the same way that punishment regulates legal relationships (although there are of course differences between the two).[19] In other words, blame both creates and sustains order between individuals by letting them know what can be expected of them and letting them know that if they do not comply, they will be hurt either by our admonishments or by the negative reputation which they develop in the rest of society.

Paradoxically, in regulating personal and social relationships, blaming often undermines them. For blaming cannot help but create divisions between those being blamed and those doing the blaming, especially if in blaming individuals we threaten to exclude them from our community. Since the practice of blaming is divisive, it would seem best for us to avoid blaming when possible if we are at all concerned about communal harmony. But could we ever eliminate the practice of blaming altogether?[20]

P. F. Strawson, who also chooses to view blameworthiness not as an aspect of free will, but as part of our reactive attitudes, is skeptical about the extent to which we can leave these reactive attitudes behind. Strawson argues not only that we as human beings need to express indignation and hostility in situations where we have been violated, but that "a life without reactive attitudes is barely conceivable and wholly repellent."[21] Likewise, he makes clear that the objective approach to blameworthiness shared by those who claim the necessity of rationally evaluating the mindset of others is "unfortunate."[22]

19. I discuss the significant differences between social blame and legal punishment below.

20. By asking the question in a straightforwardly practical way, my analysis clearly diverges from most discussions of blameworthiness, which focus on whether or not blame is *deserved* rather than practical. For an excellent discussion of why the question "Ought we to retain praise, blame, etc.?" is a fundamentally practical question rather than one based on free will, see both Strawson, "Freedom and Resentment," *Free Will and Resentment,* 2–4; and Bennett, "Accountability," 30.

21. Strawson, "Freedom and Resentment," 9.

22. Ibid.

Strawson makes both claims on the basis of a sharp distinction between reactive and objective attitudes (the latter being defined as the ability to see another human being not as part of a participating relationship, but as an "object of social policy; as a subject for what, in a wide range of sense, might be called treatment").[23] According to Strawson, the objective attitude can be emotionally toned in many ways, but not in all ways. It can include repulsion and fear, pity and love, but it cannot include the range of reactive attitudes that evolve within participatory relationships, attitudes such as resentment, gratitude, forgiveness, anger, and reciprocal love. According to Strawson, "if your attitude towards someone is wholly objective, then though you may fight him, you cannot quarrel with him, and though you may talk to him, even negotiate with him, you cannot reason with him."[24]

By drawing a sharp distinction between reactive and objective attitudes in this context, Strawson is able to underscore the importance of participatory relationships to the practice of blaming and to make clear what is at stake in doing away with blame altogether. But he is not able to articulate how the two attitudes relate to each other in practice, since he views them as mutually exclusive. Nor is he able to take into consideration the possibility of incorporating an objectivist attitude into our practice of blaming as a way of tempering its more hurtful aspects.

Presumably, if we were to show how some individuals now juggle their reactive and objective attitudes in practice, we might be able to develop a more tolerant attitude towards others within our practice of blaming. In other words, we might be able to interject a modicum of understanding into our reactive attitudes without leaving our relationships to others behind altogether or becoming the cold and emotionless beings that Dostoyevski warned us about in his own apology for resentment.[25]

But could we ever do away with blaming altogether? On the one hand, our need to convey to others that we disapprove of their actions might be fulfilled just as well by other forms of indignation, although it is not clear that other forms of indignation would be any less divisive than blaming. Likewise, we might lessen the need for blaming and

23. Ibid.
24. Ibid.
25. Dostoyevski asks in *Notes from the Underground* (London, 1972): "What can I do if I don't even feel resentment? . . . My anger, in consequence of the damned laws of consciousness, is subject to chemical decomposition. As you look, its object vanishes into thin air, its seasons evaporate, the offender is nowhere to be found, the affront ceases to be an offence and becomes destiny, something like a toothache, for which nobody is to blame" (27).

other forms of indignation if we were to become more tolerant and supportive in our relationships with others. But even so, there would not seem to be any way of eliminating the practice of blaming altogether. For toleration presupposes that we already blame individuals on some occasions, and supportiveness after a certain point can become very oppressive. (Indeed, since supportiveness may be less expressive and more consciously manipulative than blame, we might find it to be more oppressive than blame when taken to extremes.)

Moreover, something like our social practice of blaming might be absolutely necessary to any rule-following activity. How, we have to ask, could we make sense of the practice of law-abidingness if we did not have a way of backing laws up with punishment? And how could we expect conventions to be maintained and social rules followed if we did not have a system of negative incentives to associate with their infringement? Presumably we will have to retain something like our social practice of blaming.

How might we solve the problem of divisiveness that often accompanies blame? One way would be to legalize relationships which we now consider to be purely social or personal. In particular, we might render violations of these relationships punishable by law. The advantage of doing so presumably would be that punishment, unlike blaming, is impersonal, at least from the standpoint of those inflicting the pain. Although the introduction of legality in this context could not, for obvious reasons, be universalized, it might prove to be effective in areas which are not purely social to begin with, e.g., the economy and the bureaucracy. But even in these cases, the individual's freedom would be curtailed in a much more serious way than if she had simply been blamed.

While blaming individuals may lead them to change or restrict their behavior, it does not close off avenues of action in the way that legal punishment does. Individuals can always reject blame by claiming either that their actions were not wrong or that the expectations that we have imposed on them are too stringent. Moreover, if they are effective in their rejections of blame, i.e., if they are able to persuade others of the correctness of their own standards of behavior, they may be able to change the more general criteria of blameworthiness that the rest of us invoke as members of a blaming community.

Whether they will be able to do so will depend, presumably, not only on the particular standards of behavior that they themselves embrace, but on the amount of power that they have at their disposal. If blame is not backed up by a sufficient amount of social power, it will not be taken seriously. Nor will it be effective in the alteration of our communal standards. Take, for instance, the case of a child who blames her parents for behaving badly at a social gathering. Although the child may have all sorts of social conventions on her side, she does not have the power to hold her parents accountable. Hence, she will most likely be told that it is not her place to blame them, and her judgments of blame will probably not carry much weight in her community.

In cases such as this, we cannot help but notice that blame is intimately connected with power and authority in two important respects. First of all, individuals must have a certain amount of power and authority in the community to have their ascription of blame taken seriously. While blame is much more accessible to individuals than legal punishment, in that almost everyone is in the position to blame others at some point in time, it is clear that some individuals are able to make their ascriptions of blame stick more than other individuals are. This is not always because they wield power directly in society either. They may, for instance, be able to obtain support from others on the basis of principle or else by playing on the guilt feelings of those who themselves wield power. Presumably members of the civil rights movement could not have made their ascriptions of blame stick as much as they did without both principled support and the guilt feelings of those who had profited from racism in the past.

Second, the standards of appropriate behavior that ground those judgments of blameworthiness that receive the most attention in society will probably reflect the interests and values of those doing the blaming. As such, we might want to take into consideration the possibility that blame serves more purely social and political interests in the cases about which we have been concerned, although these interests may not themselves be well defined. It is to this possibility that I now turn.

Blaming, Interests, and the Maintenance of Power

The social and political aspects of blaming become most apparent when we acknowledge that the action for which we blame a particular individual is never objectively defined. It is instead defined partly according to our social and political norms, norms which take on a special place in our definition of an individual's action in cases where the action involves bringing about harm. In these cases, whether or not we are willing to define an individual as causing the suffering of others depends on, among other things, our expectations of the individual and her relationship to those suffering.

If we were to place the relativity of our action descriptions at the center of our analysis of blame, we would have to acknowledge that our social practice of blaming serves two further functions which are neither purely expressive nor psychologically manipulative. The first involves the individuation of actions, or in other words, the construction of a relationship between individuals and an external state of affairs. The second involves the reinforcement of our own values and expectations of individuals, as well as the distribution of power in society which renders our description of the individual legitimate, or at least politically acceptable.

Both of these functions are politically charged and hinge on the relationship between the two judgments that we have been focusing on: causal responsibility and blameworthiness. The first enables individuals to understand what they are doing on a very basic level by connecting them causally with an external state of affairs. The second ensures that those who take our blame seriously will also take seriously both our social and political norms and the communal structures with which they are associated.

What do our judgments of causal responsibility and blameworthiness have to do with the individuation of actions? Presumably individuals need to have some sense of the effects that they are having on the world in order to conceive of themselves as acting. Likewise, since there are so many different effects that their actions might have on the world, individuals need to be presented with a more limited selection, a selection which we articulate for them (and which they articulate for themselves) by deeming particular states of affairs the consequences of their actions.

By connecting individuals with external states of affairs in general, we both reinforce an individual's sense of connectedness with the outside world and underscore her own particular role in it, a role that is presumably necessary to the construction of her personal identity. Likewise, by connecting her with particular states of affairs and not others, we not only create a space for her to withdraw from the world, but help her to sustain a sense of identity as an individual with a self that is distinct from other events in the world.

Since our judgments of causal responsibility and blameworthiness are caught up with such fundamental processes as those associated with the creation of a self, we should not be surprised to discover that the expectations that we bring to bear on them are fairly well entrenched and difficult to change. Nor should we be surprised to discover that individuals have a great deal at stake in seeing that our descriptions of them do not change over time (or at least not too quickly). John Harris may have been able to change his description of the affluent in an academic journal. But if he had tried to do so in social and political practice, he would presumably have run into a great deal of resistance, not only because of the threat that his description poses to the interests of the affluent but because of the threat that it poses to their sense of self.

Nevertheless, our descriptions of particular individuals do change over time in many cases. Moreover, such changes often signal a shift in the individuals' self-understandings. In cases where we increase the amount of harm for which they can be held causally responsible, we in effect extend their involvement in the world. In cases where we restrict the amount of harm for which they can be held causally responsible, we in effect increase the isolation of their existence (which is not necessarily a bad thing).

The fact that we are able to extend or contract an individual's involvement in the world in this way suggests, among other things, that by deeming harm the consequence of an individual's actions we not only enable the individual to understand what she is doing according to our expectations of her and our standards of acceptable behavior, but reinforce the very expectations and standards of acceptable behavior on which our descriptions of her are based. Certainly this appears to be true in the cases with which we have been concerned, all of which involve harm to others.

By holding individuals causally responsible for actions of the form "X brought about harm", we in effect insure, if we are powerful enough to do so, that the interests of those being harmed will be better protected in the future. Likewise, by *not* blaming individuals for such an action, or by not describing them as responsible in the first place, we in effect let such harm occur. In both sorts of cases, we end up either supporting or challenging the existing hierarchy of values in society, as well as the distribution of power on which that hierarchy is based.

The practice of blaming plays a very important role in these cases. By holding the tire manufacturer blameworthy for the deaths resulting from his having sold the city bad tires, we support our assumption that the life interests of city schoolchildren are more important than the manufacturer's business interests. By not holding the textile manufacturer blameworthy for the illnesses of his workers which result from, say, an excessive amount of cotton fibers in the air, we (or some among us) reinforce the assumption that the health interests of these workers can be trumped by the business interests of the textile manufacturer when the two sets of interests clash.

While our judgments of causal responsibility are crucial to the reinforcement of such an assumption, we would not be able to reinforce the assumption if we were not also able to associate it with a judgment of blameworthiness, i.e., with a judgment whose moral associations render it more powerful than a mere causal explanation. What is the relationship here between our judgments of causal responsibility and blameworthiness? On the one hand, our judgments of blameworthiness, if taken seriously, effectively reinforce our judgments of causal responsibility, as well as the values and expectations on which they are based. On the other hand, we may set out to locate those individuals who are causally responsible for external harm in the first place only because we participate in our social practice of blaming, a practice which takes causal responsibility as one of its primary conditions. In this sense, our judgments of causal responsibility and blameworthiness are mutually reinforcing.

What exactly is it about blame that enables us to reinforce our judgments of causal responsibility and take seriously others' descriptions of us as bringing about harm? Blame essentially comprises a set of negative attitudes that we take toward others when they violate what we take to be the rules of fair play. When we blame individuals we make known to them not only that they have acted badly, but that they are "bad persons," persons whom we consider to be less than worthy members of our community. Blame is thus, among other things, exclusionary: by blaming individuals for acting badly, we threaten to exclude them from our community of respect.

In most cases the relevant community comprises worldly relationships, relationships between friends, family members, comrades, business associates, and colleagues. In other cases it refers to a more abstract, indeed metaphysical, community: the community of all morally good human beings. When the community from which we are threatened with exclusion is made up of worldly relationships, we often think about the blame in question as social blame or as communal approbation. When the community from which we are threatened with exclusion is morally ideal, we often think of the blame in question as itself moral, or in other words, as an aspect of moral responsibility as traditionally understood.

Not surprisingly, the latter sort of blame is particularly effective as a way of reinforcing communal values in a liberal society, i.e., in a society which curbs the extent to which the power of the state can enter into the private sphere. Why this is so becomes clearer once we have answered two further questions: What role do our modern concepts of moral responsibility and free will play in our practical judgments of blameworthiness? And how are we able to view the latter as a purely factual discovery?

From Public Accountability to Moral Blameworthiness and Back

In viewing moral responsibility as part of our social practice of blaming, we should recognize that moral responsibility and the social practice of blaming have at least two features in common. First of all, when individuals are considered morally responsible—and blamed—for having acted badly, they are made to feel unworthy as persons, although this is more serious in the case of moral responsibility. Second, the conditions under which we hold individuals morally responsible are the same conditions under which we have always blamed them. I refer here primarily to the volitional excuses that we invoke in both blaming individuals and holding them morally responsible.

Since the social practice of blaming preceded the modern understanding of moral responsibility, we might want to characterize moral responsibility as the internalization of social blame. To do so, moreover, would be consistent with the contention of philosophers such as Jonathan Glover that "to be morally responsible for one's actions is, in a strange sense, to be accountable to oneself for them."[26] But we should also not forget that just as our modern concept of moral responsibility evolved out of our social practice of blaming, our social practice of blaming has taken on many of the same characteristics as our modern concept of moral responsibility, including an emphasis on intrinsic moral worth over mere collective censure.

Two questions arise in this context. First of all, how does collective censure become internalized as part of our modern practice of moral responsibility? Second, within what sort of context does such internalization take place? (How does our modern concept of moral responsibility fit into the worldview of an ostensibly secularized Christian society?)

If we want to understand how collective standards of blameworthiness get internalized, we need to return to both our notion of "ideal liability" and the conception of free will that we associate with it. As we have seen, our notion of ideal liability may not make sense on its own terms. But it does enable us to internalize blame by abstracting a metaphysical state of blameworthiness out of actual social relationships. Likewise, it may not have the sort of empirical referent that it would need to have in order to be considered a moral fact. But it does enable

26. Glover, *Responsibility* 29. Moira Roberts develops other aspects of this formulation in *Freedom and Practical Responsibility* (Cambridge, England, 1965).

us to think about our judgments of blameworthiness as grounded in a moral realm far removed from the contingencies of our worldly communities and to develop a much stronger practice of blaming than we would otherwise be able to develop, one whose moral stakes are higher than mere social approbation.

What is the practice of abstraction that enables us to think about our judgments of blameworthiness as far removed from worldly contingencies? Since our judgments of blameworthiness, as well as our modern concept of moral responsibility itself, rest on many of the same standards of accountability as were articulated by Aristotle, we might want to view them as an abstraction from social and political practice. But we could not understand them as a direct internalization of our collective standards of blameworthiness. For they also depend for their content on the Christian notion of moral sinfulness out of which our modern concept of moral responsibility evolved. Indeed, the notion of "ideal liability" that we associate with our modern concept of moral responsibility looks very much like the Christian notion of moral blameworthiness minus the authority of God (and even without this authority, we probably have to assume something like it in order to hold on to our absolutist moral principles).

Not surprisingly, those who believe in the Christian God generally locate the source of our modern concept of moral responsibility in the truth of Christian dogma itself. But not everyone believes in the Christian God. Hence, we might want to take into consideration the possibility that Christianity is itself a projection of human relations onto a mythical plane and that our modern concept of moral responsibility is as such a double abstraction (or an abstraction from social and political practice via the domination of Christianity for many centuries).

The form that blameworthiness has taken over the years seems to support such a hypothesis. While the Classical notion of blameworthiness was self-consciously grounded in social and political practice, the Christian notion of sinfulness viewed its source as a relationship between individuals and an external authority whose judgments were not, as it turned out, all that different from those of mere mortals. Likewise, while the modern concept of moral responsibility looks very much like the Christian notion of sinfulness minus the authority of God, it clearly abstracts itself out of such a relationship by presenting itself as a moral fact about individuals that just happens to take the form of an ideal liability relationship.

What role does the concept of free will play in the process of abstraction? Although we cannot go as far as to talk about free will as a construct *invented* to bolster our respective notions of blameworthiness, we can talk about the two as having evolved together in particular historical contexts. Aristotle, as we saw in chapter 2, was explicitly concerned to articulate the concept of voluntariness compatible with the Greek practices of blaming and punishment, and while the Christian philosophers may have thought about themselves as discovering their particular understanding of free will, they clearly shaped it according to the standards of sinfulness already set down in Christian dogma. Modern thinkers are no different from their Classical and Christian counterparts. While they may now talk about the modern notion of free will in purely scientific terms, they originally presented it as a necessary condition of modern morality, a morality which, as Kant made clear, was very closely tied up with individual moral guilt.

Since the modern notion of free will is construed as both antithetical to all forms of external determination *and* intrinsically good or bad morally, it is very well suited to the location of moral blameworthiness in an individual's own moral agency. Indeed, we might want to go as far as to view the modern notion of free will as a conceptual mechanism for internalizing the standards of social blameworthiness that we have already idealized. But we cannot ignore the fact that in practice we often substitute for the modern notion of free will a much less stringent one (even though we often continue to talk about it as contra-causal freedom).

The interesting thing about the notion of free will that we substitute for contra-causal freedom in practice is that it enables us both to locate the source of blameworthiness in an individual's own moral agency and to reinforce our sense of how much control individuals can be expected to exert over their own behavior. In the last section we saw that by imposing our own criteria of free will on individuals, we not only reinforced their sense of autonomy, but created a sense of self for them which could be considered inherently moral (as distinct from merely susceptible to our own moral judgments).

Not surprisingly, once such a notion of free will is taken for granted, it cannot help but alter our social practice of blaming both by raising the moral stakes associated with blame itself and by obscuring the extent to which blame is part of a relationship among individuals who are themselves far less than God-like in their moral judgments. How are we to understand the notion of moral blameworthiness that emerges here? While we cannot locate its source exclusively in any one historical development, we can be fairly sure of two things. One is that the modern notion of blame makes sense only in a community which has replaced collective responsibility with a more individualized form of accountability. The other is that it is most compatible with a schema of limited political authority, e.g., with one which limits the reach of political authority into the private sphere.

Both observations are supported by the actual evolution of our modern concept of moral responsibility, an evolution which is clearly part of a more general trend toward individualism. Paul Fauconnet, among others, locates in the development of individualism a shift in the nature of responsibility from external and communicable to internal and individual.[27] In a similar fashion, Karl Popper traces the movement in Western society from responsibility as a relationship between individuals and political authority to responsibility as the ability of an individual to hold himself accountable for his actions.[28]

What this suggests is that moral responsibility, as a particular form of personal responsibility, must be conceived of as having evolved within a community on the basis of a relationship between individuals and external authority. Moreover, it must also be conceived as presupposing the evolution among individuals of the ability to take responsibility not only for their own actions, but for external states of affairs as well. And finally, it must be conceived of as internalizing the relationship between individuals and external authority from which it originally evolved. But this relationship is not the only thing that individuals internalize when they accept moral responsibility for either their own actions or external harm. They also internalize the standards on which our judgments of moral responsibility are based, standards which are clearly part of our social practice of blaming and which rest on, among other things, our own conceptions of fairness and reciprocity.

What can the evolution of the concept of moral responsibility teach us? First of all, in a liberal or individualistic society such as our own, we will probably always have to rely on some form of personal responsibility. But what sort of personal responsibility is not clear. Two questions need to be answered here. How long might a secular society be expected to sustain a notion of moral responsibility that views individuals as blameworthy outside of concrete social and political relationships? And why would a secular society want to sustain such a notion of blameworthiness in the first place?

The problem raised by the first question is that individuals may not be inclined to hold themselves responsible outside the context of either religious sanctions or a relationship between them and other members of their community. As Richard McKeon points out, individuals began

27. Paul Fauconnet, *La Responsabilité* (Paris, 1920).
28. Karl Popper, *The Open Society and Its Enemies*.

holding each other responsible in practice during the late eighteenth and early nineteenth centuries, when the power of the church itself began to dwindle.[29] Moreover, it was during this period that the concept of moral responsibility first appeared in political discourse. According to McKeon, with the advent of liberal democracy it became especially important for individuals to act conscientiously on their own.[30] One way of assuring such conscientiousness was to reinforce the notion that individuals are morally responsible for their actions even in the absence of external authority.

McKeon's findings suggest that without religious standards, the internalization of blame might require another sort of external authority. How might we establish such an authority in a secular context? First of all, we might simply want to perpetuate the myth that such authority now exists and ignore the social and political considerations that ground our judgments of responsibility in the process. (Presumably philosophers and political theorists could still construe moral responsibility as the projection of our social rules of accountability, or in other words, as the "vicarious or impersonal or disinterested or generalized analogies of the reactive attitudes of blaming.")[31]

By perpetuating false consciousness in this way, they might be able to avoid the deflation of moral authority associated with other attempts to make explicit the social and political context of our moral judgments. But they could not avoid obfuscating the real nature of the differences that exist among us with regard to our judgments of responsibility. Nor could we be sure that such obfuscations would continue to be effective in a secular society.

What if we could not in a secular community keep up the facade of moral objectivity? Two possible options come to mind here. On the one hand, we could simply resign ourselves to cynicism about our moral judgments. On the other hand, we could reconstruct the concept of responsibility as part of political discourse.

What would it mean to reconstruct the concept of responsibility as part of political discourse? First of all, it would mean viewing our judgments of causal responsibility and blameworthiness as relative to our own social and political points of view rather than as moral facts to be discovered through purely factual inquiry. Second, it would mean treating the social and political considerations that ground our judgments of responsibility, e.g., those pertaining to our configuration of

29. Richard McKeon, "The Development and Significance of the Concept of Responsibility," *Revue Internationale de Philosophy* 2 (First Trimester, 1957), 34.

30. Ibid., 32.

31. Peter Strawson, *Freedom and Resentment* (London, 1974), 14.

social roles and the boundaries of our community, as open to debate on social and political grounds. Third, it would mean developing a form of accountability that falls somewhere between legal punishment, on the one hand, and intrinsic moral guilt, on the other.

While such a form of accountability is not now easy to visualize, it would presumably require that individuals be able to communicate openly with one another about responsibility and that they respect each other enough to take each other's arguments seriously. Could such a requirement be met in the foreseeable future? On the one hand, the structure of our community is not exactly a polis. On the other hand, it is much more conducive to public accountability than early Christian society. Indeed, with the increased levels of communication made possible by technology, we might be able to establish more open channels of debate about who is responsible for various sorts of harm in the world. But even then we would be confronted with the possibility that without external authority—either God's or the state's—public accountability would lose its motivational force either because we are not moved by each other's opinions or because our judgments of blameworthiness would no longer give anyone else a reason to act.

What this suggests is that if responsibility is going to be dislodged from its metaphysical premises and remain effective outside of a purely legal framework, it will have to be sustained by a community of individuals who are willing to take each other's judgments of blameworthiness seriously for reasons other than the sheer power that might be associated with them. Presumably such a community would be one based not only on the value of communal membership, but on a shared sense of the need to deliberate about questions of responsibility within the public sphere. I have not tried to establish the institutional structures of such a community in this chapter. Instead, I have tried to articulate the various considerations that we incorporate into our judgments of blameworthiness in such a way that we might be able to argue more openly about questions of responsibility in the future. I ask in chapter 10 what such an argument might look like in practice.

10

Conclusion: Morality and Power

I began this study by stating that my interests in moral responsibility are both philosophical and practical. How, I asked, can we talk about moral responsibility if the notions of free will and moral blameworthiness on which it is based are not themselves coherent? How, moreover, can we move beyond the gaps in communication that now characterize our practical discussions of moral responsibility and develop a framework for arguing openly about who is morally responsible for various sorts of harm in the world?

I have tried to answer both questions by viewing our modern concept of moral responsibility, not as a philosophical ideal to be realized in practice, but as a conceptual mechanism for bringing together two practical judgments of our own into one ostensibly factual discovery of moral responsibility. The first of these judgments, as we have seen, is that an individual is causally responsible for harm. The second is that the individual is worthy of our blame.

Neither of these judgments, I have argued, is as purely factual as we often assume it to be. Both rest on a variety of social and political considerations which we either make ourselves or inherit from others in the form of social expectations. Hence, even though we may think of ourselves as discovering the objective causes of harm, we in fact import into our causal analysis an assortment of more purely conventional attitudes about whose interests count in society. Likewise, even though we may think of ourselves as discovering whether or not an individual herself caused—freely willed—harm, we in fact bring to our psychological analysis a variety of more purely cultural assumptions about when individuals can be expected to control their own behavior.

How, we may ask, are we able to conceive of our judgments of causal responsibility and blameworthiness as purely factual if they rest on such conventions and cultural assumptions? How, moreover, if one judgment necessarily precedes the other, are we able to view the two judgments together as one factual discovery? I have tried to answer both of these questions by showing how the modern notion of free will, interpreted as contra-causal freedom, enables us to view individuals as morally blameworthy, not in virtue of a decision on our part that they are worthy of our blame, but in virtue of their having themselves caused—freely willed—harm to others.

While I have focused on the concepts of moral responsibility, free will, and blameworthiness, I have not confined myself to conceptual analysis as conventionally understood. Instead, I have focused a large portion of my attention on both the structures and the consequences of our practical judgments of moral responsibility. I have done so both by articulating the various normative and conventional expectations that ground our so-called discoveries of causal responsibility and blameworthiness in practice and by exploring the structures of power that underlie and help to maintain these expectations and the judgments of which they are a part.

Throughout the study, I have referred to and explored a variety of social and political considerations that we incorporate into our practical judgments of moral responsibility. But I have concentrated the bulk of my attention on those considerations most closely associated with both our configuration of social roles and our conception of communal boundaries. I have argued that whether we are willing to consider harm the consequence of a particular individual's actions depends not only on the causal connections that exist between the individual and harm, but on both our configuration of the individual's social role and our own sense of whether or not those being harmed are part of the individual's community.

Since social roles and communal boundaries are often talked about in static terms (recall Casey's discussion of them), we might be led to view our judgments of causal responsibility and blameworthiness as themselves static. But as I have tried to show, they are not. Indeed, in many cases these judgments have changed drastically over time in conjunction with both factual and causal discoveries and two more purely social and political phenomena. One is the existence of conflicting conceptions of both an individual's social role and her communal boundaries. The other is the ability of one group of individuals to impose their conceptions of both an individual's social role and her communal boundaries on the majority of the population, an ability that requires, among other things, the wielding of power.

In the cases upon which we have focused, the wielding of power is necessary to the alteration of our judgments of moral responsibility. But we cannot go as far as to suggest that our judgments of moral responsibility are mere *reflections* of the distribution of power in society. For as I have tried to show, the relationship between moral responsibility and power is dialectical in nature. On the one hand, our judgments of moral responsibility for external harm are grounded in, among other things, the distribution of power in our society. On the other hand, these same judgments help to shape our configuration of social roles and our conception of communal boundaries, as well as the distribution of power on which both are based.

How do they do so? Key here are the notions of causation and blameworthiness inherent in our judgments of moral responsibility for external harm. While the causal relationships that we ascribe to individuals for external harm within our so-called discoveries of moral responsibility create for individuals a greater sense of connectedness to those suffering, the practice of blaming that we associate with moral responsibility can lead individuals in the future to take into consideration the interests of those suffering, a development which cannot help but alter their conception of communal boundaries—if, that is, they are motivated by the blame to which they are subjected.

In many cases our judgments of moral responsibility work to extend the boundaries of our community, as in the case of industrial diseases. But in other cases it can work to contract those boundaries by reducing the instances of harm for which we can be blamed. Take, for instance, the examples afforded by the American family. Here if relationships of mutuality, and along with them expectations of care, continue to decline in intensity with regard to extended family members, we may find that an individual's realm of causal responsibility and blameworthiness have contracted rather than expanded. Likewise, with the contraction of this realm, we may find that the individual's conception of family membership has changed to the point where she no longer feels obligated to take the interests of extended family members into consideration before acting on her own, a development that can itself be expected to alter her search for consequences in the future.

What becomes obvious here is not only the dynamic nature of our judgments of moral responsibility themselves, but the social and political contexts in which they are made. Harris, Casey, and Thompson all treated our search for consequences as guided by principles of factual discovery. But such a search is, I have suggested, politically charged in at least two important respects. First of all, it requires that we begin with a particular conception of communal boundaries, even if we are not always conscious of them. Second, it either reinforces or challenges these boundaries and the power structures on which they are based, in large part as a result of both our imposition of expectations on others and the motivational structures of blaming itself.

What does this all mean for our ability to argue openly about the moral responsibility of particular individuals for the suffering of others? It means, among other things, that if we want to understand each other's judgments of moral responsibility, we will have to become conscious of the various sorts of social and political considerations that we incorporate into them. In particular, we will have to make explicit the conception of communal boundaries with which we begin, as well as the expectations that we place on particular individuals, expectations which are frequently grounded in a variety of practical considerations, as well as in our configuration of the individual's social role and the distribution of power in society.

While we could never hope to evaluate these considerations and social structures in any objective fashion, we might, by making them explicit, be able to create a framework for arguing openly about moral responsibility in cases where our differences are largely social and political, rather than purely scientific. Presumably such a framework would allow for the expression of differences among us concerning what we should be able to expect from particular individuals, as well as provide a basis upon which we could openly disagree with each other's expectations. But it could never provide us with a formula for discovering who, in a purely factual sense, is morally responsible for particular cases of harm.

What might such a debate look like in practice? Let us take, to begin with, the case of apartheid in South Africa. Here, as we have seen, our debate has not been all that much of a debate. Instead, it has been a series of assertions backed up by the particular facts deemed relevant. What would it mean to argue openly about the moral responsibility of American capitalists for apartheid in South Africa? What exactly could we argue about?

First of all, we could argue about the various causal links that exist between American capitalists and apartheid—as long as we were also willing to acknowledge that how far back we decided to go in the causal chain would depend partly on a variety of more purely social and political phenomena. In the apartheid case, many of the causal links in question are both economic and political. Hence, we would in this case have to argue about things like the ability of American businesses in South Africa to influence the South African regime and the ability of the South African regime to sustain itself if American businesses were to shut down their South African branches.

Ironically, our willingness to acknowledge that our judgments of causal responsibility are shaped in part by our own social and political norms might enhance, rather than frustrate, the sorts of factual inquiries that are so important to an intelligent debate about moral responsibility. As things now stand, we invoke particular facts to defend our judgments of moral responsibility in cases such as apartheid. But we cannot come to terms with the differences that exist among us or defend our factual accounts against others, since we view these factual accounts as themselves objective (or at least potentially so). If, on the other hand, we were to acknowledge that our factual accounts begin with a particular understanding of, say, the role of capitalists, we might be able to come to terms with our factual differences and even learn from each other. But we could not ever hope to come up with the "correct" answer in this context. Instead, we would have to be satisfied with developing a more accurate factual account of the relationship between American capitalism and apartheid than we had access to before.

Moreover, if we were to relate this account to our judgments of moral responsibility themselves, we would have to make explicit how they are mediated by our own social and political norms. Could we ever argue openly about these norms? Presumably, if we were to do so in the apartheid case, we would have to ask ourselves questions like: "What is the proper role of an American capitalist?" "What sorts of things can we expect capitalists to take into consideration when making their investments?" "Do they need to think about the social consequences of investing in a foreign country?" "Do they need to think about South African blacks as part of their community of concern?"

All of these questions concern both the role responsibilities that we associate with American capitalists in general and the boundaries of a particular individual's community of concern. John Casey, recall, asserted that role responsibilities are absolute in an effort to show that there is only one correct description of individuals in morally controversial cases. But he was able to make such an assertion only by obscuring the variety of different roles that one individual can embody and the conflicting interpretations that we associate with such roles in our community. Presumably, if we were to take these different roles and conflicting interpretations into consideration, we would have to choose among them on the basis of our own preferences or worldviews.

Could we ever *argue* for a particular interpretation of the individual's social role or the expectations that we construe as following from it? Since social roles are grounded partly in a variety of practical considerations (such as who was in the best position to prevent harm), we might place these expectations at the center of our attention. In the apartheid case, we might ask not only "Are American capitalists capable of challenging Apartheid?" but "What sorts of sacrifices might be required by divestiture and are these sacrifices worth it?"

Likewise, we might ask how far out into the world the individual's community of concern should extend. John Harris, recall, assumed that the community of concern of the affluent extended to all of those suffering in the third world. Moreover, he characterized the communal boundaries in question as morally correct. But he was able to do the latter only by falling back on a World Moral Authority who ostensibly knew all the correct boundaries to be drawn. If such a World Moral Authority turned out not to exist, we would have to argue on more purely social and political grounds about how to weigh our interests alongside the interests of those who live in another part of the world. Presumably to do so in the apartheid case would require, among other things, that we take into consideration both the interconnections that already exist between us and those suffering in South Africa and the sort of community that we ourselves value.

While such an argument might never be "won," it might at the very least lead us to make explicit the normative assumptions that ground our judgments of causal responsibility in the divestiture controversy, assumptions that range from the proper role of a capitalist to the value that we attach to national boundaries. Likewise, it might lead us to alter some of these assumptions if they were shown to be inconsistent with other values that we hold dear. And finally, it might lead us to understand the differences that exist among us with regard to the moral responsibility of particular individuals for the suffering of others.

None of these developments is negligible. While we may be aware, say, if we are antiapartheid activists, that our causal judgments have something to do with our politics, we may not be aware of the various assumptions that we have made about the role responsibilities of an investor or about the boundaries of her community. Moreover, if we were to make these assumptions explicit, we might discover that they clashed with other values that we take seriously, e.g., the value that we attach to free choice or to national boundaries. And even if we did not discover such a clash, we would presumably be better equipped to understand the differences that exist between us and those who argue against ascribing causal responsibility to capitalist investors for apartheid.

In the apartheid case, the differences between us are both factual and normative. Moreover, because the causal connections that exist between American investors and apartheid are so complex, they are not as readily grasped as other sorts of connections with which we have been dealing. Hence, we should not expect our debates over moral responsibility in this case to be crystal clear, even if we are able to make explicit the social and political norms that ground our various judgments of causal responsibility.

In other cases the causal connections in question are more obvious and hence less controversial. Take, for example, the case of an industrialist who dumps chemicals into the public water supply. In this case we can locate a fairly straightforward causal connection between the dumping of chemicals and the pollution of public waters. But we will not necessarily agree on whether or not the industrialist should be held causally responsible for the water's pollution. Presumably some of us would do so. But others might hold the town's filtering system causally responsible (for not picking up the chemicals) or simply assume that water pollution is natural and hence not the sort of thing for which anyone can be held causally responsible.

Since in this case we all agree on the facts of the situation and generally assume that all members of our town are also part of our community of concern, we will probably center our debate on the role responsibilities of the industrialist, a debate which will most likely take into consideration who is in the best position to prevent water pollution and how valuable it is to regulate industries in a free-market system. Likewise, since the interests of the company and the town are clearly at odds in this case, we may have to articulate the conflicting interests that ground our respective judgments of causal responsibility.

Could we ever argue with each other openly about whose interests should take precedence in this context? While we might be able to argue about whose interests are overriding or more general, we would presumably be held back from constructing an ideal hierarchy of interests by the fact that interests are themselves valued according to the power of those who hold them. While we might be able to talk openly about what the ideal distribution of power should be as a way of prioritizing interests in this context, to do so might not be all that effective, since power itself is now often construed in zero-sum terms (according to which one person's gain is another's loss).

Presumably, if we could show that everyone's power would be enhanced and everyone's interests realized by a particular judgment of causal responsibility, we might be able to debate about causal responsibility without regard to our own interests. While such cases are clearly not the norm, they do arise in situations where everyone is potentially causally responsible for a harm which is itself universal. Take, for example, the case of resource depletion. If we were to hold all Americans who use aerosol spray cans causally responsible for the decreasing levels of ozone in the atmosphere, we might increase the amount of blame in society. But we would not lead one group to become more powerful than others (although aerosol can producers would probably suffer). Moreover, we might help provide for everyone's better health in the future. Hence, we might feel free to argue openly about causal responsibility in this case without fear of losing power ourselves.

But such cases are admittedly rare and arise only in situations where we can talk about a very general interest that everyone realizes together. In most cases we are confronted with a conflict of interests in our judgments of causal responsibility that renders open debate very difficult. Indeed, in some cases, we are forced to acknowledge that our judgments of causal responsibility are not only *relative* to power but *about* power.

Take, for example, the controversy surrounding Daniel Patrick Moynihan's assertions that black women are causally responsible for the low morale and sense of inferiority experienced by black men (as a result of their position of strength in the family). While Moynihan couched his assertions in the neutral-sounding language of the social sciences, he clearly incorporated into them his own normative assumption that a black woman's role is to be subordinate to her man, or at least to buck up his morale. Likewise, feminist critics of the Moynihan report did not simply question Moynihan's social science methodology. Instead, they argued that his assumption about the role of black women was both insulting and designed to disempower black women as a way of empowering black men.

Moynihan could have of course simply been wrong about the causal responsibility of black women for black men's disempowerment. (He might, for instance, have pointed to white racism as the source of the problem.) But even so, the differences between Moynihan and feminists cannot be viewed in purely factual terms. Instead, they have to be viewed in terms of the different expectations that each party has of black women in the family. What would it mean to argue about these expectations openly? Presumably it would mean, among other things, arguing about the relationship between husband and wife and whether one should be construed as subordinate to the other.

In this case, the roles of husband and wife are politically charged to the extent that they embody power relations. Moreover, any alteration of them would presumably signal a shift in power between the two groups. But we could still imagine a conflation of interests such that both groups were able to come to terms with judgments of causal responsibility concerning the low morale of black men, especially if the causes were to be located in white racism rather than in the strength of black women.

In other cases the interests associated with one judgment of causal responsibility appear, at least at first glance, to be diametrically opposed to the interests associated with other judgments. Take, for example, the case of unemployment among American males. While some individuals now hold employed American women causally responsible for the unemployment of American men, others deny such causal responsibility on the grounds that women should not be expected to give up jobs because of male unemployment. Presumably, if both groups were to argue about their judgments of causal responsibility, they would have to argue about, among other things, whether or not men should have precedence over women on the job market.

Interestingly enough, in cases where individuals are confronted with their normative assumptions about "men's jobs," they often change their minds and blame, not women, but someone else, either their employer or the job market in general. In other cases, where, say, the employed are not American women but "foreigners," views are less likely to change quickly. Take, for instance, the disputes in Texas between American and Vietnamese fisherman. While the Vietnamese cite decreasing numbers of fish or Texans' own laziness as the source of the latter group's recent failures, many Texas fishermen blame the Vietnamese for their plight (because of the success of the Vietnamese as fishermen). In this case the normative assumptions grounding each judgment of causal responsibility are made explicit. Texas fishermen claim that the Vietnamese have invaded their territory; the Vietnamese retort that they have just as much right as any American to fish off the Texas coast. Both groups make clear that behind their differing judgments of causal responsibility there are conflicting conceptions of who belongs to the community in power.

By making these conflicting conceptions explicit, we might, at the very least, be able to understand each other's judgments of causal responsibility better than we do now, as well as the conflicting expectations that we bring to bear on particular individuals' actions. Likewise, if we were to evaluate critically both the judgments of causal responsibility and the expectations on which they are based, we might be led to change each other's minds about each. But we could not do so, presumably, without raising a host of more general questions concerning what kind of community we want to live in, questions such as "Do we want to open our borders to foreigners and give them equal rights?" or "Do we want to give priority to those groups who have lived in the United States for many years?"

Not surprisingly, the answers that we give to these questions will determine to a large extent whether or not we view the Vietnamese as having directly caused the failures of others. If we expect them to stay out of the waters, then we will surely view their fishing as at least partly responsible for the smaller number of fish that others are able to catch. If, on the other hand, we assume that they have as much right to fish in the waters as fishermen who have been there for a longer period of time, we will most likely look elsewhere, for example, to those who pollute the waters or to nature itself, for our causal explanation.

What this suggests is that even directness of causal relations is something that we might be able to argue about in terms of our expectations of individuals, expectations which are grounded not only in cultural traditions and practical considerations, but in both our configuration of social roles and our conception of communal boundaries. But we could not do so without acknowledging two further things. One is the extent to which all of these factors help shape our sense of what kinds of actions are a standard means of bringing about harm. The other is the importance of this sense to our judgments of both directness and causal responsibility.

In the case of the Vietnamese fishermen, we see two different opinions about whether "foreigners moving in" is a standard means of causing harm. Likewise, we see two different sets of judgments about how causally responsible foreigners are for others' economic losses. In the case of working women, we are confronted with a similar situation. On the one hand, there are those who view the employment of women as a standard means of keeping men unemployed. On the other hand, there are those who view the employment of women as normal (and/or good) and hence not as the sort of thing for which women can be held causally responsible.

The employment of women has also been viewed by some as a standard means of breaking up the two-parent family. Hence, we should not be surprised to discover that working women are often judged causally responsible for the high divorce rate. Nor should we be surprised to discover such judgments being rejected by those who view the employment of women as normal and good.

In both of these cases, what we take into account in deciding whether or not a particular action is a standard means of bringing about harm is bound up not only with our own traditions and cultural backgrounds, but with highly personal preferences concerning gender relations. Hence, to argue about them openly with others might be difficult to the extent that our evaluative criteria are themselves different. But in other cases, we might argue more openly about whether or not particular actions are standard means of bringing about harm, especially if we are talking about public policies.

Take, for instance, the case of apartheid in South Africa. In this case we are confronted with two closely related possibilities. One is that international capitalism is a standard means of legitimating existing regimes. The other is that international capitalism is a standard means of exploiting the masses. Both possibilities are controversial, the second more obviously so. But each can be argued about by asking a series of questions whose answers have more to do with economics and politics than with personal preferences, questions such as: "Does international capitalism necessarily (or frequently) reproduce the status quo in non-Western countries?" "Does capitalism exploit workers more than other economic systems? (Might other economic systems not exploit workers more extensively?)" "Are there positive contributions that capitalism makes that we need to talk about alongside its possible harms?"

Presumably, if we discover that capitalism makes positive contributions to both our community and other communities in which we invest, we will not go as far as to deem capitalism a standard means of bringing about harm. (Marxists very rarely ask the question in positive terms.) But we might still be willing to say that capitalist investors are causally responsible for particular cases of harm around the world on the grounds that they did not take into consideration particular negative consequences of their actions.

In the apartheid case, we are able to argue about the standard means of bringing about harm because we generally agree on the harm in question. While we might not all think that fighting apartheid is as important as economic accumulation, most of us value both. Hence, even though we place different expectations on different individuals, we are able to argue about the consequences of particular institutions and practices. In other cases, such as those involving the breakdown of the American family or the unemployment of American males, we differ with respect to our understanding of harm. Most of us would prefer to see happy families and full employment. But not all of us would view the repression of women as a harm. Nor would we all think about happy families in the same way. Hence, a means-ends analysis might be more difficult.

Likewise, a means-ends analysis might be difficult in cases where we differ with respect to the sorts of ends that might be used to justify means that we all view as ugly. Two sorts of scenerios come to mind here. One includes disagreement about whether or not violent means can ever be justified by ends deemed valuable. The other includes disagreement about the value of the particular ends in question.

Both sorts of disagreement are common during wartime and were especially strident during the recent war between the United States and

Iraq. During this war, we were confronted with sharply different opinions about whether war was worth fighting, differences of opinion that led to sharply different understandings of particular wartime activities and to conflicting ascriptions of responsibility. While critics of the war were not willing to view the bombing of Baghdad as a necessary means to the freedom of Kuwait, supporters of the war certainly were.

The two groups may have based their judgments of responsibility on different information about the war. But the major differences between them in this context were largely a matter of normative expectations. Since antiwar activists did not support the war, they were not willing to view the Baghdad air raids as necessary for a more positive end. Likewise, since supporters of the war were willing to view these raids as necessary for a more positive end, they were not as likely to view the raids as a standard means of killing, even though killing obviously took place. Nor as such were they willing to blame the United States government for the deaths of Iraqi citizens in the way that critics of the war were willing to do.

Two things become clear here. One is that means and ends are not self-evident, but are constructed along a continuum on the basis of what our own goals are (or what we advertise them as being). The other is that how we construct the relationship between means and ends will determine in part whether or not we judge particular individuals to be causally responsible for harm. Both points are especially clear in wartime scenarios because of the shifting boundaries between aggressive and defensive actions and because wars are made between communities with obviously conflicting goals and perspectives. But each point is also relevant in less-obvious cases such as international capitalism, where what one group takes as the means to a greater good another group takes as either an end in itself or the means to further destruction.

How might we argue about the judgments of causal responsibility that result from such differing means-ends perspectives? First of all, we could at the very least question the sincerity of those who use particularly destructive means to justify more general goods or who try to justify aggressive actions as self-defensive in all cases. (Can we really believe that Iraq entered Kuwait to save the Kuwait people or the Arab world?) Second, we could ask whether or not the means used are in fact necessary to the end in question. (Might other, less destructive, means have not worked better?) Third, we could become more self-conscious about how our means are also ends, if not to us, then to those who experience them as such.

In all of these cases, arguing about causal responsibility requires not only that we get the facts of the situation straight, but that we become self-conscious about the norms and expectations that we incorporate into our judgments of causal responsibility. While neither of these processes enables us to discover the "correct" judgment of causal responsibility, both help us in situations where we want to figure out whether or not our judgments of causal responsibility are based on values that we really accept. Likewise, each is necessary if we want to counter judgments of causal responsibility which we oppose.

What would it mean to counter another's judgment of causal responsibility in this context? It might mean simply that we bring up facts of the situation that our opponent has not taken into consideration or that we challenge her means-ends analysis. It might mean that we question her interpretation of an individual's social role by showing that it is impractical or that it leads to the development of bad character. Or it might mean that we dispute her conception of the individual's moral business by showing that it does not jibe with the causal connections that exist between the individual and those suffering or that it violates other moral principles, e.g., universal humanity, that she or we take seriously.

Since all of these considerations are controversial, we should not expect consensus to prevail. Likewise, we should not be surprised to discover that our arguments become even more complex in cases where we disagree about the individual's state of mind as well as the causal responsibility of her actions. In the cases cited above, we take it for granted that the individual was in control of her actions. In other cases we cannot take such control for granted, especially if the individual herself pleads either ignorance or compulsion. Take, for example, the case of a particular investor who, when told that she was causally responsible for the maintenance of apartheid, claimed that she didn't know it at the time. How can we come to terms with such a plea? We cannot, I suggested in chapter 9, decide whether her plea is acceptable on the basis of some ideal criteria of knowledge. Instead, we will have to ask ourselves how much we can expect investors to think about the consequences of their actions and how far out into the realm of consequences they can be expected to take their analyses.

Both questions are extremely difficult to address, since they require us to think not only about how we should interpret particular roles, but about how we should distribute the requirements of knowledge among particular individuals. Presumably, we could never come up with an ideal distribution in this context, even if we did agree on how to prioritize our goals. But we could argue about why it might be more productive in particular cases either to expand or to shrink the range of consequences that an investor should be expected to think about when investing her money.

The same sort of argument would have to be established about excuses of the form "I was not in control over myself when I acted." Excuses of this sort are not all that common in industrial management or the investment of capital funds. But they are common in cases involving drug use or combat fatigue. In these cases we are confronted with a decision about whether or not a particular individual's mental impairment was such that she can be excused from blame. How do we decide? In most situations we rely on intuitions about when it is fair to say that an individual was sufficiently in control of herself to be blamed for her actions. Hence, in arguing openly about blameworthiness in this context, we might want to ask ourselves: "Under what conditions can we fairly expect individuals to exercise control over themselves?"

Since we now disagree among ourselves about whether or not, say, drug use or combat fatigue or professional stress are valid excuses, we would presumably not always come up with the same criteria. But in expressing what we think is fair to expect from individuals, we might, at the very least, come to see the extent to which our criteria of fairness are based not only on scientific evidence pertaining to various psychological processes, but on cultural norms such as those associated with transcending pain or controlling one's environment. Likewise, we might come to recognize that whether or not we construe an individual as having been free enough to be blamed also depends on our conceptions of sympathy and forgiveness, as well as on our sense of when it is practical to blame or to refrain from blaming.

While we would probably not be able to come up with one cultural norm to agree upon, we might, by openly recognizing the place of such norms in our judgments of control, become more sensitive than we now are to the fact that in blaming others we impose on them cultural norms that they themselves might not share. (While an Englishman might expect a great deal of self-control from those around him, an Italian might question the repression that such self-control entails.)

What about levels of compassion and sympathy? Since both are in many respects highly subjective, we might not be able to scrutinize them in the same way that we scrutinize, say, the scientific evidence now surrounding junk food stress. But as the arguments of Thomas Sowell and Benjamin Hooks clearly demonstrate, we could argue about the effects of "too much" or "too little" sympathy on the initiative of those being blamed, and try to locate a healthy mean between total indulgence of them, on the one hand, and rigid assumptions of free will, on the other. Moreover, we could take more seriously than we now do the effectiveness of support, as opposed to blame, and even try to develop a more positive concept of moral responsibility itself.

And finally, even if we could not agree on how much self-control to expect from individuals in this context, we could try to be consistent between different groups who might, for example, experience stress differently or become stressed as a result of different sorts of experiences. As things now stand, we often sympathize with those whose experiences we share. If we are professionals, we will probably be able to grasp more readily than others the pressures associated with the "fast track." But we might not be able to grasp at all the sorts of pressures that confront someone who is living in extreme poverty or who is under constant bombardment in a war. Moreover, we might, as a result, leave out of our criteria of fairness the experiences of these others—or in other words, develop criteria that were biased toward one particular group over other groups.

How might we avoid such biases? By noting their existence, we would take one important step. But such a step is clearly not sufficient, especially if those acknowledging the biases are the same as the group who develops the criteria, a group that will in many circumstances comprise the most powerful members of the community. Moreover, as I have suggested, while we are capable of becoming much more conscious of our own perspectives than we now are and of thinking about them in light of more general goals, we can never transcend them altogether as moral agents. Hence, unlike utilitarians, we cannot entertain the possibility of developing a universal or ideal or neutral practical analysis. Nor should we try to do so, since the so-called universals that we would discover would presumably reflect our own points of view.

Instead, we would be much better off both making our own perspectives explicit as they ground our judgments of moral responsibility and creating a forum in which others were able to do so themselves. Presumably, creating such a forum would be feasible only if we were also able to establish social and political institutions capable of sustaining the free, i.e., noncoercive, flow of opinions about who is morally responsible for the suffering of others. I have not attempted to establish such institutions in this study. Instead, I have concentrated on articulating the grounds of debate that would occur within them.

What if such institutions turned out not to be politically feasible? Presumably the sort of pragmatic analysis that I have begun here would not be as important to pursue as I have suggested. But we still might want to retain such an analysis as a way of becoming self-conscious about our own moral judgments. Moreover, if nothing else, such an analysis would enable us to move beyond several more purely philo-

sophical dilemmas that contemporary thinkers confront in their efforts to make sense of moral responsibility.

The most widely acknowledged of these dilemmas is that the notion
of free will entailed by moral responsibility appears to be incompatible
with determinism. Since most contemporary philosophers insist on retaining the view of moral responsibility as independent of social and
political practice, they are forced to choose between two untenable
positions: either determinism is valid and moral responsibility is not
possible, or else moral responsibility is possible and determinism is not
valid. But if they were to view moral responsibility as part of social and
political practice, they might be able to hold both that determinism is
valid and that moral responsibility is possible, albeit in a different form
from that generally envisioned.

Second, by viewing moral responsibility as part of social and political
practice, they might be able to make room in their analysis for what has
come to be known as moral luck. As things now stand, moral and political theorists find it necessary to develop a series of contorted arguments in their efforts to sustain the more general assumption that
moral worth is independent of the contingencies of daily life. But if
they were willing to concede that moral worth as we now know it is not
an aspect of contra-causal freedom, they might be able to accept the
role that such contingencies play in our evaluation of an individual—
contingencies that range from the circumstances in which an individual acts to those interventions by other individuals which lead us to
change our minds about what the individual is herself doing.

Third, if they were to view moral responsibility as part of social and
political practice, they might be able to treat these contingencies as
more than mere "luck." Since Thomas Nagel, Bernard Williams, and
others conceive of these contingencies within a discussion of moral responsibility as traditionally understood, they are led to view them, not
as potentially explicable, but as the absence of individual control or
mere randomness. If, on the other hand, they were to view these contingencies as part of the context in which we judge each other to be
morally responsible, they might be able to discover in these supposed
instances of moral luck a more systematic set of socially determined
practices. This, in any case, is what I have tried to suggest by articulating the contexts in which we construct and evaluate each other's actions
from the point of view of blame.

But undoubtedly, by taking a pragmatic approach to the study of
moral responsibility, they too would be confronted with the sorts of arguments that critics invoke to undermine the value of pragmatism as a
moral and political theory. These arguments are many and varied, but

three of them stand out as potentially damaging. The first holds that by working within existing practices, moral and political theorists necessarily reproduce the ills of contemporary society. The second holds that by eschewing principles external to social and political practice, moral and political theorists lose any critical edge which they may have had at one time. The third holds that once our values are conceived of as part of social and political practice, they lose their moral authority—and hence become less helpful in the regulation of our community.

The first argument is generally made by Marxists and others who assume that all moral practices in contemporary society are determined in some fashion by the needs of a system which is itself corrupt. While I have not challenged this argument directly, I have provided two reasons why our practices of causal responsibility and blaming may be necessary to any society—or at least to any that we can imagine. First of all, without our practice of causal responsibility, we would not be able to intend our own actions or to understand what other individuals were doing. Second, without our practice of blaming, we would not be able to sustain communication with others or to function within institutions of any sort.

The second critical point suggested above—that we cannot move beyond the status quo as pragmatists—is made not only by foundationalists, but by nonfoundationalists who do not want to become trapped by a conservative methodology. Three points are in order here. First of all, as Richard Rorty makes clear, revolutionary activity of all sorts takes place within social and political practice. Hence, we cannot rule out the possibility that our judgments of moral responsibility will change over time. Second, social practices can, and sometimes do, themselves change when applied to new situations. Third, even though it is difficult to imagine how the practices of causal responsibility and blaming might change when applied to new situations, it is *not* difficult to imagine how these two practices might be used to bring about social and political change. Nor is it difficult to locate cases in which such change has already taken place within our practices of causal responsibility and blaming as a result of conflicting social and political norms.

The third critical point—that once our values are construed as part of social and political practice, they lose their moral authority—is, I think, the most potentially damaging to any pragmatic analysis of our moral values. I have not tried to counter it empirically. For to do so would require knowing something about the future that we cannot know. But I have tried to show that if we accept the argument now, we are obliged to concede two further points: one, that we are incapable of adhering to nonmetaphysical, i.e., communal values; the other, that moral agency is threatened by the level of self-consciousness entailed by pragmatic inquiry. I have not been willing to concede either of these two points, although I fully acknowledge that both may in the future turn out to be true. Instead, I have left open the possibility that pragmatic reconstructions such as the one that I have provided here may some day become part of public deliberation.

Select Bibliography

Adams, Robert. "Involuntary Sins." *Philosophical Review* 94 (1985), 3–31.

Adkins, A. W. H. *Merit and Responsibility: A Study in Greek Values.* Cambridge, England, 1959.

Altman, Andrew. "Pragmatism and Applied Ethics." *American Philosophical Quarterly* 20 (1983), 227–35.

Andre, Judith. "Nagel, Williams, and Moral Luck." *Analysis* 43 (1983), 202–7.

Anscombe, G. E. M. *Intention.* Oxford, 1957.

———. "Modern Moral Philosophy." *Philosophy* 33 (1958), 1–19.

———. *Causality and Determinism.* Cambridge, England, 1971.

———. "Soft Determinism." In *Contemporary Aspects of Philosophy,* ed. Gilbert Ryle. Boston, 1976.

Apel, Karl-Otto. "Transcendental Semiotics and the Paradigms of First Philosophy." *Philosophical Exchanges* 2 (1978), 3–22.

———. *Charles S. Pierce: From Pragmatism to Pragmaticism.* Amherst, Mass., 1981.

Aquinas, Thomas. *Summa Theologica,* part 1, question B. *Basic Writings of Saint Thomas Aquinas,* ed. A. C. Pegis. New York, 1945.

Aristotle. *Nicomachean Ethics,* trans. Martin Ostwald. Indianapolis, 1962.

———. *Eudemian Ethics,* trans. J. Solomon. *Complete Works of Aristotle,* ed. Jonathan Barnes. Princeton, 1984.

Audi, Robert. "Moral Responsibility, Freedom, and Compulsion." *American Philosophical Quarterly* 11 (1974), 1–14.

———. "Responsible Action and Virtuous Character." *Ethics* 101 (1991), 304–21.

Augustine. *City of God.* New York, 1950.

———. *On Free Choice of the Will,* trans. Ann S. Benjamin and H. L. Hackstaff. Indianapolis, 1964.

———. *On Two Souls Against the Manichees.*

Austin, J. "A Plea For Excuses." *Proceedings of the Aristotelian Society* 57 (1956–57), 1–30.

Ayer, A. J. "Freedom and Necessity." *Polemic* 5 (1946).

———. *The Concept of a Person and Other Essays.* New York, 1963.

Babcock, William. "Augustine on Sin and Moral Agency." *Journal of Religious Ethics* 16 (1988), 28–55.

Baier, Kurt. *Moral Point of View: A Rational Basis of Ethics*. Ithaca, 1958.

———. "Could and Would." *Analysis Supplement* 23 (1968), 20–29.

Baker, G. P., and P. M. S. Hacker. *Wittgenstein: Rules, Grammar, and Necessity*. Oxford, 1985.

Barnes, Wriston H. F. "Intention, Motive, and Responsibility." *Proceedings of the Aristotelian Society*. Suppl. vol. 19 (1945), 230–48.

Bates, Stanley. "The Responsibility of Random Collections." *Ethics* 80 (1971), 343–47.

Beardsley, Elizabeth. "A Plea For Deserts." *American Philosophical Quarterly* 6 (1969), 33–42.

Beardsly, Monroe. "Actions and Events." *American Philosophical Quarterly* 12 (1975), 263–76.

Beck, Lewis White. *A Commentary on Kant's Critique of Practical Reason*. Chicago, 1960.

Benett, W. *Religion and Free Will*. Oxford, 1913.

Bennett, Jonathan. "Whatever the Consequences." *Analysis* 26 (1965), 83–102.

———. "Accountability." *Philosophical Subjects*, ed. Z. van Straaten. Oxford, 1980, 14–47.

Bentham, Jeremy. *An Introduction to the Principles of Morals and Legislation*. Oxford, 1967.

Berlin, Isaiah. *Four Essays on Liberty*. London, 1969.

Bernstein, Richard. *Praxis and Action: Contemporary Philosophies of Human Action*. Philadelphia, 1971.

———. *The Restructuring of Social and Political Theory*. New York, 1976.

———. *Philosophical Profiles: Essays in a Pragmatic Mode*. Philadelphia, 1986.

———. "One Step Forward, Two Steps Backward." *Political Theory* 15 (1987).

Berofsky, Bernard. "Determinism and the Concept of a Person." *Journal of Philosophy* 61 (1964), 461–75.

———. *Free Will and Determinism*. New York, 1966.

———. *Determinism*. Princeton, 1971.

———. *Freedom From Necessity*. New York, 1987.

Blizek, William. "The Social Concept of Responsibility." *Southern Journal of Philosophy* 7 (1971), 107–11.

Bohlen, F. H. "The Moral Duty to Aid Others on the Basis of Tort Liability." *University of Pennsylvania Law Review* 56 (1908), 217–44, 316–38.

Boonin, Leonard. "Guilt, Shame, and Morality." *Journal of Value Inquiry* 17 (1983), 295–304.

Bradley, R. D. "Ifs, Cans, and Determinism." *Australasian Journal of Philosophy* 40 (1962), 146–58.

———. "Causality, Fatalism, and Morality." *Mind* 72 (1963), 591–94.

Brand, Myles. "The Language of Not Doing." *American Philosophical Quarterly* 8 (1971), 45–53.

Brandt, Richard. "A Utilitarian Theory of Excuses." *Philosophical Review* 78 (1969), 337–61.

Bronaugh, Richard. "Freedom As the Absence of an Excuse." *Ethics* 74 (1964), 161–73.

Brown, D. G. *Action.* Toronto, 1968.

Brown, Peter, and Henry Shue. *Boundaries: National Autonomy and Its Limits.* Totowa, N.J., 1981.

Brown, Peter, and Henry Shue, eds. *Food Policy: U.S. Response to Life and Death Choices.* New York, 1978.

Burnet, John. *Nichomachean Ethics: Text and Commentary.* London, 1900.

"Business Opposes Divestiture." *New York Times,* 25 April 1988, 2.

"Business Should Stay in South Africa." *New York Times,* 4 May 1989, 5.

Campbell, C. A. "Free Will: A Reply to R. D. Bradley." *Australasian Journal of Philosophy* 36 (1958), 46–56.

———. "Moral Libertarianism: A Reply to Mr. Franklin." *Philosophy* 2 (1962), 337–47.

Casey, John. "Actions and Consequences." In his *Morality and Moral Reasoning.* London, 1971.

Chinn, Ewing. "Intentional Actions and Their Side Effects." *Southern Journal of Philosophy* 13 (1977), 461–67.

Chisolm, R. "The Descriptive Element in the Concept of Action." *Journal of Philosophy* 61 (1964).

Cohen, Gerald. "Beliefs and Roles." *Proceedings of the Aristotelian Society* 67 (1966–67), 17–34.

Cohen, L. J. "Who Is Starving Whom?" *Theoria* 47 (1981), 65–81.

Collingwood, R. G. *An Essay On Metaphysics.* Oxford, 1940.

Compton, John. "Responsibility and Agency." *Southern Journal of Philosophy* 11 (1973), 85–89.

Cooper, D. E. "Collective Responsibility." *Philosophy* 43 (1960), 258–69.

Cooper, Neil. "On Evading Responsibility." *Journal of Applied Ethics* 4 (1987), 89–94.

Craig, William. "Augustine on Foreknowledge and Free Will." *Augustine Studies* 15 (1984), 41–63.

D'Arcy, Eric. *Human Acts.* Oxford, 1963.

Danto, Arthur. *Analytic Philosophy of Action.* Cambridge, England, 1973.

Davidson, Donald. "Actions, Reasons, and Causes." *Journal of Philosophy* 60 (1963), 685–700.

———. "Agency." In *Agency, Action, and Reason,* ed. R. Brinkly, R. Branaugh, and A. Morrass. Oxford, 1971.

Davis, Jennifer. "America's Conscience." *New York Times,* 2 March 1988, 23.

Dector, Midge. *The New Chastity and Other Arguments against Women's Liberation.* New York, 1972.

Delumeau, Jean. *Sin and Fear: The Emergence of a Western Guilt Culture, Thirteenth–Eighteenth Centuries.* New York, 1990.

Dennett, Daniel. *Elbow Room: The Varieties of Free Will Worth Having.* Cambridge, Mass., 1984.

———. "I Could Not Have Done Otherwise—So What?" *Journal of Philosophy* 84 (1984), 553–65.

"Developing Maternal Liability Standards for Prenatal Injury." *Saint John's Law Review* 61 (1987), 592–614.

Dewey, John. *Ethics*. New York, 1908.

———. *Reconstruction in Philosophy.* New York, 1937.

———. *Logic of Inquiry.* New York, 1938.

———. *Public and Its Problems.* New York, 1946.

———. *Outline of a Critical Theory of Morality.* New York, 1957.

Dihle, A. *The Theory of Will in Classical Antiquity.* Berkeley, 1982.

Donoghan, Alan. *The Theory of Morality.* Chicago, 1977.

Dostoyevski, F. *Notes from the Underground.* London, 1972.

Dover, K. J. *Greek Popular Morality in the Time of Plato and Aristotle.* Oxford, 1974.

Downie, R. S. "Social Roles and Moral Responsibility." *Philosophy* 39 (1964), 29–36.

———. "Roles and Moral Agency." *Philosophy* 39 (1968), 39–42.

———. *Roles and Values.* London, 1971.

Dworkin, Gerald. *Determinism, Free Will, and Moral Responsibility.* Englewood Cliffs, N.J., 1970.

Dworkin, Ronald. *Law's Empire.* Cambridge, Mass., 1986.

Emmet, Dorothy. *Function, Purpose, and Powers.* London, 1958.

———. *Rules, Roles, and Relations.* London, 1966.

Epstein, R. A. *Modern Products Liability Law.* Wesport, Conn., 1980.

Evans, E. P. *The Criminal Prosecution and Capital Punishment of Animals.* London, 1987.

Ewing, A. C. *Ethics.* London, 1953.

Fauconnet, Paul. *La Responsabilité.* Paris, 1920.

Feinberg, Joel. *Doing and Deserving.* Princeton, 1970.

———. *Harm To Others.* Oxford, 1984.

"Fetal Alcohol Syndrome: Liability for Failure to Warn—Should Manufacturers Pick up the Tab?" *Journal of Family Law* 28 (1989–90), 71–85.

Fischer, John Martin. "Responsibility and Control." *Journal of Philosophy* 89 (1982), 24–40.

———. "Responsibility and Failure." *Proceedings of the Aristotelian Society* 86 (1985–86), 251–70.

Fischer, J. M., ed. *Moral Responsibility.* Ithaca, 1986.

Fischer, John Martin, and Mark Ravizza. "Responsibility and Inevitability." *Ethics* 101 (1991), 258–78.

Fishkin, James. *The Limits of Obligation.* New Haven, 1982.

Fisk, Milton. *Ethics and Society: A Marxist Interpretation of Value.* Sussex, 1980.

Fitzgerald, P. J. "Acting and Refraining." *Analysis* 4 (1967), 133–39.

Flathman, Richard. *Political Obligation.* New York, 1972.

———. *Concepts in Social and Political Philosophy.* New York, 1973.

———. *The Practice of Rights.* Cambridge, England, 1976.

———. *The Practice of Political Authority.* Chicago, 1980.

———. *The Philosophy and Politics of Freedom.* Chicago, 1987.

Flores, Albert. "Collective Responsibility and Professional Roles." *Ethics* 92 (1983), 537–45.

Frankena, William. *Ethics*. Englewood Cliffs, N.J., 1963.

Frankfurt, Harry. "Alternative Possibilities and Moral Responsibility." *Journal of Philosophy* (1969), 829–39.

———. "Coercion and Moral Responsibility." In *Essays on Freedom of Action*, ed. Ted Honderich. London, 1973.

———. "What Are We Morally Responsible For?" in *How Many Questions? Essays in Honor of Sidney Morgenbesser*, ed. L. Carman. Indianapolis, 1982.

Franklin, R. L. "Dissolving the Problem of Free Will." *Australasian Journal of Philosophy* 39 (1961), 111–24.

———. "Moral Libertarianism." *Philosophical Quarterly* 12 (1962), 24–35.

Freedman, Benjamin. "A Meta-Ethics for Professional Morality." *Ethics* 89 (1978), 1–19.

French, Peter. "Senses of 'Blame.'" *Journal of Southern Philosophy* 14 (1976), 443–45.

French, Peter, ed. *Individual and Collective Responsibility*. Cambridge, Mass., 1972.

Freund, Ludwig. "Responsibility—Definitions, Distinctions, and Applications." *Nomos III: Responsibility*. New York, 1960.

Fried, Charles. *Right and Wrong*. Cambridge, Mass., 1978.

Friedman, Milton. *Capitalism and Freedom*. Chicago, 1962.

Furley, David. "Self-Movers." In G. E. R. Lloyd and G. E. L. Owen, eds., *Aristotle on the Mind and Senses*. Cambridge, 1978.

Gallop, D. "On Being Determined." *Mind* 71 (1962), 181–96.

Geach, P. T. "Ascriptiveness." *Philosophical Review* 69 (1960), 221–26.

Gershonowitz, A. "What Must Cause Injury in Products Liability?" *Indiana Law Journal* 62 (1986), 701–33.

"Getting Away with Murder: Federal OSHA Preemption of State Criminal Prosecutions for Industrial Accidents." *Harvard Law Review* 101 (1987), 535–54.

Gibson, Roger F. "Corporations, Persons, and Moral Responsibility." *Journal of Thought* 21 (1986), 17–86.

Giddings, Paula. *When and Where I Enter: the Impact of Black Women on Race and Sex in America*. New York, 1984.

Ginet, C. "Can the Will Be Caused?" *Philosophical Review* 71 (1962), 49–55.

Glascow, W. D. "On Choosing." *Analysis* 17 (1956), 135–39.

———. "The Concept of Choosing." *Analysis* 20 (1959–60), 63–67.

Glover, Jonathon. *Responsibility*. London, 1970.

Goldman, Alvin. *Theory of Human Actions*. Englewood Cliffs, N.J., 1970.

Gomperez, H. "Individual, Collective, and Social Responsibility." *Ethics* 49 (1939), 329–42.

Goodin, Robert. *Protecting the Vulnerable*. Chicago, 1985.

———. "Apportioning Responsibilities." *Legal Philosophy* 6 (1987), 167–85.

Gossein, Phillip. "Is There a Freedom Requirement for Moral Responsibility?" *Dialogue* 18 (1979), 289–306.

Greene, Theodore M. Introduction to *Kant's Religion*. New York, 1960.

Haines, Nicholas. "Responsibility and Accountability." *Journal of Philosophy* 30 (1955), 141–51.

Halton, Eugene Rochberg. *Meaning and Modernity: Social Theory in the Pragmatic Attitude.* Chicago, 1986.

Hampshire, Stuart. *Freedom of the Individual.* New York, 1965.

Hampshire, Stuart, ed. *Public and Private Morality.* New York, 1978.

Handy, R. "Determinism, Responsibility, and the Social Setting." *Philosophy and Phenomenological Research* 20 (1960), 469–76.

Hardie, W. F. R. *Aristotle's Ethical Theory.* Oxford, 1968.

Hardin, Garrett. "Life Boat Ethics: The Case against Helping the Poor." *World Hunger and Moral Obligations,* ed. William Aiken and Hugh La Follette. Englewood Cliffs, N.J., 1977, 11–21.

Harman, Gilbert. *A Theory of Morality.* New York, 1977.

———. "Relativistic Ethics: Morality As Politics." *Midwest Studies in Philosophy* 3 (1978).

Harris, John. "The Marxist Conception of Violence." *Philosophy and Public Affairs* 3 (1973–74), 192–220.

———. "Williams on Negative Responsibility." *Philosophical Quarterly* 24 (1974), 265–73.

———. *Violence and Responsibility.* London, 1980.

Hart, H. L. A. "The Ascription of Responsibility and Rights." *Proceedings of the Aristotelian Society* 49 (1948–49), 171–94.

———. "Legal Responsibility and Excuses." in *Determinism and Freedom in the Age of Modern Science,* ed. Sidney Hook. New York, 1958.

———. "Variations of Responsibility." *Law Quarterly* 83 (1967), 346–64.

———. *Punishment and Responsibility.* Oxford, 1968.

Hart, H. L. A., and A. Honore. *Causation in the Law.* Oxford, 1959.

Hartshorne, C. "Freedom Requires Indeterminism and Universal Causality." *Journal of Philosophy* 55 (1958), 793–811.

Hayden, Graham. "On Being Responsible." *Philosophical Quarterly* 28 (1978), 46–57.

"Hazards in the Workplace: What is the Employer's Duty?" *Trial* 24 (1988), 24–27.

Held, Virginia. "Can a Random Collection of Individuals Be Morally Responsible?" *Journal of Philosophy* 67 (1970), 471–81.

Henderson, J. A., and T. Eisenberg. "The Quiet Revolution in Products Liability: An Empirical Study of Legal Change." *UCLA Law Review* 37 (1990), 479–553.

Hertzberg, Lars. "Blame and Causality." *Mind* 84 (1974), 500–15.

Hoffman, Joshua, and Gary Rosenkrantz. "On Divine Foreknowledge and Human Freedom." *Philosophical Studies* 37 (1984), 414–34.

Holborrow, L. C. "Blame, Praise, and Credit." *Proceedings of the Aristotelian Society* 72 (1971–72), 85–100.

Holdcroft, David. "A Plea for Excuses." *Philosophy* 44 (1969), 314–29.

Hook, Sidney, ed. *Determinism and Freedom in the Age of Modern Science.* New York, 1958.

Hooks, Benjamin. *Go Tell It!* New York, 1979.

Hornsby, Jennifer. *Actions.* London, 1980.

Hospers, John. "Blame and Excuses." In his *Human Conduct,* 469–93. New York, 1961.

Hume, David. "Of Liberty and Necessity." In an *Inquiry Concerning Human Understanding.* New York, 1907.

———. *Treatise of Human Nature.* Oxford, 1956.

Hunter, J. F. M. "Acting Freely and Being Held Responsible." *Dialogue* 12 (1973), 233–45.

Husak, Douglas. "Omissions, Causation, and Liability," *Philosophical Quarterly* 30 (1980), 318–26.

Irwin, T. H. "Reason and Responsibility." In *Essays on Aristotle's Ethics,* ed. A. Rorty. Berkeley, 1980, 117–56.

———. *Aristotle's First Principles.* Oxford, 1988.

Jensen, Henning. "Morality and Luck." *Philosophy* 59 (1984), 323–30.

Johnson, Chalmers. *The Politics of Productivity: The Real Story of Why Japan Works.* New York, 1989.

Jones, J. W. *The Law and Legal Theory of the Greeks.* Oxford, 1956.

Jonsen, Albert. *Responsibility in Modern Religious Ethics.* Washington, D.C., 1968.

Kagen, Shelly. "Causation, Liability, and Internalism," *Philosophy and Public Affairs* 15 (1986), 41–66.

Kant, Immanuel. *Religion within the Limitations of Reason Alone.* New York, 1960.

———. *Groundwork of the Metaphysics of Morals.* New York, 1964.

Kenner, Lionel. "On Blaming." *Mind* 76 (1967), 238–49.

Kenny, Anthony. *Aristotle's Theory of the Will.* New Haven, 1979.

———. *Free Will and Responsibility.* Oxford, 1984.

Lacey, A. R. "Free Will and Responsibility." *Proceedings of the Aristotelian Society* 58 (1957–58), 15–32.

Lehrer, Keith. "Decisions and Causes." *Philosophical Review* 72 (1963), 224–27.

Lehrer, Keith, ed. *Free Will and Determinism.* New York, 1966.

Lerner, Gerda. *The Creation of Patriarchy.* Oxford, 1986.

Levy-Bruhl, Lucian. *L'Idee de Responsabilité.* Paris, 1884.

Lewis, H. D. *Morals and the New Theology.* London, 1947.

———. "Collective Responsibility." *Philosophy* 23 (1948), 3–18.

———. *Freedom and History.* London, 1962.

"Liability for the Transmission of AIDS and Herpes." *1987 Annual Survey of American Law* (February 1989), 523–47.

Lipton, Merle. *Capitalism and Apartheid: South Africa, 1910–1984.* New York, 1985.

Lloyd, G. E. R., and G. E. L. Owens, eds. *Aristotle on Mind and the Senses.* Cambridge, England, 1978.

Locke, David. "Ifs and Cans Revisited." *Philosophy* 37 (1962), 245–56.

Lucas, J. P. *Freedom of the Will.* Oxford, 1971.

Lyons, David. "On Sanctioning Excuses." *Journal of Philosophy* 66 (1969), 649–60.

Lyotard, Jean François. *The Postmodern Condition.* Minneapolis, 1984.

————. *Just Gaming.* Minneapolis, 1985.

Mabbot, J. D. "Free Will and Punishment." *Contemporary British Philosophy,* ed. H. D. Lewis. New York, 1956.

MacIntyre, A. C. "Determinism." *Mind* 6 (1951), 28–41.

Mack, Eric. "Bad Samaritanism and the Causation of Harm." *Philosophy and Public Affairs* 10 (1980), 230–59.

Mackay, D. M. "On the Logical Indeterminacy of Free Choice." *Mind* 15 (1960), 31–40.

Mackie, J. L. "Responsibility and Language." *Australasian Journal of Philosophy* 33 (1955), 143–59.

————. *Cement of the Universe.* Oxford, 1974.

————. *Ethics: Inventing Right and Wrong.* New York, 1977.

Mangum, G. L. "Murder in the Workplace: Criminal Prosecution vs. Regulatory Enforcement." *Labor Law Journal* 39 (1988), 230–31.

"Maternal Tort Liability for Prenatal Injuries." *Suffolk University Law Review* 22 (1988), 747–77.

Mayo, Bernard. "Downie On Roles." *Philosophy* 29 (1969), 108–19.

McGinn, Colin. *Wittgenstein on Meaning: An Interpretation and Evaluation.* Oxford, 1984.

McKeon, Richard. "The Development and Significance of the Concept of Responsibility." *Revue Internationale de Philosophie* 2 (First Trimester, 1957), 3–32.

McLaughlin, C. A. "AIDS: Current State of the Law—An Overview." *Journal of Law and Health* 3 (1988–89), 77–115.

Mead, George Herbert. *Mind, Self, and Society.* Chicago, 1974.

————. *The Individual and the Social Self.* Chicago, 1982.

Melden, I. A. *Free Action.* London, 1961.

Mellema, Gregory. "On Being Fully Responsible." *American Philosophical Quarterly* 21 (1984), 189–93.

————. "Groups, Responsibility, and the Failure to Act." *International Journal of Applied Ethics* 2 (1985), 57–66.

Mendelbaum, Maurice. "Determinism and Moral Responsibility." *Ethics* 70 (1960), 204–19.

Meyer, Robert N. *The Consumer Movement: Guardians of the Market Place.* New York, 1989.

Mill, J. S. *An Examination of Sir William Hamilton's Philosophy.* London, 1867.

Morgan, Edmund S. *The Puritan Family.* New York, 1966.

Morgenbesser, S., and J. Walsh, eds. *Free Will.* Englewood Cliffs, N.J., 1963.

Morillo, Carolyn. "Doing, Refraining, and the Strenuousness of Morality." *American Philosophical Quarterly* 14 (1977), 29–37.

Moynihan, Daniel Patrick. "Negro Family: The Case for National Action." U.S. Labor Department Report. Washington, D.C., 1965.

Muller, K. B. *Ideology and Moral Philosophy.* New York, 1971.

Myers, C. Mason. "Free Will and the Problem of Evil." *Religious Studies* 23 (1987), 289–94.

"Nabisco Rejects Divestiture." *New York Times,* 25 March 1988, 5.

Nagel, Thomas. "Moral Luck." In *Mortal Questions.* Cambridge, England, 1979.

Nicholson, Linda, ed. *Feminism/Postmodernism.* London, 1990.

Nowell-Smith, P. H. "Free Will and Moral Responsibility." *Mind* 57 (1948).

———. "Determinism and Libertarianism." *Mind* 63 (1954), 317–37.

Nussbaum, Martha. *The Fragility of Goodness: Luck and Ethics in Greek Tragedy and Philosophy.* Cambridge, 1986.

O'Connor, D. J. "Possibility and Choice." *Proceedings of the Aristotelian Society,* Suppl. vol. 34 (1960), 1–24.

Offstead, H. "Can We Produce Decisions?" *Journal of Philosophy* 56 (1959), 89–94.

———. "Recent Work on the Free Will Problem." *American Philosophical Quarterly* 4 (1967), 179–207.

"OSHA's Turnabout." *National Journal* 21 (November 1989), 289–92.

Oughton, D. "Liability for Economic Loss Suffered by the Consumer of Economic Goods." *Journal of Business Law* (September 1987), 370–77.

Parker, Richard. "Blame, Punishment, and the Role of Result." *American Philosophical Quarterly* 21 (1984), 269–76.

Pears, David. *Freedom of the Will.* New York, 1963.

Peers, William. *The My Lai Inquiry.* New York, 1979.

Pennock, J. R. "The Problem of Responsibility." In Carl Friedrich, ed, *Nomos III: Responsibility.* New York, 1960.

Perry, R. B. *General Theory of Value.* Cambridge, Mass., 1954.

Philips, Michael. "Rationality, Responsibility, and Blame." *Canadian Journal of Philosophy* 17 (1987), 141–54.

Pike, Nelson. "Divine Omniscience and Voluntary Action." *Philosophical Review* 74 (1965), 27–46.

———. "Of God and Freedom." *Philosophical Review* 75 (1965), 369–79.

———. "Over-Power and God's Responsibility for Sin." In his *Existence and Nature of God.* Notre Dame, 1983.

Pitcher, George. "Hart on Action and Responsibility." *Philosophical Review* 69 (1960), 226–35.

———. "'In Intending' and Side Effects." *Journal of Philosophy* 67 (1970), 659–68.

Pitkin, Hanna. *The Concept of Representation.* Berkeley, 1967.

———. *Wittgensein and Justice.* Berkeley, 1972.

Prior, A. N. "The Consequences of Actions." *Proceedings of the Aristotelian Society* 30 (1956), 91–95.

"Punitive Damages Recoverable in a Strict Products Liability—Failure to Warn Action Based on Exposure to Asbestos." *Rutgers Law Journal* 18 (1987), 979–93.

"Pursuit of the Corporate Criminal: Employer Criminal Liability for Work-Related Deaths as a Method of Improving Workplace Safety and Health." *Boston College Law Review* 29 (1988), 451–80.

Quinton, Anthony. "On Punishment." In H. Acton, ed., *The Philosophy of Punishment.* New York, 1969, 55–64.

Raphael, D. D. "The Consequences of Actions." *Proceedings of the Aristotelian Society* 30 (1956), 100–19.

Rawls, John. *A Theory of Justice.* Cambridge, Mass., 1971.

———. "Kantian Constructivism in Moral Theory." *Journal of Philosophy* 77 (1980), 215–72.

———. "Justice As Fairness, Political Not Metaphysical." *Philosophy and Public Affairs* 15 (1985), 223–51.

———. "Priority of the Right and the Good." *Philosophy and Public Affairs* 17 (1988), 251–71.

"The Real Fatal Attraction: Civil and Criminal Liability for Sexual Transmission of AIDS." *Drake Law Review* 37 (1988), 657–97.

Richards, Norvin. "Luck and Desert." *Mind* 95 (1986), 198–209.

Richman, R. *God, Free Will, and Morality.* Boston, 1983.

Roberts, Jean. "Aristotle on Responsibility for Action and Character." *Ancient Philosophy* 9 (1989), 23–36.

Roberts, Moira. *Freedom and Practical Responsibility.* Cambridge, England, 1965.

Robertson, Pat. "Understanding South Africa." *New York Times,* 13 February 1988, 19.

Rorty, Richard. *Philosophy and the Mirror of Nature.* Princeton, 1979.

———. *Consequences of Pragmatism.* Minneapolis, 1982.

———. "Postmodernist Bourgeois Liberalism." *Journal of Philosophy* 80 (1983), 583–89.

———. "Solidarity and Objectivity." *Nanzen Review of American Studies* 6 (1984), 1–19.

———. "The Priority of Democracy to Philosophy." In *The Virginia Statute for Religious Freedom,* ed. Merrill D. Peterson and Robert C. Vaughan. Cambridge, England, 1988, 257–81.

———. *Contingency, Irony, and Solidarity.* Cambridge, 1989.

Ross, W. D. *Aristotle.* London, 1960.

Ryle, Gilbert. *Concept of Mind.* London, 1949.

Sartre, Jean-Paul. *Being and Nothingness.* New York, 1956.

Saunders, John Turk. "Of God and Freedom." *Philosophical Review* 75 (1966), 219–25.

Saxonhouse, Arlene. "Aristotle: Defective Males, Hierarchy, and the Limits of Politics," *Feminist Interpretations of Political Theory,* ed. Mary Lyndon Shanley and Carole Pateman, 32–52. Cambridge, England, 1991.

Schauer, Fred. *Playing by the Rules: A Philosophical Examination of Rule-Based Decisionmaking in Law and Life.* Oxford, 1991.

Scheid, J. H. "Affirmative Duty to Aid in Emergency Situations." *John Marshall Journal of Practice and Procedure* 3 (1969).

Schlick, Moritz. "When Is Man Responsible?" In his *Problems in Ethics.* New York, 1939.

Schneider, H. W. *The Puritan Mind.* Ann Arbor, 1958.

Schoeman, F., ed. *Responsibility, Character, and the Emotions.* Cambridge, England, 1987.

Schwartz, A. "Proposals for Products Liability Reform: A Theoretical Synthesis." *Yale Law Journal* 97 (1988), 353–419.

Scriven, Michael. "Causes, Connections, and Conditions in History." In *Philosophical Analysis and History,* ed. William Dray. New York, 1966.

"Setting the Standard: A Mother's Duty during the Prenatal Period." *University of Illinois Law Review* 189 (1989), 493–516.

Shklar, Judith. *Legalism: Law, Morals, and Political Trials.* Cambridge, Mass., 1964.

———. *The Faces of Injustice.* New Haven, 1990.

Simm, Arthur. *Bread for the World.* New York, 1975.

Singer, Peter. "Famine, Affluence, and Morality." *Philosophy and Public Affairs* 2 (1972), 229–43.

Skinner, Quentin. "Action and Context." *Proceedings of the Aristotelian Society* 8 (1978), 57–70.

Sleeper, R. W. *The Necessity of Pragmatism.* New Haven, 1986.

Smart, J. J. C. "Free Will, Praise, and Blame." *Mind* 70 (1961), 291–306.

Smiley, Marion. "Pragmatic Inquiry and Social Conflict: A Critical Reconstruction of Dewey's Model of Democracy." *Praxis* 9 (1990), 365–80.

Smith, H. M. "Intercourse and Moral Responsibility for the Fetus." In *Abortion and the Status of the Fetus,* ed. W. B. Bondeson et al. Dordrecht, 1983, 229–45.

Smith, Holly. "Varieties of Moral Worth and Moral Credit." *Ethics* 101 (1991), 279–303.

Smith, John. *Purpose and Thought: The Meaning of Pragmatism.* Chicago, 1978.

Sober, Elliot. "Apportioning Causal Responsibility." *Journal of Philosophy* 85 (1988), 308–19.

Sorabji, Richard. *Necessity, Cause, and Blame.* Ithaca, 1980.

Sowell, Thomas. *Affirmative Action Re-Considered: Was It Necessary?* Washington, D.C., 1975.

———. *Compassion vs. Guilt and Other Essays.* New York, 1987.

———. *A Conflict of Vision.* New York, 1987.

Sprigge, T. L. S. "Punishment and Moral Responsibility." In *Punishment and Human Rights,* ed. Milton Goldinger. Cambridge, Mass., 1974, 73–98.

Squires, J. E. R. "Blame." In *Philosophy of Punishment,* ed. H. B. Acton London, 1969, 204–11.

Stern, Lawrence. "Freedom, Blame, and Moral Community." *Journal of Philosophy* 71 (1974), 72–84.

Stewart, Thomas A. "The Resurrection of Ralph Nader: After Ten Years in the Shadows." *Fortune* 119 (May 1989), 106–8.

Stohl, Johan. "St. Paul and Moral Responsibility." *Free Inquiry* 10 (1990), 30–31.

Stoljar, S. "Ascriptive and Prescriptive Responsibility." *Mind* 68 (1959), 350–60.

Stone, Lawrence. *The Family, Sex, and Marriage in England, 1500–1800.* New York, 1977.

Strawson, Peter. *Freedom and Resentment and Other Essays.* London, 1974.

Suzman, Helen. "Why Sanctions Don't Work." *New York Times,* 4 October 1988, 23.

Tennant, F. R. *The Concept of Sin.* Cambridge, England, 1912.

Thayer, H. S. *Meaning and Action: A Study of American Pragmatism.* Indianapolis, 1973.

Thompson, Dennis F. "Moral Responsibility of Public Officials: The Problem of Many Hands." *American Political Science Reviews* 74 (1980), 905–16.

————. "Ascribing Responsibility to Advisers in Government." *Ethics* 93 (1983), 546–60.

————. "Moral Responsibility and the New York City Fiscal Crisis." In Joel Fleishman et al., eds., *Public Duties.* Cambridge, Mass., 1981.

————. *Political Ethics and Public Office.* Cambridge, Mass., 1987.

Thompson, Paul. "Collective Responsibility and Professional Roles." *Journal of Business Ethics* 5 (1986), 151–54.

Thomson, J. J. "Individuating Actions." *Journal of Philosophy* 68 (1971), 774–80.

"To Have and to Hold: The Tort Liability for the Interpersonal Transmission of AIDS." *New England Law Review* 23 (1988–89), 887–917.

Tooley, Michael. "Abortion and Infanticide." *Philosophy and Public Affairs* 2 (1972–73), 37–65.

"Tort Liability for Sexual Transmission of Disease: A Legal Attempt to Cure 'Bad' Behavior." *Willamette Law Review* (Fall 1989), 807–27.

Trammell, J. "Saving Life and Taking Life." *Journal of Philosophy* 72 (1975), 131–41.

Trusted, Jennifer. *Free Will and Responsibility.* Oxford, 1984.

Vendler, Zeno. "Effects, Results, and Consequences." In *Analytic Philosophy.* ed. R. J. Butler. Oxford, 1962.

Walzer, Michael. *Just and Unjust Wars.* New York, 1977.

Wasserstrom, Richard. "Roles and Morality." In *The Good Lawyer,* ed. D. Luban. Totowa, N.J., 1984.

Watson, Gary. "Free Agency." *Journal of Philosophy* 72 (1975), 205–20.

Watson, Gary, ed. *Free Will.* Oxford, 1982.

Weinryb, Elazer. "Omissions and Responsibility." *Philosophical Quarterly* 30 (1980), 1–18.

Wihely, N. J. "Industrial Disease and the Onset of Damage." *Law Quarterly Review* 105 (1989), 19–24.

"Will Divestiture Work?" *New York Times,* 4 June 1989, 18.

Williams, Bernard. *Morality: An Introduction to Ethics.* New York, 1972.

————. "Moral Luck." *Moral Luck.* Cambridge, 1981.

————. *Ethics and the Limits of Philosophy.* Cambridge, England, 1985.

Williams, Gardner. "The Natural Causation of Human Freedom." *Philosophy and Phenomenological Research* 19 (1958–59), 529–31.

Wolf, Susan. "Asymmetrical Freedom." *Journal of Philosophy* (1980), 151–56.

————. "The Importance of Free Will." *Mind* 90 (1981), 386–405.

Yack, Bernard. *The Problems of a Politicl Animal: Community, Conflict, and Justice in Aristotelian Political Thought.* Forthcoming, Berkeley, 1992.

Yolton, John. "Acts and Circumstances." *Journal of Philosophy* 59 (1962), 337–50.

Young, Iris. *Justice and the Politics of Difference.* Princeton, 1990.

Zimmerman, Michael. "Luck and Moral Responsibility." *Ethics* 96 (1987), 374–86.

————. *An Essay On Moral Responsibility.* Totowa, N.J., 1988.

Index